Llewellyn's 2020

Sabbats

ALMANAC

Samhain 2019
to
Mabon 2020

Rituals • Crafts • Recipes • Folklore

Llewellyn's Sabbats Almanac:
Samhain 2019 to Mabon 2020

Cover art © Carolyn Vibbert
Cover design by Shira Atakpu
Editing by Annie Burdick
Interior Art: © Carolyn Vibbert, excluding illustrations on pages 37, 73, 76, 109, 111, 146, 148, 182, 216, 219, 254, 256, 290, which are © Wen Hsu

You can order annuals and books from *New Worlds*, Llewellyn's catalog. To request a free copy, call toll free: 1-877-NEW WRLD toll-free, or order online by visiting our website at http://subscriptions.llewellyn.com.

ISBN: 978-0-7387-4947-1

Llewellyn Worldwide Ltd.
2143 Wooddale Drive
Woodbury, MN 55125-2989
www.llewellyn.com

Printed in the United States of America

2019

JANUARY
S	M	T	W	T	F	S
		1	2	3	4	5
6	7	8	9	10	11	12
13	14	15	16	17	18	19
20	21	22	23	24	25	26
27	28	29	30	31		

FEBRUARY
S	M	T	W	T	F	S
					1	2
3	4	5	6	7	8	9
10	11	12	13	14	15	16
17	18	19	20	21	22	23
24	25	26	27	28		

MARCH
S	M	T	W	T	F	S
					1	2
3	4	5	6	7	8	9
10	11	12	13	14	15	16
17	18	19	20	21	22	23
24	25	26	27	28	29	30
31						

APRIL
S	M	T	W	T	F	S
	1	2	3	4	5	6
7	8	9	10	11	12	13
14	15	16	17	18	19	20
21	22	23	24	25	26	27
28	29	30				

MAY
S	M	T	W	T	F	S
			1	2	3	4
5	6	7	8	9	10	11
12	13	14	15	16	17	18
19	20	21	22	23	24	25
26	27	28	29	30	31	

JUNE
S	M	T	W	T	F	S
						1
2	3	4	5	6	7	8
9	10	11	12	13	14	15
16	17	18	19	20	21	22
23	24	25	26	27	28	29
30						

JULY
S	M	T	W	T	F	S
	1	2	3	4	5	6
7	8	9	10	11	12	13
14	15	16	17	18	19	20
21	22	23	24	25	26	27
28	29	30	31			

AUGUST
S	M	T	W	T	F	S
				1	2	3
4	5	6	7	8	9	10
11	12	13	14	15	16	17
18	19	20	21	22	23	24
25	26	27	28	29	30	31

SEPTEMBER
S	M	T	W	T	F	S
1	2	3	4	5	6	7
8	9	10	11	12	13	14
15	16	17	18	19	20	21
22	23	24	25	26	27	28
29	30					

OCTOBER
S	M	T	W	T	F	S
		1	2	3	4	5
6	7	8	9	10	11	12
13	14	15	16	17	18	19
20	21	22	23	24	25	26
27	28	29	30	31		

NOVEMBER
S	M	T	W	T	F	S
					1	2
3	4	5	6	7	8	9
10	11	12	13	14	15	16
17	18	19	20	21	22	23
24	25	26	27	28	29	30

DECEMBER
S	M	T	W	T	F	S
1	2	3	4	5	6	7
8	9	10	11	12	13	14
15	16	17	18	19	20	21
22	23	24	25	26	27	28
29	30	31				

2020

JANUARY
S	M	T	W	T	F	S
			1	2	3	4
5	6	7	8	9	10	11
12	13	14	15	16	17	18
19	20	21	22	23	24	25
26	27	28	29	30	31	

FEBRUARY
S	M	T	W	T	F	S
						1
2	3	4	5	6	7	8
9	10	11	12	13	14	15
16	17	18	19	20	21	22
23	24	25	26	27	28	29

MARCH
S	M	T	W	T	F	S
1	2	3	4	5	6	7
8	9	10	11	12	13	14
15	16	17	18	19	20	21
22	23	24	25	26	27	28
29	30	31				

APRIL
S	M	T	W	T	F	S
			1	2	3	4
5	6	7	8	9	10	11
12	13	14	15	16	17	18
19	20	21	22	23	24	25
26	27	28	29	30		

MAY
S	M	T	W	T	F	S
					1	2
3	4	5	6	7	8	9
10	11	12	13	14	15	16
17	18	19	20	21	22	23
24	25	26	27	28	29	30
31						

JUNE
S	M	T	W	T	F	S
	1	2	3	4	5	6
7	8	9	10	11	12	13
14	15	16	17	18	19	20
21	22	23	24	25	26	27
28	29	30				

JULY
S	M	T	W	T	F	S
			1	2	3	4
5	6	7	8	9	10	11
12	13	14	15	16	17	18
19	20	21	22	23	24	25
26	27	28	29	30	31	

AUGUST
S	M	T	W	T	F	S
						1
2	3	4	5	6	7	8
9	10	11	12	13	14	15
16	17	18	19	20	21	22
23	24	25	26	27	28	29
30	31					

SEPTEMBER
S	M	T	W	T	F	S
		1	2	3	4	5
6	7	8	9	10	11	12
13	14	15	16	17	18	19
20	21	22	23	24	25	26
27	28	29	30			

OCTOBER
S	M	T	W	T	F	S
				1	2	3
4	5	6	7	8	9	10
11	12	13	14	15	16	17
18	19	20	21	22	23	24
25	26	27	28	29	30	31

NOVEMBER
S	M	T	W	T	F	S
1	2	3	4	5	6	7
8	9	10	11	12	13	14
15	16	17	18	19	20	21
22	23	24	25	26	27	28
29	30					

DECEMBER
S	M	T	W	T	F	S
		1	2	3	4	5
6	7	8	9	10	11	12
13	14	15	16	17	18	19
20	21	22	23	24	25	26
27	28	29	30	31		

Contents

Introduction

NEARLY EVERYONE HAS A favorite sabbat. There are numerous ways to observe any tradition. This edition of the *Sabbats Almanac* provides a wealth of lore, celebrations, creative projects, and recipes to enhance your holiday.

For this edition, a mix of writers—JD Hortwort, Michael Furie, Jason Mankey, Laura Tempest Zakroff, Suzanne Ress, and more—share their ideas and wisdom. These include a variety of paths as well as the authors' personal approaches to each sabbat. Each chapter closes with an extended ritual, which may be adapted for both solitary practitioners and covens.

In addition to these insights and rituals, specialists in astrology, history, cooking, crafts, and family impart their expertise throughout.

Daniel Pharr gives an overview of planetary influences most relevant for each sabbat season and provides details and a short ritual for selected events, including New and Full Moons, retrograde motion, planetary positions, and more.

Charlynn Walls explores the realm of old-world Pagans, with a focus on traditional gravestone symbols we often associate with Samhain, as well as some unique sabbat festivals tied to the Nordic culture.

Mickie Mueller conjures up a feast for each festival that includes an appetizer, entrée, dessert, and beverage.

Ember Grant offers instructions on DIY crafts that will leave your home full of color and personality for each and every sabbat.

Charlie Rainbow Wolf presents a favorite crystal or stone for each holiday season and provides background and hands-on uses for each.

About the Authors

Blake Octavian Blair is a shamanic practitioner, ordained minister, writer, Usui Reiki Master-Teacher, tarot reader, and musical artist. Blake incorporates mystical traditions from both the East and West, with a reverence for the natural world, into his own brand of spirituality. Blake holds a degree in English and religion from the University of Florida. He is an avid reader, knitter, crafter, pescatarian, and member of the Order of Bards, Ovates and Druids (OBOD). He loves communing with nature and exploring its beauty whether it is within the city or hiking in the woods. Blake lives in the New England region of the USA with his beloved husband. Visit him on the web at www.blakeoctavianblair.com or write him at blake@blakeoctavianblair.com.

Kate Freuler lives in Ontario, Canada, with her husband and daughter. She owns and operates www.whitemoonwitchcraft.com, an online witchcraft boutique. When she isn't crafting spells and amulets for clients or herself, she loves to write, paint, read, draw, and create.

Michael Furie (Northern California) is the author of *Supermarket Sabbats, Spellcasting for Beginners, Supermarket Magic, Spellcasting: Beyond the Basics*, and more, all from Llewellyn Worldwide. A practicing Witch for more than twenty years, he is a priest of the Cailleach. He can be found online at www.michaelfurie.com.

Ember Grant has been writing for the Llewellyn Annuals since 2003. In addition, she is the author of three books: *Magical Candle Crafting, The Book of Crystal Spells*, and *The Second Book of Crystal Spells*. She lives in Missouri with her husband and two very spoiled feline companions. Visit her at EmberGrant.com.

JD Hortwort resides in North Carolina. She is an avid student of herbology and gardening. She has written a weekly garden column since 1991. She is a professional, award-winning author, journalist, and magazine editor, as well as a frequent contributor to the Llewellyn annuals. Recently retired from journalism, she continues to write on topics as diverse as gardening and NASCAR. When not at the keyboard, she spends time in her own landscape, taking trips with friends wherever the road leads, and with her nose buried in a book.

James Kambos is a writer and artist from Ohio. He has written many articles and essays about the folk magic traditions of Appalachia, Greece, and the Near East. He also designs cards and calendars. James has a degree in history and geography from Ohio University.

Jason Mankey is a Wiccan-Witch who lives in Northern California with his wife, Ari, and two cats. He's the author of *Transformative Witchcraft: The Greater Mysteries*, along with several books in The Witch's Tools series. He writes online at the blog Raise the Horns.

Mickie Mueller explores magic and spirituality through art and the written word at her home studio and workshop in Missouri. She is the author/illustrator of *The Voice of the Trees*, the illustrator of *The Mystical Cats Tarot* and *The Magical Dogs Tarot*, and the author of *The Witch's Mirror* and *Llewellyn's Little Book of Halloween*. Since 2007, Mickie has been a regular article and illustration contributor to Llewellyn's almanacs and annuals and many Llewellyn books. Her art has been seen as set dressing on SyFy's *The Magicians* and Bravo's *Girlfriend's Guide to Divorce*. Visit her online at MickieMuellerStudio.etsy.com

Daniel Pharr was born and raised in the desert Southwest, and knew his path was a Pagan one after being introduced to the ancient ways of the goddess almost twenty years ago. He has studied extensively with several nationally recognized Pagan institutions and learned the arts of healing (including Reiki, reflexology, therapeutic touch, and massage), tarot, astrology, intuitive counseling, and herbalism. As a healer and psychic, he believes his experience in these areas have brought him in touch with the lunar energies he writes of in this book. It is the knowledge and use of these energies which make him successful, and his private practice extends to corporations and organizations as well as individuals. Pharr is also a scuba instructor, a martial arts teacher with a Black Belt in Kenpo Karate, and a Certified Firewalker Instructor.

Suzanne Ress has been practicing Wicca for about twelve years as the leader of a small coven, but she has been aware of having a special connection to nature and animal spirits since she was a young child. She has been writing creatively most of her life—short stories, novels, and nonfiction articles for a variety of publications—and finds it to be an important outlet for her considerable creative powers. Other outlets she regularly makes use of are metalsmithing, mosaic works, painting, and all kinds of dance. She is also a professional aromatic herb grower and beekeeper. Although she is an American of Welsh ancestry by birth, she has lived in northern Italy for nearly twenty years. She recently discovered that the small mountain in the pre-alpine hills that she inhabits with her family and animals was once the site of an ancient Insubrian Celtic sacred place. Not surprisingly, the top of the mountain has remained a fulcrum of sacredness throughout the millennia, and this grounding in blessedness makes Suzanne's everyday life especially magical.

Charlynn Walls is an active member of her local community. A practitioner of the craft for over twenty years, she currently resides in Central Missouri with her family. She continues to share her knowledge by teaching at local festivals and producing articles for publication with Llewellyn Worldwide.

Charlie Rainbow Wolf is happiest when she is creating something, especially if it's made from items that others have discarded. Pottery, writing, knitting, astrology, and tarot ignite her passion, but she happily confesses she's easily distracted; life offers such wonderful things to explore! A recorded singer-songwriter and published author, she champions holistic living and lives in the Midwest with her husband and special needs Great Danes. Visit her at www.charlierainbow.com.

Laura Tempest Zakroff is a professional artist, author, dancer, designer, and Modern Traditional Witch. She is the author of *Weave the Liminal*, *Sigil Witchery*, and *The Witch's Cauldron*, and the co-author of *The Witch's Altar*. Laura blogs for Patheos and Witches & Pagans, contributes to *The Witches' Almanac* and edited *The New Aradia: A Witch's Handbook to Magical Resistance*. Visit her at www.LauraTempestZakroff.com.

Samhain

Samhain: The Cat

Suzanne Ress

BLACK CATS HAVE LONG been associated with witches. But why a black cat rather than a black dog, rabbit, or snake? Do cats really have a magical connection to the spirit world? I've heard people say that cats can see ghosts, and that they know when someone is about to die.

Cats have been kept as domesticated animals for as long as sheep, dogs, and goats—for over 100,000 years! They were first bred from wild cats in Mesopotamia, a useful animal for keeping rats and mice out of the grain. The popularity of cats spread to ancient Egypt, where felines were so treasured by human beings that they earned their own revered fertility goddess, Bastet, keeper of hearth and home, keeper of secrets, and guardian against evil spirits and disease. Killing a cat in ancient Egypt was punishable by death.

A cat who died was deeply mourned by her human keepers, no different than the death of a human family member. Many cats were embalmed or mummified, and buried in the family crypt.

As happens with most animals that humans keep and develop affection for, the cat began to be seen as being imbued with special, not quite *animal*, properties. She was believed to be able to see beyond what is readily apparent.

Cats were brought with travelers throughout the ancient world, and, in most civilizations, were welcomed and highly thought of because of their vermin-controlling ability. However, when cats were brought to ancient Greece, which had already domesticated the native weasel for rodent control, people were a little less enthusiastic about them.

At some point after the domesticated cat had reached Europe, she became associated, intentionally or not, with Hecate. The reason for this is unclear, but could possibly have been a misinterpretation of the meaning of polecat (a type of weasel), which was one of Hecate's animal familiars. Another possibility is that the Hecate myth was mixed up with the myth of the Norse goddess of fertility and death, Freya, whose chariot was pulled by two black cats. Anyway, something went askew for cats with the advent of Christianity. The cat undeservedly became associated with darkness, the devil, and black witchcraft.

In the thirteenth century, Pope Gregory declared that all cats were evil and had associations with Satan. As a result, many cats were senselessly killed throughout the Christian world. People who chose to keep cats anyway, especially older women, were often condemned as witches.

Although times changed, and peoples' opinions of cats greatly improved, the erroneous belief that the black cat is the consort of witches has kept its grip in modern imagery.

Some years ago, I had an inexplicable encounter with a cat that I've never been able to satisfactorily explain. My husband and I and our kids decided to make the drive to his ancestral mountain home in the Apennines for Samhain weekend. In Italy, October 31 has only recently begun to be celebrated, but November 1 has long been celebrated as All Saints' (Hallows) Day, and November 2 is the Day of the Dead, when a trek to the cemetery bearing flowers or other grave-top decorations is in order.

In the car, we brought pumpkins to carve, and our costumes—black ragged clothes, pointy hats; my husband had a grim reaper mask—and we brought our little black dog Lorniken. On the way out of the house, I also grabbed the latest issue of a magazine I subscribed to.

We were headed for the tiny village of San Benedetto in Alpe, where my husband had spent all the summers of his youth, in the house built by his great-great grandfather. It was a large, old stone construction, heated by a single wood-burning stove. Between the two long windows in the living room was a portrait of the long-gone forefather and his wife. I thought it fitting that we were spending Samhain with these ancestors.

The house was cold, so we lit the wood-burning stove and walked down the street to the village restaurant for dinner, bringing Lorniken along on her leash, as she seemed nervous about staying in the house alone.

Afterward, we carved the pumpkins into grinning jack-o'-lantern faces at the kitchen table, one for each of us, as protection against marauding evil spirits, but unfortunately I had forgotten to bring one, even a small one or a turnip, for Lorniken.

I set the four jack-o'-lanterns outside on the front step and lit them, then went inside to warm myself, and began to read an article in the magazine I'd brought along about the physiological process of dying. The rather morbid article described exactly what happens to a human or other mammalian body in the moments leading up to death, and in the period immediately following, from the slowing of blood circulation to the body's vital organs, to the final choking breaths that make "the death rattle," to cardiac arrest, brain death, and on to livor mortis, algor mortis, and, finally, rigor mortis, after which the only thing left for the body to do is decompose. The article was quite detailed and was getting too gruesome for me, so I made a suggestion.

"Why don't we put on our costumes and go out for a walk?"

"Okay!" "Yes!" The kids were happy to be doing something to celebrate the holiday.

We changed our clothes, which put us all into a more fun-loving mood, and walked out the front door, past the glowing lantern faces. At the moment I thought, "Surely animals don't need their souls protected from evil spirits; I have never carved Lorniken a jack-o'-lantern before!"

We walked up the steep cobblestone alley through the middle of the village. It was all uphill to the ancient abbey at the top, too narrow for cars to travel on. My husband had not remembered to bring along Lorniken's leash, but we often did without it, as she was obedient about staying at our sides during walks.

There were no other humans around. At the small square in front of the abbey we encountered a gorgeous black cat, a tom with a white star on his chest, and for some reason he decided to follow along with us.

I thought at the time that the cat resembled a Cat Sidhe—a shape-shifted witch! Lorniken was a timid, black mutt who had never paid any attention at all to cats. She had never chased or barked at them, nor had she been friendly to them. But to this big, healthy-looking tom following her she was neither neutral nor blind. It crept up close behind her and whipped out a sharp-clawed paw, swiping the air just millimeters from her face, causing our shy dog to run for protection next to my husband's leg, her tail low. At first, we were all intrigued by the cat's bold behavior, wondering why he seemed to be trying to convey some special message to our dog, but after a while it began to get creepy. The cat followed us away from the piazza, through the abbey village at the top, and then crept through the hedges in the berm as we began our descent down the main road back to the village, his eye constantly on our dog.

In Irish and Scottish lore, it is believed that a Cat Sidhe can steal a person's soul, and can be especially vengeful on Samhain Eve, if a saucer of cream is not left on one's doorstep for him.

Every time we thought he had gone away, the cat would suddenly leap or pop out again from behind a rock or a bush. I had never seen a cat act that way toward a dog, and I could not stop thinking that this really was a genuine Cat Sidhe, and it scared me.

After a while, as we continued walking down the hill in the center of the curving asphalt road, it seemed the cat had finally grown tired of his game and left us.

Then suddenly we heard a car approaching from uphill, and, as it rounded the curve, aware that we were all dressed in black and walking at night on an unlit black road, I pulled my daughters way over to the side berm with me to wait for the car to pass. My husband and Lorniken stood on the other side of the road. The car's headlights shone on the dark pavement and I thought the driver probably had no idea there was a family waiting on the sides. I stared across the road at Lorniken, nearly invisible even to me, willing her to stay put by my husband's leg. But just a hair of a second before the car crossed her path, Lorniken ran across the road to me and my daughters. Seemingly in slow motion and silence, she was struck by the car, run over by the car, and then the car continued on down the hill, oblivious that anything unusual had happened.

We ran to her in the dark. She lay on her side in the middle of the road, her eyes closed. I spoke some words to her, and my daughters began to cry. And then I heard the death rattle of her final breath and she shuddered and died.

"She's dead," I said. My children wailed.

I saw the tomcat slink away on the other side of the street, back in the direction of the abbey, and I shivered.

We moved Lorn's body to the side of the road and covered her with fallen leaves. In shock, we returned home. Passing the jack-o'-lanterns by the door, it seemed to me their grins were more like smirks. My daughters and I went inside, not knowing what to do, while my husband found a shovel, and, still wearing his Grim Reaper mask, dug a grave in the small front yard of the old house.

I suggested we just all go to bed early, and my daughters, still sobbing, went upstairs to the chilly bedrooms. My husband returned to where Lorniken had been struck down and carried her stiffened body back to the house to place it in the grave, which he covered over with dirt.

We were all much too sad and upset to enjoy the long weekend, so we chose to leave the next morning. Not knowing what to do with the carved jack-o'-lanterns, I carried them, two at a time, into the woods and, after extinguishing their flames, left them under the trees to rot back into the earth. I tossed my magazine with the article on the death process into the dumpster.

Once we were back home, and for several days afterward, whenever I would go for a walk in the woods, alone or with a friend, I felt Lorniken's spirit following behind me, as she had done in life. And then she disappeared. I was still distraught about her absence and especially about the circumstances of her death, but it seemed that her spirit had found peace and moved on.

I have gone over the events of that Samhain night often in my mind and I am always still mystified by the tom cat's behavior. He chose our dog, a dog he had never seen before, to follow and tease, and it really did seem that he had a mission. But was it to protect our dog, or to drive her to her death?

Peoples' ideas of cats have oscillated throughout the centuries between benevolence and maleficence, largely depending on the way they think of Pagans, and especially of witches, as, for mysterious reasons, the two continue to go hand in hand.

Cats have been revered as protectors of human beings, especially able to protect a selected human from hidden enemies. And they have been killed en masse because of their supposed association with the devil.

Probably the most reasonable way to think of cats, though, is as the separate, sometimes unreadable, species that they are, peacefully coexisting with human beings for over 100,000 years.

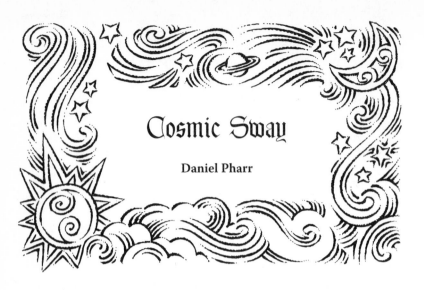

Cosmic Sway

Daniel Pharr

PLEIADES HAS RISEN. SAMHAIN will bring the winter's darkness and hibernation. Each Full Moon since Lughnasadh has been a harvest Moon, providing additional light into the hours of the night for the harvest. These are the food stocks that will sustain life through spring's first day on Imbolc, until the warmth of summer is renewed at Beltaine. As with most goings on, the metaphor is as important as the actuality.

The time between worlds, Samhain is the Otherworld, the place of the ethereal self, with aspirations and anchors, successes and failures, lives and deaths, all standing in opposition and contrast, for interaction and self-understanding. The Otherworld is a place of adventure without consequence; losing a battle with a dragon yields wisdom and a story and no actual physical damage.

Dark Moon

The dark Scorpio Moon of October 27 at 11:39 p.m. is a spirited opportunity to connect with the Otherworld. Visiting the Otherworld is most easily accomplished at this time of the year, and the dark Moon in Scorpio will enhance the experience with its strong connection to Pluto, the ruler of the underworld. Scorpio will add passion and intensity to the experience, positively or negatively.

Lessons of the dark Moon are profound and difficult, angry and misunderstood. Sit quietly with a candle, set a steady drumbeat, tap your sternum with two fingers like a drum, or do it for another. Forgive transgressions and the transgressors, lost friends, family, and parents. Forgive the Goddess, the path of lessons, and the self. Release fear, then judgement. Release emotions claiming righteousness. Sit with forgiveness, speak into the ether, feel the release and acceptance.

Samhain Moon

Under the comfortable Sagittarius Moon, Samhain's free-spirited celebration will warm in the fire of spontaneity, exhilaration, and carefree romantic feelings and encounters, beginning at sunset, about 5:53 p.m. on October 31. The Moon is void-of-course when Samhain begins, giving the Capricorn Moon a foothold in the evening's festivities, but more like an angel on the shoulder, easily overshadowed by the devilish Sagittarius Moon on its way out. Merriment will ensue, but not without payment to come later.

Mead

This would be grand time to set next year's vintage of mead to ferment. Be sure to make enough mead to lubricate the celebrations from Litha next year through to Litha the year after. The mead cycle begins with fermenting a new batch after Samhain and opening the first bottle the following Litha. The process is simple and only a few items are needed. Keep present in the mind while mixing next year's sacrament that the Celts considered mead a gift from the Goddess.

Full Moon

The Taurus Full Moon on November 12 at 8:34 a.m. provides a wonderful opportunity to luxuriate in the coziness and comfort of home. A hot cup of tea or coffee, a nice read in a comfy chair, a long warm bath, an afternoon nap, a massage—these are but a few of the earthly restorations leading to a perfect day culminating in relaxation. A couple of rejuvenating days under the Taurus Moon will be power-enhancing and internally strengthening, but the year has only just begun and this not the time to get carried away with a rather substantial power of will. Allow the inner Venus to calm the bull. This may well be the last opportunity for rejuvenating recreation for some time to come. Holidays with family, friends, or even strangers could be challenging.

November Dark Moon

The dark Moon will be in Sagittarius at 10:06 a.m. on November 26, heading into the Thanksgiving holiday. The tendency will be to revisit the memories and impulsiveness of Samhain's past, recklessly tempting fate while preparing for travel, traveling, or shopping for the holiday. As the Celts would have said, we can never truly go home. Time is a spiral, not a circle, and what once was can never be relived, if for no other reason than time has passed. This Sagittarius Moon will manifest as optimism in utopian ideals, and the inspirations of others. Desires of family understanding or acceptance and hopes of joy or connection will be dashed quickly if held to a utopian standard of excellence. Pressure building from the coming societal holidays might couple with unmet desires, causing quick words to burn their recipient. Compensate any feelings of being trapped by planning the next winter holiday, thereby avoiding this seemingly perpetual reoccurrence.

Thanksgiving

The Capricorn and Aquarius Moons shining on the Thanksgiving holiday weekend will provide plenty of opportunity for familial strife, the breaking and enforcing of rules, and need for freedom and independence. Thursday and Friday, under a Capricorn Moon, will be endured under the mantle of rules and responsibilities. Pliability, emotional openness, and general receptivity may appear to have manifested in family and others, but the actual level of openness will vary wildly. Share openly, without expectation. Don't take offense to the misunderstanding of others. Breathe.

Saturday and Sunday will chill under the Aquarius Moon. People will be more in their heads and less in their hearts or bodies. After two days of Capricorn's rules and regulations, having a relaxed and lengthy conversation with the like-minded will seem a dream that must be made manifest. Freedom and the open road will beckon, but if their calling is to be denied, a desire to create new rules will abound. The power dynamic of subordination and discipline will not work for more than a very select few.

Six Days

Six days after the dark Moon on November 26 will be the evening of December 2 and the morning of December 3. Ideally, after the Moon leaves the void-of-course in Aquarius and enters the emotional, lovelorn Pisces at 2:10 a.m., cut the mistletoe for the Yule celebrations, using a golden sickle if one is available, or a boline, or any knife or scissor if need be, and keep the cutting fresh in water (like cut flowers). Mistletoe is best harvested from oak trees, but again, use what you can find. Lunar energies will support helping and sacrificing for others, but don't give yourself away.

Full Moon

The next Full Moon will be the last Full Moon before Yule. This Moon will feel uncontrolled, hopping back and forth between Gemini and Cancer. The Moon becomes Full at the moment it goes void-of-course in Gemini, 12:12 a.m., and then moves into Cancer at 6:23 p.m., both on December 12. The cheery, quick-witted demeanor that fosters intellectuality and sociability will compete with and ultimately give way to emotional sensitivity and vulnerability. Groups will not be a good idea. The crab will crawl into its shell, bury itself in the sand of the ocean floor, and ride out the storm that is the Cancer Full Moon.

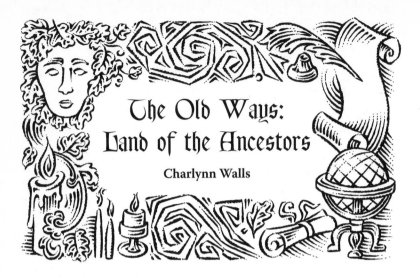

The Old Ways: Land of the Ancestors

Charlynn Walls

VISITING CEMETERIES ON SPECIAL OCCASIONS was something my family did on a regular basis when I was a young child. I often recall going with my great-grandmother, grandmother, and great-aunts to the cemetery to clean the headstones and to leave small tokens to honor our dearly departed. This was done a couple of times a year, usually on the birthdate of the one who had passed and near holidays like Samhain. This was a rite that was done with reverence. During these times I felt connected to those that had passed on.

Samhain is the spiritual observance that marks the end of the harvest season and the transition into the winter months. It is observed on the thirty-first of October or soon thereafter. This was the Celtic New Year. As such, it is a time when the veil between the worlds is at its thinnest and the spirits of the dead can comingle with the living.

The Celts

The Celtic people, who eventually settled in the British Isles, emerged around 400 BCE. With them came a unique outlook on life, death, and the interaction of the two. The Celtic culture had a special reverence for the land. Their worldview was that of animism. The land, trees, water, animals—everything had its own spirit that either worked in harmony with the people or actively worked against them.

Great importance was placed on the family groupings of the ancient Celtic people. They were bound together in clans, their basic family unit. The clans organized into larger familial groups, which Sirona Knight noted as "tuath," and today we would recognize as a tribe (Knight 2000). The ancestral lineage was revered, and there was a connection between family and land that became intertwined in death. Those that have passed from this life were returned to the land though burial. And in turn the land became imbued with spiritual essence of those who passed, and they were reunited with the Mother Goddess. It held special importance for the living and showed the continuity of life.

The connection and cycle of life was reaffirmed during Samhain when the dead could return to the land of the living and commune and celebrate the end of autumn and beginning of the new year. Due to Samhain's placement in the calendar, it sits alone, which causes it to exist outside of the natural conventions of time and space.

Connecting with the Ancestors

The Celts followed the turning of the seasons as part of their agrarian culture. They followed the same processes their ancestors did. They would sow the fields, which in return would produce food for the coming year. The land showed that it could be renewed year after year. Because the land provided, people were able to meet their basic needs with the bounty of the harvest, including food, a means to create clothing, and a way to provide shelter.

Death was a part of life. When the bodies of the dead were buried they rejoined the land. Burial sites became sacred sanctuaries that were revered by the living. These areas were thought to be spiritual eddies of power, since they possessed the power of those that had passed, joining with the spirits of the land.

The ancient Celts would often visit the sacred burial sites of their dead. As noted by Barry Cunliffe, they would visit consistently, "over a period of time, perhaps on a seasonal basis or when a particular event, past or pending, demanded a propitiatory response." (Cunliffe 1997)

They would bring with them offerings that would nourish and appease their ancestors. The connection and communion with the spirits of the ancestors was continual. The visits would span the seasons, a give and take that would allow for a reciprocal relationship between the living and the dead.

Celebrating the Land of the Ancestors

When the Wheel of the Year again turns to Samhain we can bring the same reverence to our ancestors that the ancient Celts did. Here are a few ways to bring the past and present together in a manner that the Celts would see as reminiscent of the ancient ways.

Offerings

The Celts would often leave offerings of food for the deceased to show their respect and reverence. To do the same, you can visit your loved ones where they rest and leave offerings of your own there. These gifts can be anything—food, a note, or a memento that has special meaning to you and the deceased. The purpose is to reaffirm your connection and bond to the ancestors.

Another practice could be to invite the spirits to dine with you. When you set the table, create an extra place setting. Small pieces of what the diners are having should be placed on the plate and then buried after the feast has concluded. This would be like the Dumb Feast, where practitioners set an extra spot at the table, but the diners would forgo any form of verbal communication throughout the meal. Small gestures to the spirits have meaning to those on both sides of the veil.

Creating Places of Power

The Celts, through honoring their ancestors, created places of power. You can create your own places of power. You will want to find a grave, grove, spring, or space that you visit or can visit frequently. On your first visit, place a quartz crystal in the space—one that was charged on Samhain with the energies of your beloved dead. Each time you visit this space bring with you an offering. The token you provide will reconnect you with the land and your ancestors. By doing so you build the connection each time, making it stronger.

References

Cunliffe, Barry. *The Ancient Celts*. Oxford: Oxford University Press, 1997.

Green, Miranda. *Animals in Celtic Life and Myth*. London: Routledge, 1992.

Knight, Sirona. *Celtic Traditions: Druids, Faeries, and Wiccan Rituals*. New York, NY: Citadel Press, 2000.

McCoy, Edain. *The Sabbats: A New Approach to Living the Old Ways*. St. Paul, MN: Lewellyn Publications, 1994.

Morgan, Sheena. *The Wicca Book of Days*. London:Vega, 2002.

Nichols, Mike. *The Witches' Sabbats*. Albany, CA: Acorn Guild Press, 2005.

Ravenwolf, Silver. *Halloween: Customs, Recipes & Spells*. Woodbury, MN: Lewellyn Publications, 2013.

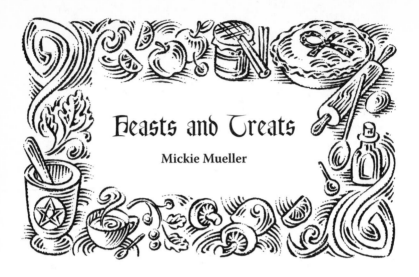

Feasts and Treats

Mickie Mueller

THE TRADITIONAL CELEBRATION OF Samhain and its secular counterpart Halloween (celebrated alongside Samhain in the northern hemisphere) have developed many flavors specific to this fall season. The air grows crisp in the evening and we yearn for something warming as the days grow shorter. Traditional and seasonal foods this time of the year include pumpkins, winter squash, beans, nuts, kale, and, of course, sweets of all kinds. The flavors of Samhain are a deep part of our food memories.

Walnut Cauliflower Stuffed Kale Leaves

You can also use browned chorizo sausage for this recipe, but even the omnivores in our house fell in love with this healthy version using cauliflower and walnuts. Kale is a Samhain/Halloween tradition from Victorian times and was often used in love divination. It's said that a walnut tree was sometimes used as a meeting place for witches' rituals, perfect for the Witch's New Year!

Prep time: 20 minutes
Cooking time: 50 minutes
Servings: 16–20 leaves

½ head of cauliflower (or 1/2 pound cooked chorizo)
1 cup walnuts
1 chipotle pepper in adobo sauce
½ tablespoon chili powder
½ teaspoon cumin
½ teaspoon cayenne pepper
½ teaspoon salt
1–2 tablespoons olive oil
½ cup cooked rice
2 bunches of kale leaves

Preheat oven to 375° F (245° C). Place the cauliflower (or cooked chorizo), walnuts, chipotle pepper, and spices in a food processor and pulse until the mixture has the texture of sausage. As it's blending, slowly drizzle the olive oil through the chute until well mixed. Spread mixture evenly on a parchment-lined baking dish and bake for 30 minutes, stirring halfway through.

Fill a large pot with water and bring it to a boil. Fill a separate large bowl with ice and water. Drop 5–6 leaves of kale in the pot for about 1½ minutes. Scoop them out with a slotted spoon and plunge into ice water for 1–2 minutes, then dry on paper towels. Repeat with all the kale. Fold each kale leaf in half along the stem and remove about 2 inches of the stem with a knife, leaving a V-shaped notch in the leaf.

When the walnut and cauliflower mixture is ready to come out of the oven, mix it with the cooked rice. Place a spoonful of the mixture in the middle of a kale leaf. Roll the leaf over the mixture, starting from the bottom of the leaf and rolling toward the pointed end. Fold the sides in as you go; the curly edges of the leaves help keep the filling in. Roll each one up into a cigar shape. Place it seam side down into an oven-safe baking dish. Repeat with each piece of kale. Bake 16–20 minutes and serve warm.

Black and Orange Samhain Chili

Hearty soups and chilis are always popular at the Samhain open houses I have every year. When you eat too much candy, it's nice to have a high-protein meal, and this black and orange chili fits the bill. Black beans, according to folklore, drive away baneful spirits. The color scheme of the Samhain needfires of old included dark figures silhouetted against an orange fire and setting sun, which is still seen in the modern Halloween aisle. Then we pull in a hint of chocolate to craft this magical chili. You can add browned ground beef, chorizo, or veggie crumbles to this chili if you want to, but we found it was really good as-is.

Prep time: 30 minutes
Cooking time: 3–4 hours
Servings: 6–8

1 white onion, diced
2 tablespoons olive oil
1 orange bell pepper, diced
4 cloves of garlic, minced
3 tablespoons chili powder
1 teaspoon smoked paprika
½ teaspoon ground cumin
½ teaspoon cayenne pepper
4 (16-ounce) cans of black beans, undrained
1 can diced tomatoes, drained
6 sun-dried tomatoes, sliced
3 chipotle peppers in adobo sauce, sliced
Optional: browned ground beef or vegetarian crumbles
½ ounce dark chocolate
1 small butternut squash, peeled and diced into ½-inch pieces
Shredded cheese, sour cream, cilantro, and tortillas for garnish and topping

In a skillet, sauté the diced onion in olive oil. Cook 2–3 minutes, then add garlic and bell pepper and cook until tender. Add chili powder, smoked paprika, ground cumin, and cayenne pepper Cook 1 minute. Add the mix to a slow cooker with black beans, diced tomatoes, sun-dried tomatoes, chipotle peppers, browned ground beef if you're using it, and chocolate (trust me, it's subtle but adds depth). Cook in the slow cooker on low for 3–4 hours.

Poke the butternut squash several times with a fork and microwave for 2–3 minutes. Slice the top and bottom ends off, then cut it in half, slicing the base away from the neck. Set the sliced flat end on a cutting board and use a serrated vegetable peeler or paring knife in a downward direction to remove the skin, then repeat on the other end. Scoop out the seeds. (You can roast those seeds like pumpkin seeds, delicious!) Cut the squash into ½-inch squares. Add the squash to the slow cooker 20 minutes before the chili is done. If you're using vegetarian crumbles instead of ground beef, add it at this time as well. When butternut squash is tender, turn the slow cooker down to warm and serve the chili. Feel free to top or serve with cheese, sour cream, cilantro, or tortillas.

Savory Pumpkin Bruschetta

I know there's pumpkin everything this time of year. While the sweet pumpkin spice "everything" can quickly turn into pumpkin overload, I like using pumpkin for a savory dish as a nice way to experience the flavors of autumn without being redundant.

Prep time: 15 minutes
Cooking time: 5 minutes
Servings: 16–26 slices

2–3 teaspoons olive oil
Small 1-pound pumpkin, peeled and cut into ½ inch cubes (about 4–5 cups total)
½ cup fresh grated parmesan, divided (or sub vegan cheese)
1 teaspoon red pepper flakes, or to taste
2–3 teaspoons balsamic vinegar
1 tablespoon fresh rosemary sprigs, roughly chopped

Garlic salt to taste

1 loaf of crusty bread, such as French bread (sub gluten-free bread if you prefer)

Heat olive oil in a skillet and sauté the cubed pumpkin until it's soft and the exterior caramelizes. Put half of the pumpkin in a food processor or blender with ¼ cup of parmesan and, while blending, drizzle in ¼ cup of olive oil. Mix until smooth.

In a large bowl, gently toss the remaining pumpkin cubes with salt and pepper, rosemary, red pepper flakes, a small drizzle of olive oil, and balsamic vinegar. Slice bread about an inch thick; you'll get 16–26 slices depending on the length of your loaf. Brush both sides with olive oil and sprinkle with garlic salt. Toast the bread on a grill or in a skillet, on both sides, just until golden brown. Arrange bread slices on a baking sheet. Spread the pureed pumpkin on the top of each slice of bread, top with the seasoned pumpkin cubes and fresh parmesan, and put under the broiler for about 1 minute. Serve warm.

Porcelain Sugar Skull Cookies

This is a simple sugar cookie recipe, but if you really want a shortcut, you can use premade sugar cookie dough (although sugar cookies are easy to make yourself). Samhain is a time to remember our ancestors sweetly. These cookies are delicious and the icing looks like painted porcelain. Sugar skulls are used on the offrenda altars of those who celebrate Dia de los Muertos from October 31 through November 2. You can paint these cookies using traditional Dia de los Muertos sugar skulls as inspiration or paint them in any style that you like.

Prep time: 15 minutes (plus 30 minutes for the dough to chill)

Cooking time: 10–12 minutes per cookie sheet

Servings: 24 or more cookies, depending on the size of your cookie cutter

2 ½ cups all-purpose flour or gluten-free flour mixture
1 teaspoon baking soda
¼ teaspoon salt
¾ cup white sugar
1 cup butter (2 sticks), softened to room temperature
1 egg or vegan egg substitute
1 teaspoon vanilla extract
½ teaspoon almond extract

Preheat oven to 350° F (177° C). Mix flour, baking soda, and salt with a wire whisk. In a separate large bowl, use an electric mixer to blend together the egg, butter, sugar, vanilla extract, and almond extract until creamy. Add the dry ingredients and mix with a wooden spoon until well blended. Flatten the ball of dough to about 2 inches thick and wrap with plastic wrap. Flattening it helps it to cool faster. Refrigerate for 30 minutes. This step solidifies the butter, making it easier to roll out, and helps the cookies keep their shape and spread less while cooking than room temperature dough would.

Place chilled dough on a floured countertop and roll it to about ¼ inch thick. Cut with a skull-shaped cookie cutter or cut into shapes with a knife and place the cookies on a parchment-lined baking sheet. Bake 10–12 minutes or until golden on the edges. Cool for a couple minutes on the baking sheet, then transfer to wire cooling racks.

Porcelain Icing

1 cup powdered sugar
1 tablespoon + 1 teaspoon water

Mix ingredients together with a spoon until smooth. Spread icing on cooled cookies evenly using a butter knife, small rubber spatula, or the back of a spoon. Allow cookies to set at least 5 hours, until the icing is hard (24 hours is best). Use brand-new paintbrushes and food coloring to decorate the skulls as you'd like; you can also use edible cookie decorating pens.

Crafty Crafts

Ember Grant

THESE CRAFTS ARE ALL about celebrating "witchiness" by indulging one of the most popular witchy motifs—the potion bottle. Real "witch bottles" that are hundreds of years old have been found in Europe, and they are still created by witches today. And we all know that potions and brews are stereotypical of witchcraft culture—but I've never met a witch who didn't enjoy a decorative bottle, even if only to use it as a vase. For Samhain, we're going to make both. And there are plenty of ways to personalize them so you can get exactly what you need.

Witch Bottle

Historically speaking, these bottles were found buried in homes in England and New England, typically beneath fireplaces or in the home's foundation. Folklore from the times describes a bottle that would contain nails, pins, and even urine, and was intended to repel a curse directed at the bottle's owner. The urine provided the personalization needed to link the bottle to its owner; hair, fingernails, blood, or saliva could also be used. Of course, you don't have to include these items in your bottle—especially if you're making one that will be visible to others! While the classic witch bottle was intended to be hidden, modern practitioners of the craft often make ones that can be openly displayed—either for decoration, or for a specific spell. The choice is yours.

Materials

Glass bottle or jar with cork stopper ($3–$10)
Candle/wax for sealing
Items to put inside your bottle
> *Cost:* $10+
> *Time spent:* Less than an hour

Choose items to put in your bottle: salt, nails (bent and rusty are best), thorns, bent straight pins, a piece of fingernail or strand of hair, crystals or stones, bits of broken glass, dried herbs and flowers, a pendant or charm, shells, feathers, or anything else that appeals to you. Your purpose will help determine what you put in the bottle.

The most important things you need to decide first are 1) your bottle's purpose (for a spell or simply decorative) and 2) if you plan to display it or hide it. Obviously you'll want to display a decorative bottle; a spell bottle can be either hidden or left out where people can see it.

A decorative bottle might focus more on including colorful and interesting items—a variety of broken glass, for example, or multi-colored salts and stones. If you want your bottle to serve a specific magical purpose—protection, for example—you will need to choose stones, herbs, etc. that are appropriate for your needs.

The amount of each is up to you; it depends on bottle size and how you want it to look. For example, you could have lots of salt with other items sprinkled in, or just a few grains of coarse sea salt. You can certainly make a bottle that's both decorative and serves the purpose of protecting the bottle's maker (as well as home and family).

You can also make a combination bottle. Include a bit of hair from everyone in your family—including pets—and add protective herbs and stones; even include ones that promote good fortune.

Speak your own words over the bottle as you drip wax on the top to seal the cork. You can hide your bottle or display it.

Carve or press a sigil or symbol into the soft wax or tie a ribbon around it. Ideally, assemble your bottle on the full moon.

Decorative Potion Bottle or Jar

The apothecary look is popular Halloween decor these days—making labels and creative bottles to display on shelves. Here's an easy way to give an ordinary glass bottle or jar an ancient, creepy look.

Materials

Bottle or jar (prices vary)

Activ-Clay—air dry ($5–$15, depending on the package size)

Acrylic paint ($2–$3 per bottle)

Optional, for decoration: rubber stamps, embellishments such as beads or rhinestones, decorative ribbons or symbols

Cost: $10+

Time spent: at least 1 day, to allow drying time

Look for bottles and jars with interesting shapes. Some wines are sold in four-packs of single-serving containers—these miniature wine bottles make great potion bottles, even if they're plastic. Just make sure you have enough clay to completely cover the outside (and the bottom) as well as just inside the top opening.

Roll out the clay—the thinner the clay, the more likely it will crack, which may be a decorative feature you desire. Stick the clay to the bottle. Apply it in pieces and press them together with your fingers. Don't forget about the top, bottom, and inside the top, if applicable. Wide-mouth jars, for example, need to have a layer of clay just inside the opening. Once the entire jar or bottle is covered, you can get really creative for the next stage of the process.

While the clay is still soft, you can make impressions in it—write words or draw symbols and sigils into the clay using a toothpick. You can also use rubber stamps. On one small jar I made, I used a rubber stamp of a Celtic spiral and covered the jar with imprints,

but then rolled the jar around in my hands so the imprints would appear worn down. So many things can be used as imprints; in addition to rubber stamps, you can use fabric, stone, paper towels, jewelry, leaves (real or silk), tree bark, cookie cutters, decorative plates and ceramics, and more—basically, anything with a texture. You can use leaves here, too, to make impressions in the clay.

Or you can use a sponge to give it a rough look. I rolled one of my bottles in sand and this gave the clay an interesting texture.

You can also press a stone cabochon into the clay, or even encrust the entire piece, or parts of it, with beads, crystals, pearls, or even shells; just make sure the clay is thick enough to hold them. If any fall out later, you can glue them back on.

Try making shapes out of clay and press them to the clay that's already covering the bottle. I made a small ivy leaf (like the fall leaf project on page 290) for one of mine. You may want to roll some clay so it looks like a snake and wrap it around your bottle, or fashion a skull and crossbones shape.

Make it ornate and beautiful or old and creepy. Don't worry about making it look perfect—the more imperfect it appears, the better. You want to create something that looks old, ancient, and mysterious.

Because the clay shrinks a little as it dries, it may crack here and there during the drying process. Personally, I like that effect. It gives the bottle even more character. You can reduce the cracking by using a thicker layer (½ inch or more) of clay.

Let the bottle dry—it may take a day or two. Then you can paint it. You may want to stick with earthy tones—brown or gray—for a real stone look, but you don't have to. You can even use a sponge to further accent the "stony" appearance. Then, as with the fall leaf project, add a protective coat of Mod Podge.

When the paint is dry, you can still continue to add embellishments. Consider adding a label, or tie a string around the bottle's neck with an ornate pendant. These bottles can be used as a vase for real plants or you can make them into spooky decorative pieces by adding fake spiderwebs, or plastic bones or bugs. Depending on the size of the bottle, you can even use it as a taper candle-holder. However you use them, these bottles evoke mystery and magic.

A Crystal for Every Season: Obsidian

Charlie Rainbow Wolf

THIS IS THE LAST of the harvest festivals and marks the beginning of winter in the northern hemisphere. Where Beltane fires are fires of fertility, Samhain flames are cleansing and protective. Many believe that this is the time of year when the veil between the physical world and the spirit world is the thinnest. Some see it as the end of the old year and the beginning of the new one.

Divination is popular at Samhain because of the ethereal and enigmatic atmosphere that shrouds this time of year in mystery. When I was a kid we would peel an apple and throw the long rind over our left shoulder to see who we'd marry. In my case, it turned out to be correct! Tarot, playing cards, rune stones, tea leaves, and scrying are just some of the other ways divination might be used to pry into the darkness and glimpse the potential future.

It's possible to do divination with stones, too. I have a huge bag of crystals and stones; some are semi-precious and polished, while others are river rocks brought to me from friends who went on holiday, or interesting pebbles I picked up on my own travels. They all mean something. For example, malachite is an indication that some balance and tranquility are necessary, turquoise is the bringer of good luck, and rose quartz indicates the need for compassion and understanding or the possibility of a new romance or relationship.

Stones that are appropriate to use in your Samhain festivities include all colors of calcite, fire opal, all forms of jasper, jet, hematite, moldavite, and tektite. My favorite stone for Samhain is obsidian. It fascinates me because it's actually a form of volcanic glass and ranges in color from the palest translucent smokey gray to the darkest of black, with nearly every shade and hue in between.

Through the ages, obsidian has been used for both magical and practical purposes. It's been napped into knife blades and weapon points, polished for scrying, and cut into jewelry and other items. It's a 5 on the Mohs scale, putting it halfway between soft and hard. Obsidian, like glass, has no crystalline structure, so it's technically not a stone, but it's still valued by diviners, healers, carvers, and jewelers alike.

Apache Tear

These are small pebbles of obsidian, translucent and usually light gray or amber. Healers use them to balance the emotions and heal wounds from the past. Because of their name, these stones are sometimes used when dealing with grief or loss. Many energy workers use it as a stone of protection, while shamans and medicine people find it an asset when traveling between the realms.

Black Obsidian

The name says it all with this one. It's black as black can be, unless it's napped or carved thinly, when it will be more of a translucent brown. Healers work with black obsidian to get right to the heart of the matter. It's thought to be the strongest and most intense of all the obsidians. This makes it the most protective—but sometimes a bit overpowering—ally.

Mahogany Obsidian

This stone contains iron, giving it a rusty-red glow. It's not as harsh or intense as the black obsidian, and in healing it's used to bring past hurts to the surface, so they can be dealt with and released. In particular, it's a root chakra stone, and helps you to find your anchor and build your foundation in this life. If you're looking to leave the past behind and embark on a new path, mahogany obsidian is an excellent companion.

Peacock Obsidian and Rainbow Obsidian

Both of these stones have inclusions of blue, gold, green, red, orange, and indigo, and they are both solid allies for those who do pathworking and dreamwork, as well as for healers who delve into other realms for guidance and answers. It's a potent and protective stone, and in the hands of an experienced energy worker has been known to help novices open up to their authentic self and start to manifest their powers. Peacock obsidian displays its colors in random whorls and patterns, while rainbow obsidian is banded and orderly. They both work with all chakras, and encourage optimism and focus.

Sheen Obsidian

This stone reveals a deep golden aura emanating from its core when it catches the light just so. It's a popular stone with scryers, and like black obsidian, also allows you to cut through the chaff and reach the heart of the matter. It's not a healing stone as such; sheen obsidian is more a companion to open the pathway to healing, and then another stone is used for the actual energy balancing. Sheen obsidian has also been used to activate a person's latent talents and bring them to the surface so they can be explored.

Snowflake Obsidian

This stone is black with white crystals that look like snowflakes once it's been polished. It's a yin and yang stone, bringing balance and harmony to the physical and the subtle body. Use this stone when you're adapting to changes, so that you don't fall into any patterns of negative behavior or thinking. Keep one handy where you're working to help you to stay fresh and enthusiastic regarding the task at hand.

Samhain Divination Crystals

For this exercise you'll need a total of eight stones or crystals. I highly recommend you get natural tumbled stones, but it's entirely possible to do this with eight pebbles painted different colors:

White (or clear, if you are using natural stones) for purity

Red for passion, survival, life force

Orange for balance, creativity, focus

Yellow for confidence, self-esteem, a hunger for knowledge

Green for connecting to the earth and her children, for compassion and understanding

Blue for understanding and communication, for hearing others as well as your inner self

Indigo for intuition, insight, spiritual growth

Purple for enlightenment, movement (physical or metaphorical), spiritual understanding

(You'll also need an opaque bag in which to place the stones.)

Each of these stones has a meaning, as listed above. Quiet your mind, open your heart, and ask the stones what you need to know. When you feel ready, draw one out of your bag. Think about the keywords above as they apply to your current situation. Do you see what the universe is trying to tell you? If you're doing this as a group activity, ask others in your circle for their input on the situation, or maybe draw a stone for someone else to interpret. If you're working by yourself, jot a few thoughts down in a notebook to read later. You might be surprised at how recurring themes appear once you start probing around in your inner being!

Samhain Ritual for Departed Animals

Suzanne Ress

ALTHOUGH IT IS CUSTOMARY to remember and honor the spirits of dead human beings at Samhain, there is no reason why the spirits of our departed animal friends should be neglected. Our animal companions, so beloved whilst alive, rarely enjoy such long lifespans as we do, so, if you have or have had a pet, you will probably experience his or her death.

Honoring the spirits of our dead animal friends at Samhain, when the veil between this world and the afterworld thins and even opens up, is a way for us to accept death, even of those we love, as a natural, always recurring, part of the wheel of life.

Dumb suppers are a traditional way to celebrate Samhain, but this one has a new twist: it's a dumb supper for departed pets.

On the evening of October 31, members of the coven (and their guests, if desired) shall meet once the sun has set and the sky grown dark, at the abode of one of the members. This ceremony is to be centered on a full evening meal. Participants are invited to bring a sweet or savory dish of some sort to share with all, but only nine— no more and no less—dishes may be placed upon the table and served, so if there are to be more than nine participants, some may bring wine or mulled cider instead, and if there are to be fewer than nine, some participants will have to bring two or more dishes each. The number of dishes includes dessert, as well as any appetizer or tidbit, such as olives, nuts, and whatnot. The host, who is in charge of planning, must make certain that there are exactly nine dishes of food for the table.

Whilst preparing a dish for this ritual supper, you should remain in complete silence, from the moment you enter your kitchen until the dish, however simple or elaborate it is, is made. It may be more challenging to accomplish this if you choose something that has a long baking time—au gratin potatoes, for instance, which may need two hours in the oven—so choose carefully what and also when you will prepare your dumb supper contribution.

The host's table shall be laid with a black, indigo, or purple cloth, and thirteen white candles. The number of chairs around the table shall be the same as the number of participants times two.

Before beginning the supper, the dining area should be sanctified, either by drawing down the quarters and forming a sacred circle around the table and chairs, or by thoroughly censing the area with bay and rosemary incense.

Make sure that all cellular phones are switched off and left well outside the dining area.

In addition to the food, each participant is asked to bring a memento of his or her departed pet. This could be a photograph of the pet in life, a toy, a cushion or blanket the pet once drew comfort from, or some bits of the pet's fur or other shed matter kept in a silken bag or a decorated box. It could also be some article worn by the pet—a collar or sweater—or even the scrap of such an article. What is most important is that the memento embodies the spirit of the lost pet. These mementos will be placed like name cards on the chair to the left of each pet owner's place.

In case there are participants present who have never lost a pet, these people shall remember another now dead animal they have seen or known of, whether it be a wild bird flown against a glass window in a storm or a great buck struck down by a hunter's bullet.

Participants shall arrive at the host's home dressed entirely in black, wearing also black head coverings. The only jewelry permitted shall be of black iron and jet.

The doors and windows of the abode should be left unlocked and unlatched, and if the outside air temperature is not too cold, windows and doors should be left ajar, making it easier for animal spirits to enter. If the windows and doors are left open, take care to provide the candles with hurricane lamps.

The nine dishes are to be arranged on the table, the thirteen white candles lit, and all other lighting extinguished. Participants will all be seated around the table, each with an empty chair and place setting to his left.

The host shall be the last person to sit down at the table, and once she is seated, the ritual has begun. From this moment on there shall be complete silence.

In silence, the dishes shall be passed around the table widdershins, from person to person. Each participant shall first serve their own pet, placing some of each of the nine foodstuffs on the plate to their left, and then serve themselves and pass the dish onward to their right.

When every plate at the table has some of each of the nine foods upon it, the host shall raise a silent toast to the spirits of all the departed pets. Make sure that each pet's glass is full, too. After a sip of libation, the host may commence eating, and all present shall enjoy their dinners in silence.

Suggested dishes are special occasion foods that your departed pet may have enjoyed in life, or else foods that would have enticed your pet to the table, such as herring in cream sauce for a lost cat, roast pork ribs for a lost dog, a carrot salad with raisins for a departed horse, seeded rolls or crackers for a bird, etc. Since the human participants will be eating the same dishes, some modification may have to be made in the case of departed pet reptiles or amphibians.

Like a séance for departed spirits, the goal of the dumb supper is to attract and entice specific spirits that may be lingering near on this night when the afterworld is open to the living world.

As you eat, try to feel the presence of your departed friend beside you, by looking at and touching the memento if it helps. Meditate on the feeling of your pet's presence, as you remember it from your daily life. In some cases, such as a very old and decrepit animal who was euthanized out of kindness, or a pet that died very long ago, the pet's spirit may have wholly integrated into the afterworld, and will be impossible to contact. In such cases it is best to leave the spirit in peace and spend the time at the dumb supper silently reminiscing on his or her life and feeling thankful for the time you had together. In other cases, especially pertaining to violent, premature, or unexpected deaths, the animal's spirit may be lingering nearby, and, if enticed, will gladly make her presence known beside you at the table.

If your pet does show up, don't expect her to consume any of the food on her plate. This is a symbolic offering only.

When all participants have finished eating, the candles should be extinguished and the group will remain in silence and darkness for as long as the host deems necessary to allow for the arrival of any animal spirits who, perhaps frightened by the light, might now arrive in complete darkness.

When the host deems that a sufficient amount of time has passed—it may be ten minutes or it may be thirty—they shall carefully rise from the table, and, moving slowly, find the nearest light switch, preferably not a very bright light, and turn it on.

It is at this moment that attentive participants might see small, brisk shadows moving toward and out the windows and doors. Silence must be maintained for a little longer, however. If a sacred circle has been drawn, it must now be undrawn.

Finally, the host may break the silence, offering some words to the departed pets, along the lines of these:

"We offered to you, our dear animal companions, a place in our lives while you were living, and this evening we have welcomed you back again. Know that your presence was treasured by us, each one of you, and know that you will never be forgotten. May your spirits find peace and joy over the next few days as you wander. Feel free to visit with us again if you so desire."

The mementos, now having been made sacred, should be kept in a safe place by each one's owner. These can be used in future ceremonies over the course of the year, as talismans of the afterworld, adding power to spellcasting.

The food remaining on the departed animals' plates shall be disposed of sacredly, presenting it as an offering to the god of death, the Horned God, the Grim Reaper, what you will. It can be left outdoors for stray and wild animals, or given to living pets, or certain items can be composted to return to the earth from which they came.

Notes

Yule

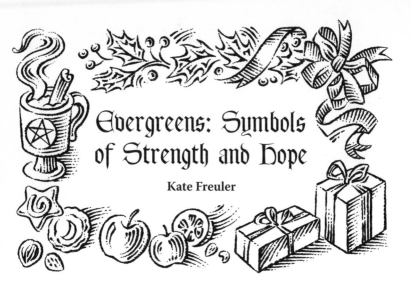

Evergreens: Symbols of Strength and Hope

Kate Freuler

YULE, OR THE WINTER Solstice, is the longest night of the year in the northern hemisphere. On this day, one side of the planet is plunged into darkness for more consecutive hours than at any other time on the yearly calendar. There's a fitting saying that says "the darkest hour is just before dawn"; this sabbat focuses not only on the total darkness, but on the return of the light that comes afterward. From now on, the days will begin to lengthen bit by bit as the earth slowly rotates, exposing us to more sunlight each day. Yule honors the return of the Sun God in his many names and guises. However, Yule also marks the beginning of the hardest and coldest months. Many gray, barren days are yet to be endured before spring graces us with its warmth. So while we celebrate the returning solar energies and steady restoration of the sun, at this time we also ask for fortitude and strength to face coming trials.

Symbolism of the Evergreen

One of the most well-known decorations for Yule has always been the evergreen. People bedeck their houses inside and out with the green boughs of pine, spruce, and holly, as well as all shapes and sizes of pine cones. Many folks do this for the sake of tradition, without realizing the meaning behind it. These plants are the only ones that stay green during this sometimes-treacherous season, and therefore are brought into the home as a reminder of strength, prosperity, fortitude, and joy. Evergreens remind us that we have the ability to love and hope in the coldest of times. This practice of decorating with evergreens has survived from pagan to modern times, which only reiterates the staying power of these mighty trees. Pine trees in magic are associated with protection, prosperity, and fertility. Add to this their reputation of resilience and strength and they're a wonderful ingredient to add to spells and crafts in the magical household, especially during the Winter Solstice when their hopeful energy is needed most.

Hope and Strength

There's more to the evergreen's connection with this sabbat than meets the eye. Sure, its greenery is festive, but if we look deeper into the nature of evergreen trees, how and why they flourish, and the ways they protect themselves from the climate, we can see that they have some admirable traits—humans could learn a few things from these trees! Conifers such as pine and fir stay green and lively throughout the entire winter. They withstand the adversity of freezing temperatures, shortened exposure to sun, and merciless ice storms. While leafy trees go dormant every fall and essentially sleep through the cold season, the resilient evergreen continues to tough it out despite what it's up against. Their innate strength and bravery, and how they have developed to protect themselves against the odds, is an admirable feat of evolution. Wise and resourceful, they store water and energy all year to ensure they can survive winter. In the midst of a stark, freezing landscape, these trees proudly stand out, bright green and thriving. Not to mention, they are amongst the oldest kind of trees on earth! They are certainly a symbol of eternal life and longevity.

Fertility

Many coniferous trees, such as cedar, fir, hemlock, and spruce, produce cones. Cones have a long history of being associated with fertility, which makes sense, as these interesting objects act as the tree's reproductive organs. The female cones, which are larger and thicker than the males, carry seeds inside their scales. The smaller, softer male cones have yellow pollen inside. The wind carries the pollen to the female cones, which fertilizes the seeds, and then the fertilized seeds drop to the ground to grow more trees. Thus continues the cycle of life. Fertility, magically speaking, doesn't always have to be physical: it can mean fruitfulness of ideas, career goals, prosperity, and many other things. For this reason, pine cones both male and female can be made into Yule crafts and decor to represent bright beginnings, rebirth, and fresh starts with the return of the sun. The female cones are usually larger and more durable for crafting purposes.

The Third Eye

The bottom of the pine cone displays a mandala-like pattern known as the Fibonacci Spiral or the Golden Ratio Spiral. This spiral is the same sacred geometry that's present throughout the natural world and exists in our third eye, in a tiny gland in our brain called the pineal gland. This pineal gland is shaped just like a pine cone, and is even named after it (pine-al). The pineal gland is associated with enlightenment and the spiritual awareness connected to the third eye chakra in the forehead. Pine cones can be used in spells or meditations to open the third eye or strengthen psychic senses.

Yule Spell Crafts with Evergreens

Gathering Evergreens

Go out into nature and find an evergreen tree. Spend a moment standing underneath it, feeling its strong presence and acquired wisdom. Think about how it has been rooted there for many years, possibly longer than you've been alive! Consider all it has witnessed beneath its boughs—the continuous life cycles of animals who have lived and died in its branches, the insects and birds it has provided a home for. Look at the ground and you will see twigs that have fallen, many with needles still intact. Preferably you can take a piece that is already shed upon the ground, but if not, ask the tree permission and unobtrusively clip only one piece. You may leave an offering of thanks beneath the tree, such as a handful of bird seed for the wildlife.

The Wreath

Wreaths of pine and other evergreens are a universal and popular decoration for the season, almost as prevalent as the Yule tree itself. The wreath, being round, symbolizes the unending cycle of life, death, and rebirth that is seen in the seasons and in our lives. Constructing a wreath out of evergreens is a long-standing tradition for many people of both religious and secular persuasions. It doesn't have to be a huge wreath for a front door; it can be a small charm, as explained below. The best trees for this craft are of the short needled variety, like spruce or fir.

This craft will help you create a decorative wreath of your own.

You Will Need:

A flexible length twig, 6 inches or longer. A fresh stick is best, as these bend easiest.

About 6 inches of green ribbon

Jingle bells and glitter (optional)

Take your length of pine and contemplate its strength, resilience, and protective powers. Also consider its associations with abundance for the coming season. Bend the twig into a circle shape and tie the ends together with the length of green ribbon. As you bind the circle by wrapping the ends with ribbon, imagine you're catching the magical energies of the plant inside the circle shape of the charm. Tie a bow and add bells, glitter, or other embellishments if you wish. Hang this somewhere in your home to attract strength, health, and abundance, and to act as a protection charm in hard and trying times.

Prosperity on the Doorstep

Find some boughs of evergreens with the needles still attached. Place some flat twigs underneath the doormat of your home to cleanse the energy of all who enter your residence. Also place three coins with the branches, to welcome prosperous energies into your house. Every time the boughs are walked over, their scent and their energy will be activated and brought in through your front door. You can also place a couple of pine needles in your wallet or purse to attract money and abundance.

Yule Potpourri

Make a seasonal potpourri to attract positivity as the sun returns to the sky. Potpourri is a mixture of dried herbs, plants, and sometimes oils, which is placed throughout the home to spread its fragrance. It can be left dry in decorative bowls, simmered with water on the stovetop, or heated in a special potpourri warmer to activate its scent. Pine has a wonderful, fresh aroma that, according to aromatherapy experts, can lift your spirits and boost your mood.

Ingredients
Dried cinnamon sticks or powder
Dried orange peels
A handful of pine or evergreen needles
Several drops of pine oil (optional)

On the night of the Winter Solstice, mix these items together in a bowl with your hands while envisioning yourself content and peaceful in your home. Imagine a sense of lighthearted warmth settling over you as you mix the potpourri. See the sun coming back into your life, and with it, bright blessings. Place the fragrant, dry mixture in bowls around the home to spread the pleasant scent, or put a handful in a pot of water and simmer on low heat on the stove. Make sure you do not let it boil dry. You can also place this herb mix around the base of Yule candles or sprinkle it around your property to attract positive new beginnings.

A Strengthening Brew

This brew is very simple in construction but powerful when created with intent. On the night of the solstice, place three handfuls of evergreen needles in a pot on the stove, with two cups of spring water, over high heat. Stand before it and envision how the evergreen stands tall, fierce, and alive against the gales and gusts of ice storms, never backing down. As the water starts to bubble, imagine it steaming with strength, willpower, and resilience. After the water boils, reduce to a simmer for five minutes and then remove from heat. Let it cool, strain it, and place it in a jar for up to two weeks. Add this strength brew to your bathwater when you're feeling drained by life, before facing a situation that requires fortitude, or when you need a general pick-me-up. You can add some to your bucket of water when mopping floors, or a very small amount to a load of laundry to infuse your clothing with the strength of the evergreen. You could also dab some on your skin over your heart or on your chakra points when your energy feels low.

Winter Solstice Divination

The spiral pattern on the base of the pine cone means it can be used as a point of meditation for the third eye. The third eye, located in the center of the forehead, is the energy center for psychic ability, intuition, and spirituality. This being the longest night of the year, it's theoretically a time associated with inner wisdom and dreams. Select a pine cone that has a distinct spiral formation on its base. Place it on your altar and put three drops of lavender oil on it. As you inhale the soothing scent of lavender, gaze at the spiral and make an energetic connection between your third eye chakra and the spiral, like of a beam of indigo light joining them.

Sleep with it under your pillow on the longest night of the year. Before falling asleep, ask for information or guidance for the coming season. Make sure you write your dreams down!

Cosmic Sway

Daniel Pharr

THE MIDPOINT OF THE winter season and shortest day of the year, Yule is seldom the coldest of winter days, even though reason would suggest that shorter days would also be colder days. The coldest days of winter are usually in January, or even in February after Imbolc, the first day of spring. However, this is the time of year when folks hope for snow. The Yule celebration always seems perfect when giant snowflakes are gently falling on a windless moonlit night. A fire is a must on this high holiday, as it symbolizes the rebirth of the Sun, although many find an indoor fire more appropriate for the more intimate gathering that usually happens on the solstice. Dinner and the exchange of gifts are simply easier in the warmth of dry indoors.

Scorpio Moon

The Scorpio Moon will arrive at 7:57 the morning of December 21 and hang out for two days, but will go void after just a day and a half, on the twenty-second at 11:27 p.m. During the time that the Moon is in Scorpio, emotions may feel intense and prove to be a challenge. Envy and avarice will be on the rise, especially in groups, making this a less-than-favorable time to exchange gifts. Sexual energy will be running with little regard for subtlety, which will further add fuel to the covetousness already present. Unless big drama is the desire, keep the gathering intimate.

Yule Log

Light the yule log with coals saved from last year's log. Oak is the traditional Yule wood for the ritual fire, but as always, use what can be found. Draw a figure of an old woman on the new log with chalk, or by other means, and burn it to ashes as a metaphor for the death and rebirth of the Goddess. Make the fire's complete consumption of the wise crone depiction a group priority and ask for volunteers to take turns holding a vigil on the pyre. The total destruction of the figure bodes well for the total avoidance of misfortune in the coming year. Play games and enjoy the celebration while she burns.

Make a wassail for the celebration. Always appropriate for the Yule feast are soup and bread, and that which is gathered from nature, such as nuts, meats, and apples. Recent harvest stores will provide the ingredients for pies and cakes, cheeses, anything roasted, and eggnog, mulled wine, or mead to wash it all down.

The Yule candle burns all night. The flame is sacred to the Goddess and was kept burning all year long by the ancient Druids, and, likewise, secretly by the nuns of Glastonbury to honor the Goddess, even though the flame had been ordered to be extinguished by the Church. Be sure to place it in the confines of something non-combustible that cannot be inadvertently tipped or covered by dancing dogs or curious kitties.

Christmas

Once the Moon fully enters Sagittarius at 11:34 a.m. on December 23, a more frisky energy will arrive, although those more sensitive to her energies might feel the Moon's movement to void-of-course late on the twenty-second. This Sagittarius Moon will be more conducive to fun and frolic. Take this opportunity to gather with friends and read the tarot or cast the stones, for this Moon will be all about giving advice. Folks will be interested in travel, foreign and domestic, and any outdoor activities, if anyone needs gift ideas. This playful Moon will carry through until Christmas morning at 6:18 a.m., when the Moon goes void and makes its journey out of Sagittarius and into stern and ordered Capricorn. If Christmas celebrations are planned, Christmas Eve might be better suited, especially if the celebrations will extend into the wee hours of the twenty-fifth. Christmas morning will best experienced drinking coffee and lazing in pajamas, while the afternoon, especially after 4:45 p.m. when Capricorn imposes its rules, will be best utilized cleaning up from the night before. If everyone gets involved, quick work will be made of it.

Dark Christmas Moon

The Capricorn dark Moon will arrive Christmas night, but not fully culminate until twelve minutes after midnight on the twenty-sixth. The black night will provide the perfect opportunity to become one with the lunar energies and have some downtime. Take a "me" day. The twenty-sixth is in the middle of the week, so if work is a must, try to avoid taking on any new projects until the Aquarius Moon arrives on the twenty-eighth.

New Year

The conventional New Year's Eve will be consumed under a pleasant Pisces Moon coming into play at 10:41 p.m. on December 30. Connection will be the catchphrase of this holiday. Increased approachability and receptivity will bring people closer more quickly, allowing for less awkwardness when the time arrives for the midnight kiss. The body will also be more greatly affected by cocktails and the like.

Full Moon

The Leo Full Moon will arrive at 2:21 p.m. on January 10 but will not last long, as the Moon will void its course four hours later at

6:58 p.m. The sun will set at 4:47 p.m., leaving a very short opportunity for a Full Moon ritual before the energies shift into unpredictability. If magical business is to be done during the Full Moon ritual, plan ahead to take advantage of the Leo influence.

Dark Moon

The dark Aquarius Moon at 4:21 p.m. on January 24 will provide an excellent opportunity for time alone and inner exploration, although it is not so much a time for introspection and growth as it is for planning, the analysis of past interactions, and understanding the now and how it might lead to the future. Knowledge is power, as they say, and this Moon will help to uncover knowledge hidden by previous circumstance. A personal retreat for a day or even a long weekend could do wonders.

Gardening

Plenty of food has been stored from the harvests, and the gardens are just now giving up their last grip on their bounty. Black radish, leeks, kale, carrots, broccoli, and Brussels sprouts are finishing the season.

Work the ground. Pull the weeds and grass that took root during the last season. Remove rotting and finished plants. Burn the weeds, grass, and diseased plants. Compost all heathy organic matter. Cover the garden and let it hibernate. Seeds that dropped will freeze over the winter and crack open. These will become volunteers next spring and sprout as soon as the earth is warm again. Now the garden gets time to rest after preparation for the next growing season.

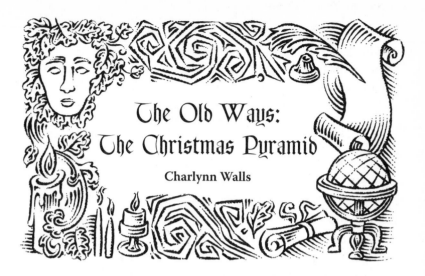

The Old Ways: The Christmas Pyramid

Charlynn Walls

I HAVE VERY DISTINCT memories of the Christmas/Yule season when I was a child. Many of my family members had been stationed in Germany at some point in their military careers, so we incorporated many customs and foods that were traditional in that part of the world. However, my fondest memories are of watching the small flickering lights from the candles that sat ensconced in a fantastically carved wooden pyramid. The carved figures on the carousel would spin as the heat rose to turn the leaves of the fan at the top of the structure. This was the Weihnachtspyramiden (Grimm 1970), or Christmas Pyramid. It captured my imagination and provided hours of entertainment on those long evenings leading up to Yule.

Yule, or the Winter Solstice, is the shortest day and longest night. It marks the return of the sun as the days begin to get longer from this point forward. Yule is the coldest and darkest time of the year. The festivities often utilize candles or other means of illumination as sympathetic forms of magic that beckon the return of the sun, which gives its life-bringing warmth back to the earth.

Evergreens and Light

Yule is intrinsically linked with the well-known Christmas tree. It seems that everywhere there is the image of twinkling lights and stings of popcorn or tinsel draped in the branches of the evergreen tree with packages of all shapes and sizes nestled at its base. Evergreen boughs and trees were brought into the homes during the Yule season because they symbolized everlasting life. These trees were able to survive harsh conditions and not only lived but thrived. Their use can be traced back to Greek and Roman origins when bay was hung throughout homes to entice Apollo to continue his chariot ride through the heavens. The use of the Christmas tree as we know it is thought to have begun in Germany during the eighth century. There are conflicting accounts of how the tree became an integral part of the Christmas holiday, but it is thought that they were brought into the homes to help convert Pagans to Christianity.

Candles were added to the trees to provide light and decoration during the sixteenth century in Germany. The story goes that Martin Luther was out walking through the woods one day. He caught the glittering light shining from the ice crystals on a pine tree. He considered the sight inspiring and he sought to recreate that for his family so that they could experience it as well. He brought a tree indoors and wired candles to the tree. The illumination that the candles produced could also be seen to correspond to the returning light of the sun. The concept took root and soon spread across the world. However, the cost of having a tree with lights was an extravagance that most common folk could not afford.

German Origins

The Christmas Pyramid was first created in the Ore Mountains of Germany (History.com Editors 2009). These wooden decorations were a low-cost substitute for a Christmas tree. They were built to resemble a tree in shape. The pyramids were anywhere from one to five tiers high. The base, the lowest tier, was constructed with four to eight spaces for candle holders built in. The heat generated from the candles would rise, turning the leaves of the fan-like structure at the top. The fan began to spin, which rotated the carved scenes within the middle tiers.

These are popular items in Germany and in some parts of the United States where German immigrants settled. People like them due to their intricate scenes and convenient size, since they take up minimal space compared to a tree. They are also affordable.

Celebrating Yule: A Pyramid All Your Own

Not everyone has the space for a tree during the holiday season. The traditional Christmas pyramids are a great alternative if you are short on space. They are festive, easily stored, and bring together the essence of a tree and the light of the candles. It provides a festive touch that can fill your home with warmth and cheer. The great part about these is that they come in a variety of sizes and have motifs other than the traditional Christmas nativity. They can include depictions of the forest, snowmen, and even scenes right out of the Nutcracker Suite.

As Altar Decoration

You can include your pyramid on your Yule altar. The smaller pyramids are ones that have a minimum of four candles at the base, which turn the propeller on top. You can easily coordinate your candle colors to represent the four elements: earth, air, fire, and water. This can make a unique addition to your Yule festivities.

References

Grimm, Donna. "What Are Weihnachtspyramide?" Belznickle BlogSpot. http://belsnickle.blogspot.com/2012/11/what-are-weihnachteaspoon yramide.html. (no longer available)

History.com Editors. "History of Christmas Trees." History.com. Published 2009. https://www.history.com/topics/christmas/history-of-christmas-trees.

Morrison, Dorothy. *Yule: A Celebration of Light & Warmth*. St. Paul, MN: Lewellyn Publications, 2000.

McCoy, Edain. *The Sabbats: A New Approach to Living the Old Ways*. St. Paul, MN: Lewellyn Publications, 1994.

Morgan, Sheena. *The Wicca Book of Days*. London, England: Vega, 2002.

Nichols, Mike. *The Witches' Sabbats*. Albany, CA: Acorn Guild Press, 2005.

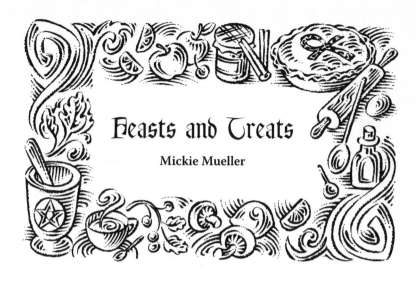

Feasts and Treats

Mickie Mueller

YULE IS A MAGICAL time of the year. We all have family favorites that we're used to enjoying during the longest days of winter; root vegetables like potatoes, yams, and onions are prominent. We love dishes that are easy to serve to a large group and that celebrate and comfort simultaneously. In Scandinavia they call this quality of coziness and contentment *hygge* (pronounced hoo-gah) and it includes enjoyment of comfy clothing, sparkling candles, tea, love and fellowship, and delicious, warming foods.

Creamy Toasted Cranberry and Bacon Baguettes

I'm not going to lie: this will ruin your diet, but it's totally worth it. It's just one day a year, or two if you have leftovers, which you probably won't. Okay, yes, you could use light or vegan cream cheese, margarine or coconut butter instead of butter, turkey or vegan bacon, or you can even make this using gluten-free bread if you prefer; it would still be darned good. I do like to use healthier versions of ingredients when I can, but every now and then it's nice to splurge.

Prep time: 10 minutes
Cooking time: 30 minutes
Servings: 16–26 slices, depending on the size of your bread

½ package of bacon (you may substitute turkey bacon or vegan
    bacon)
8 tablespoons (1 stick) soft butter
2 (8-ounce) packages cream cheese, softened
¼ cup dried cranberries, chopped
1 bunch chives, chopped
1 small red onion, finely chopped
2 loaves of baguette bread, sliced about a ½ inch thick

Preheat oven to 350° F (177° C). Fry bacon in a skillet until crisp,
and drain the slices on a paper towel. Once cool enough to handle,
chop the bacon into very small pieces. Mix the butter and cream
cheese together until well blended. Mix in the bacon, cranberries,
chives, and onion. You can also mix this topping up a few days in
advance. Spread some of the mixture on top of each slice of bread
and arrange on a parchment-lined baking sheet. Bake for 10 minutes and serve hot.

Swedish Meatballs in Mushroom Gravy with Noodles

This is the kind of a dish that's great for company, because you can
keep it warm in a slow cooker or electric pressure cooker. I make
a double batch of the gravy and divide between two slow cookers,
serving meatballs in one and pre-made veggie meatballs in the
other, so that all my guests are happy. I haven't mastered homemade
veggie burgers or meatballs yet, but there are many good pre-made
frozen brands out there, as well as plenty of recipe options if you
want to give it a go. The spices in the meatballs are traditional, although I've changed up the gravy somewhat by making it with
mushrooms. It's creamiest made with butter and half and half, but
if you can't tolerate dairy, you can substitute coconut oil and your
favorite dairy substitute.

Prep time: 15 minutes
Cooking time: 20 minutes
Servings: 6

Meatballs

4 tablespoons your choice of butter or olive oil, divided
⅓ cup minced red onion
2 garlic cloves, minced
¾ teaspoon ground allspice
¼ teaspoon nutmeg
⅛ teaspoon ginger
½ teaspoon salt
½ teaspoon ground white pepper
½ cup milk or dairy-free substitute like
coconut milk or unsweetened soy milk
1 teaspoon Worcestershire sauce
1 cup breadcrumbs, regular or gluten-free
¾ pound lean ground beef
½ pound lean ground pork
2 eggs

Heat 2 tablespoons butter or olive oil in a skillet over medium heat. Add onion, garlic, allspice, nutmeg, ginger, salt and pepper, and sauté about 5 minutes. Add milk and Worcestershire sauce and bring to a simmer. Pour the mixture into a large bowl with the breadcrumbs and mix until it becomes a thick paste. Allow it to cool. Add beef, pork, and eggs and mix with clean hands until well blended.

Form small meatballs about the size of walnuts and brown in a skillet with a couple tablespoons of olive oil or butter, turning as needed to brown all sides. You can set them aside in a covered oven-proof dish and place in the oven on warm while you make the gravy.

Mushroom Gravy

3 tablespoons butter, divided
1½ cups sliced mushrooms, white button or crimini
2 tablespoons flour (or gluten-free flour mix)

1½ cups mushroom broth
1 teaspoon Worcestershire sauce (or vegan Worcestershire)
1 teaspoon white pepper
¼ cup half and half (or substitute soy milk or coconut milk)
1 teaspoon salt
Fresh parsley, chopped for garnish

Melt 2 tablespoons butter in a large skillet and sauté mushrooms over medium heat. Add one more tablespoon butter, melt, then sprinkle in flour, salt, and pepper. Stir while cooking for 2–3 minutes. Whisk in the mushroom broth and Worcestershire and continue stirring as it comes to a simmer. Add the half and half. You can add the meatballs to the skillet and simmer for 10 minutes, then serve. Or, alternatively, add both the meatballs and gravy to a slow cooker and set it on low, cover, and cook about 1–2 hours. Serve over egg noodles, gluten-free noodles, or spaetzle. Garnish with chopped parsley.

Oven-Roasted Root Vegetables

This is a pretty easy side dish; the oven does most of the work, as the roasting really brings out the flavors of these vegetables. I've made variations on this for years. Last Yule my daughter made it with the addition of radishes. I've never used them for anything but cold dishes, but roasted they have a different flavor, and it's quite delicious!

   Prep time: 10 minutes
   Cooking time: 35–40 minutes
   Servings: 6

3–4 medium-sized potatoes
2 large sweet potatoes
1 large red onion
1 large turnip
2 parsnips
2 carrots

6 ounce bag of radishes
2 tablespoons olive oil
Salt and pepper to taste
2 garlic cloves, minced
2 tablespoons fresh rosemary

Preheat oven 425° F (220° C). Peel the carrots, parsnips, turnip, and any other veggies that you prefer peeled. I usually don't peel my potatoes or sweet potatoes, but you can if you wish. Scrub any vegetables you choose not to peel. Cut all the vegetables up into approximately 1-inch diameter chunks. Radishes just need to be cut in half.

Put all the veggies in a large bowl. Drizzle with olive oil and sprinkle with salt, pepper, rosemary, and garlic. Toss until thoroughly mixed and coated. Roast until tender, about 35–40 minutes. Remove from oven and toss halfway through cooking.

Almond Butter Bonbons

It's so nice to have something sweet at the end of a warming and comforting meal, but just because its candy doesn't mean it has to be junk food. Almonds, dark chocolate, coconut, and honey are all considered superfoods, so even though these bonbons are definitely an indulgence, they are also nutrient-rich to help your body feel good, as well as your spirit. These are not difficult to make and are better than store-bought because they're made with love, and you actually know what's in them.

Prep time: 10 minutes
Inactive: 30 minutes
Cooking time: 1–2 minutes
Servings: about 16 bonbons

⅓ cup almond butter
¼ cup honey
Pinch of salt
½ cup finely ground almond flour

1 cup dark chocolate chips or chopped chocolate
1 teaspoon coconut oil
1–2 tablespoons coarse sea salt
Shaved almonds

In a medium-sized bowl, mix the almond butter with the honey and a pinch of salt. Using a wooden spoon, start adding the almond flour gradually, a spoonful at a time, until it forms a stiff dough. Using a tablespoon, scoop up a bit of the dough and roll it into a ball about 1 inch in diameter, then place it on a wax paper-lined baking sheet. Continue until all of the dough is rolled into relatively uniform-sized balls. Chill them in the freezer for 30 minutes to set.

Melt chocolate chips and coconut oil in a microwaveable dish for about 1 minute. Mix the chocolate chunks with a spoon, even if they appear not to be fully melted; stirring them will often do the trick. Use a toothpick to dip each almond butter ball in the chocolate, turning to coat. Then return to the baking sheet. Immediately sprinkle with a pinch of coarse salt and top with a few shaved almond pieces. Repeat with all the bonbons. Keep them in the refrigerator until serving.

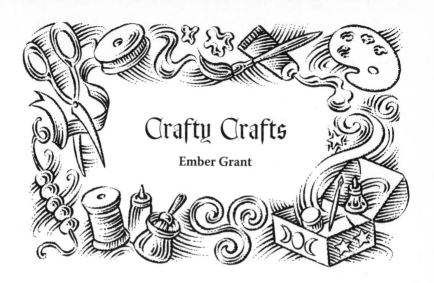

Crafty Crafts

Ember Grant

AT THE WINTER SOLSTICE we celebrate the power of renewal, as the light increases and days begin to grow longer. Honoring seasonal rhythms has been important throughout human history and this particular time of year is believed by many scholars to be one of the roots of the Christmas holiday.

20-Point Paper Star

Since the star is one of the central symbols of this holiday—the sun is a star and we welcome the sun at Winter Solstice—here's an easy paper-craft with some seasonal symbolism. This star can be used as a tree-topper or altar decoration.

In addition, this star has special significance if you consider the concept of sacred geometry. Geometrically speaking, this shape is referred to as the *great stellated dodecahedron*. It's a symmetrical design, a polyhedron (*polyhedra* means many faces) that consists of twelve pentagram (five-sided) faces.

Think of a flat pentagram shape, the center of the five-pointed star. A triangle grows from each of the five faces to create this star shape. This is called stellation. Kepler was first apply this idea to polyhedra, extending the planes of each face to form a star shape, like the one we're making here. There's both a larger and smaller version; we're making the larger one—essentially, a twenty-pointed star.

The base of this star consists of those twelve pentagrams (center of the star); then we're going to attach triangles to each pentagram. This central object is called a dodecahedron—twelve faces, thirty edges, twenty vertices. Those vertices will be the points of the star. The Pythagoreans called it "the sphere of the twelve pentagons" and believed this shape to be the "construction which God used for embroidering the constellations on the whole heaven" (Lundy 2010, 142).

Materials

Cardstock paper—greeting cards and/or scrapbook paper ($3–5)
Scissors
Glue ($2–$3)
    Cost: $5+
    Time spent: about 2–3 hours

You can use old greeting cards or thick scrapbook paper; just make sure the paper is thick enough to hold up—regular paper is too thin. Old greeting cards work well, since you end up with an interesting patchwork design. Plus, this is a great way to recycle old cards or small pieces of craft paper. You can also use plain cardstock and paint the completed star or decorate it with glitter.

There are two main designs you'll need to trace onto sturdy paper. The center will be folded and glued so you can attach the points. The other will be your model for tracing onto the paper you'll use as star points. It's important that your model for the points is sturdy enough to trace around since you'll be doing it twenty times.

First, make the center. Photocopy the base shape (Figure 1) onto plain cardstock paper; increase the size so the lines of the triangles are 2 inches long. Cut out the entire shape, fold it along the lines, and glue it together using the tabs. Next, you'll make the twenty star points. Photocopy the model shape (Figure 2) and enlarge it so the bottom line of each triangle is two inches long. Cut out the shape. You will trace this shape onto twenty cards or other pieces of sturdy paper. Using your model shape as a guide, you'll have to draw on the folding lines yourself. This can easily be done using a ruler. Cut out each star point, fold along the lines, and glue them together on the tabs. Then, when all twenty points are done, carefully attach each one to the base. The triangle shape on the bottom of each star point should line up with the triangle shapes on the base.

Allow to dry completely. When it's ready to display, it will sit up by itself or you can make a hole at one of the joints using a wooden skewer, and then glue the star to a stick. This will enable you to either attach it to a tree top or add it to a floral arrangement.

Figure 1 (for best results, scan these patterns, enlarge the images, and then print larger copies for more accessible tracing)

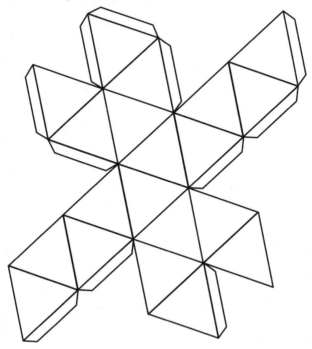

Figure 2

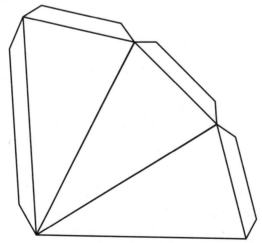

Fresh Fruit Centerpiece

Orange and cranberry is a wonderful combination for aroma, taste, and visual decoration. This fresh fruit centerpiece is simple and inexpensive. The bright red cranberries accented with orange slices make a colorful and natural sparkling centerpiece for your holiday table.

Cranberries are one of only three fruits that are native to North America and were introduced to settlers by the Native Americans in the northeast. We've come to associate cranberries with fall and winter holidays; their bright red color makes them a perfect foundation for this project.

There are many folktales about why oranges are associated with Christmas and the winter holidays. In fact, many families have a tradition of putting oranges in stockings as gifts. One story tells of the original St. Nicholas giving bags of gold to a poor man so his daughters could have dowries; the orange is said to be a symbol of this generous gesture. Other stories tell of the scarcity of fruits and vegetables during the Great Depression and that to receive an orange was a rare and special gift. Admittedly, if we consider it today, it's wonderful that in the middle of winter we can have access to such a bright, cheerful, sunny, and healthy fruit. Think about it—they come from places that receive a lot of sun! They are perfect symbols of light and good health. The scent of citrus is uplifting and welcome during the long winter months. I have strong associations with this custom as well. As a child, our high school's agricultural students sold fruit as a fundraiser at this time of year, and we always bought a box of oranges, apples, and grapefruit—the aroma filled our house. I have come to associate the smell of oranges with the Yuletide season ever since.

Materials

1 orange (price varies)
1 bag of fresh cranberries ($2–$3 per bag)
Glass jar large enough to hold all the cranberries (price varies)

Small floating candle or tea light candle (price varies)

Cost: about $10

Time spent: 20 minutes

This arrangement looks best in a tall jar, but any glass container will work, as long as it's taller than it is wide. Pick through the cranberries to remove any unsightly ones, then dump them into the glass container. Fill the container with water. Slice the orange. Slip the orange slices along the inside of the glass.

It's up to you how full you'd like your centerpiece, but there should be enough fruit so it doesn't move around too much. The water just fills in the spaces and keeps the fruit moist. Since cran-

berries float, you need to fill the jar with the berries in order for the oranges to stay in place. Place a floating candle or tea light on top of the arrangement, among the cranberries. The candle should actually be sitting in only a small amount of water.

Variations: You can use lemons and limes in addition to oranges, or instead of them. You can also make several smaller versions of this design in drinking glasses and scatter them around the house. If you want to use a bowl for this arrangement you can, but it will have a different appearance. Since cranberries float, you can simply allow the fruit—berries and orange slices—to float in a bowl alongside the candle or candles. Feel free to experiment with a variety of designs.

After you're done using the centerpiece, you can dry the orange slices and use them in crafts, or leave both the oranges and berries outside as an offering. You can string the cranberries, too, and decorate a tree outside to feed the birds and squirrels.

Reference

Lundy, Miranda, Daud Sutton, John Martineau, Anthony Ashton, Jason Martineau. *Quadrivium: The Four Classical Liberal Arts of Number, Geometry, Music, & Cosmology*. Glastonbury, UK: Woden Books, 2010.

A Crystal for Every Season: Quartz

Charlie Rainbow Wolf

YULE WRAPS UP THE sabbats for 2019. It's the time when the Oak King wrestles with the Holly King to see who will rule—but as we know, the Oak King always wins this one! The actual festival lasts from midwinter's day on December 21 through January 2, although mostly it's celebrated around the solstice. This is the longest night; the days start to lengthen from now on, as once again the wheel turns. It's the time of year when the northern hemisphere celebrates the return of the light.

Yule stones include—but aren't limited to—azurite, bloodstone, garnet, ruby, sapphire, sugilite, and my favorite, clear quartz. It reminds me of ice and snow. When meditating with quartz, I easily get drawn into its chasms and chambers and crystalline structure. I find it a good dream stone, one that helps me wander through my mind uninhibited.

Quartz comes in so many different shapes, sizes, terminations, and patterns that there's something there for everyone, each stone as different and unique as you are. It's readily available and often inexpensive. It's one of the most abundant minerals on earth. Most of the sand on the beaches in the world is made up of silicon dioxide—quartz.

Quartz is useful in manufacturing because it's piezoelectric, meaning that it creates a voltage when you apply mechanical pressure onto it. This is why it's used in computers, watches, and other electronics; quartz's frequency is known and it's predictable. It's a 7 on the Mohs scale, so it's pretty tough. In addition to its use in electronics, it's also valuable as as an abrasive (think sandpaper), in recreation (baseball diamonds and play sand), and as a gemstone.

It comes in many forms: amethyst, bloodstone, carnelian, citrine, jasper, and more. In healing, clear quartz is valuable because it is a conductor of energy. It magnifies and focuses what you pour into it, making it versatile and adaptable. The different colors influence the energy of the stone, as well as its shape and inclusions.

There's a lot of New Age hype around quartz crystals, so be careful you don't get sucked in. Go with what resonates with you, no matter what you're being told. I can't stress enough that the fundamental ingredient in any endeavor is your intent, not what someone else believes. Having said that, there are some things that feel right to me and I'm happy to share them below in case they're what you need to get started.

Crystal Cluster

In her book *Crystal Enlightenment*, Katrina Raphaell describes quartz clusters as "individual crystals who all live together in harmony and peace" (Raphaell 1985). This is an excellent Yule stone, because this is traditionally the time for the proverbial "peace on earth and goodwill toward men." Place the cluster in the center of your Yule altar to keep the energies bright and pure, or use it in a table centerpiece to create harmony and togetherness during your activities.

Double Termination

I've long been fascinated by DTs and use them often in my copper wand-making. These are stones that have naturally formed with a point at each end, so they have a mutual reception of energy, the proverbial give and take. In a wand, they shoot energy from the cosmos down the wand, to me, and then launch my energy up the wand to the cosmos. When one stone is used by two people, a bridge of energy is formed. Telepathy is enhanced when using a DT, as is healing, understanding, and cooperation.

Rainbow Quartz

This is a clear quartz stone that has a rainbow inclusion. The prismatic reflection is created because the stone has been damaged in some way. The lesson I've found it to teach is that no one is perfect. Trying times are chances to shine, to develop color and personality. Grace is born through learning to cope with trials and overcome inhibitions. I've found rainbow quartz to be a valuable talisman to carry as a reminder that something doesn't have to be flawless to be beautiful.

Phantom Crystals

Next on my list of must-have stones is a quartz phantom. This is a stone within a stone, marking the stone's growth patterns. The ghostly inclusions are usually white, but they may be a different color, depending on what the inclusion is. For me, a true phantom mimics the shape of the outer stone, and reaffirms that not everything is the same on the inside as it is on the outside. Phantoms make pretty snowscape decorations, but they are much more than that. They're keys to help you unlock your inner secrets so you can know your authentic self and appreciate your true value.

Crystal Balls and Spheres

I couldn't write an article on crystals without including the good ol' crystal ball! Of course this is a stereotype, but it's still worth exploring. Be mindful if you choose to go down this road; not everything that is sold as a crystal ball is actually stone; much of what's on the market now is glass. I'm not knocking that at all, but it's been my experience that quartz crystal balls seem much more alive. Select your sphere carefully. Clear crystal is pricey and doesn't necessarily work any better than stone that has milky inclusions or other marks.

My favorite crystal ball is nowhere near clear, but it seems to change color ever so slightly with the weather and with my mood, and that's why I like it. Every time I gaze at the dings and clouds in it, I see something new. A fun group activity when you're working with a sphere is to pass it around and ask people to share what they see in it. Even if your work is solitary, you might want to try this. Gaze into the stone at different times during your Yule activities, and jot down your thoughts in a journal. Think of it as your own seasonal "snow globe." What images lie waiting for you in its patterns?

Reference

Raphaell, Katrina. *Crystal Enlightenment: The Transforming Properties of Crystals and Healing Stones 110. Vol 1*. Santa Fe, NM: Aurora Press, 1985.

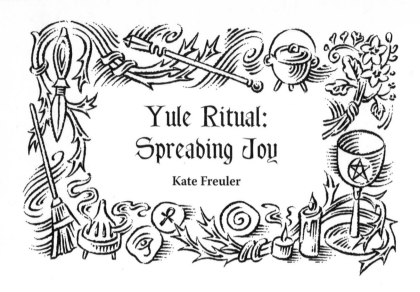

Yule Ritual: Spreading Joy

Kate Freuler

ONE OF THE MOST well-known things about Yule is that it's a time of giving. People share gifts, donate food and toys to good causes, and volunteer their time to charities. The exact origins of gift-giving at Yule are unclear, but the practice goes back centuries to a time when humble homemade presents were treasured and goodwill was spread around the community by neighbors and families. The intention that still faithfully lies at the heart of the "true meaning of the holidays" are these acts goodwill and love. Unfortunately, nowadays this generous spirit can seem hard to find in the sea of corporate greed and commercialism. Originally, people were kinder and more helpful to one another on this holiday, perhaps because they all needed community support throughout the coming hard times of winter in order to survive. This goodwill to others is not completely lost on us, even though it can seem that way during the stress and hectic nature of the holidays. The desire to spread goodness during Yuletide is still there underneath it all. We can tap into that joy and spread it around.

The following ritual can be done alone or with a group. It's a ceremony that is meant to spread love, joy, and blessings throughout your neighborhood, and is performed on the night of the Winter Solstice.

Materials

Cinnamon sticks

Various colors of biodegradable cotton thread. Choose your thread based on the meaning of the colors. A good place to start is pink for love and neighborliness. White is an all-purpose color and can be imbued with any energy. Try black for protection, green for prosperity, orange for joy, and blue for peace.

Evergreen sticks or long pine needles

Pencil

You and your circle are going to construct simple charms from the above items. The cinnamon sticks symbolize prosperity and abundance. The evergreen is present as protection. The cotton thread color is selected based on what your intent is for each of the charms. Once created, these little charms make simple triple-powered amulets to bless your community and spread good tidings in the true giving spirit of Yule.

I suggest getting sufficient materials for each participant to make at least one charm. If you're alone, you can make as many as you'd like. Since you're going to be placing these charms outside around your neighborhood, they're intentionally plain looking and inconspicuous because we don't want them to draw suspicious attention or be misinterpreted as littering. These charms, being small and natural, will most likely go unnoticed and then disintegrate throughout the cold months, passing their energy into the earth.

Divvy up the supplies and cut the required lengths of thread. Choose one person to start. They are to hold up a cinnamon stick and state something they wish to bestow upon the neighborhood, community, city, or town. Some examples of good tiding statements for community are "Safety for the children who live here," "Good vibes between neighbors," or "Protection against crime." Depending on how well you know your neighbors and community, there may be someone or something in particular that needs help or attention. Maybe you live near a hospital that would benefit from more volunteers, or a school that could use better funding. Otherwise, general well wishes are always great.

After stating the intention of the charm, the participant uses the pencil to draw a simple sun upon the cinnamon stick. Then, they bind some pine to the cinnamon with a piece of thread, the color of which matches their intent, by wrapping them together. They will knot the thread three times, and with each knot, all members of the ceremony will chant together.

On the first knot, the whole group says in unison: "We (I) see the light in the darkness."

On the second knot everyone says: "We (I) invite the light into our circle."

On the third knot say: "We (I) spread the light to others."

Continue clockwise to the next person in the circle, until everyone has stated an intention, drawn a sun, and tied a charm together. The group repeats the above chant each time a charm is knotted.

After all the charms are completed, place them in the center of your circle of people, or on your altar if you are alone. Hold hands and say together:

> *"We welcome the sun with strength and love*
> *Inside our hearts it glows*
> *Our love and joy will keep us warm*
> *And spread to all we know."*

You will then go around the neighborhood as a group on the night of the solstice, placing the charms randomly throughout the area you live in. Obviously, if it isn't safe to wander your neighborhood after dark, do this ritual in the daylight instead. If you live in an urban area, you can place the charms in any nook or cranny among the buildings. In suburbia, tuck them into a shrub or in the snow on the edge your neighbors' lawns—don't go prowling onto their property, just stick to the sidewalk. In a rural setting, you can place them anywhere along the path or road you choose to walk down. It's important to do this with intent, keeping a feeling of joy and hope in your hearts. You may wish to drink travel mugs of cocoa or cider to keep warm and cozy.

One thing you can do to bring some merry spirit into the trip is sing carols. The word *carol* means a song of praise or joy. Caroling dates back far before Christianity. You can sing songs you all know that have a message of happiness or peace. Modern carols are fine if that is what makes you feel good. If you know joyful Pagan songs, sing those. If all you can agree on are pop songs, those are fine too! The point is to feel merry, have fun, and spread good feelings. It's best not to do this in the middle of the night while people are sleeping, though. It gets dark early on the solstice, so if you are going to include singing, please do so at an appropriate time. People who are woken up by singing are unlikely to appreciate it.

An alternative to singing out loud is to bring your phone and listen to a playlist of appropriately cheerful, hopeful music that brings warmth to your heart. As you wander the neighborhood feeling this inside of you, placing your charms around, you will be spreading the joy inside of you as well.

After your trip around the neighborhood, spend time with your loved ones, friends, family, or familiars or curl up with a good book and your favorite warm snack. Settle in for the tough months knowing you've planted the seeds for bright times to come.

Notes

Imbolc

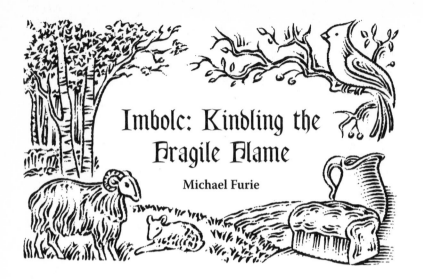

Imbolc: Kindling the Fragile Flame

Michael Furie

THIS HOLIDAY HAS ALWAYS held a certain mysterious appeal for me. It has a long history, and though it occurs during what is usually one of the coldest parts of the winter season, its magical and spiritual themes offer the promise of warmth and security, and the hope of ever-waxing light. Despite being one of the time-honored "cross-quarter days" acknowledged by ancient peoples (perhaps most notably the ancient Irish), there isn't a lot of widespread public ceremony recorded for Imbolc when compared to its associated holidays of Beltane, Lughnasadh, or Samhain. While those cross-quarter days are concerned in part with the welcoming of the light of summertime, the beginning of harvest, or the end of harvest/beginning of the dark portion of the year respectively, Imbolc is centered on the welcoming of springtime. This may seem nonsensical, since it is difficult to envision blooming flowers, colorful butterflies, and the gentle warmth of the sun heralding a new day when the ground is covered in snow or the clouds above are so thick that you cannot remember the last time you saw a clear, blue sky.

The truth is that Imbolc carries the energy of the first stirrings of spring; the acknowledgement that although the apparent conditions may remain stark and barren, the season of warmth and growth is just beginning to emerge. One of the ways that ancient peoples marked the coming of Imbolc was to take notice of when the pregnant ewes' milk came in, seeing this as a harbinger of approaching springtime. At the Winter Solstice, the rebirth of the sun is celebrated, but its influence is still muted, with the short daylight hours and often inclement weather masking its slowly increasing power. Essentially, while Yuletide can be seen as a solar renewal, Imbolc is the time of the awakening of the earth, and like the Yule sun, this growing power may not yet be fully perceived.

In my practice, one of the primary goals of any sabbat ritual is to facilitate connection and awareness of the burgeoning power present at this time. For Imbolc, that power can be reached through the primary facets of the holiday; the themes of the sabbat. For the sabbat of Imbolc, we have an overarching concept of beginnings, of growth in its initial stages, and of the preparations that need to be undergone in order to fully claim the rewards of progress. The means of preparing for the power of growth are shown as traditional practices associated with the day. There were (and are) certain customs that have been practiced, particularly in Ireland, in honor of this holiday. As I wrote in my book *Supermarket Sabbats* (Llewellyn, 2017), some important components of Imbolc that can be enacted to align with the day are:

1. Lighting a fire or using candles
2. Washing of the head, the hands, and the feet
3. Tidying up the house and overall living environment
4. Preparing a meal, particularly with milk
5. Creating amulets of protection, such as the "Brigid's Cross" so strongly associated with the holiday.

The meanings behind these simple actions are to attune to the power of Imbolc; we connect through fire, cleansing (both spiritually and practically), preparation, sustenance, and protection.

With fire, we have that warmth and rhythmic current that feels so crucial to the support and growth of life. Among the generally accepted attributes of the element of fire, there are the qualities of willpower, creation, and vitality, which align perfectly with the focus of Imbolc. For those that honor the goddess Brigid on this day, her attribute as a deity of fire can be a prominent feature of their devotion. In either case, the use of many candles or a ceremonial relighting of the "hearth fire" are great ways to tune in to the element of fire. By ritualistically cleansing the body—whether through a shower, a bath, or specifically a washing of the head, the hands, and then the feet—we not only physically clean ourselves (which of course in the days before indoor plumbing would've been crucial), but can also use this action to neutralize any disharmonious energies that may be clinging to us. In addition to ridding ourselves of negative vibes, another good practice is to clean and arrange our living environment (or at least our chosen ritual space) so that we have what we need readily available and we're not bogged down with clutter or distractions. After any mundane cleaning, a magical cleansing can be done with incense, a witch's broom, or a floor wash, if applicable.

Preparing a meal has a twofold purpose: first, a ritual feast is a frequent component of sabbat celebrations; second, one of the themes of Imbolc is sustenance, in that we have persevered through most of the barren time and are so close to sowing the seeds of springtime. We must boost our strength and also remind ourselves of the joys of abundance; it is a feast of hope and preparation for the future. One or two facets of "traditional" Imbolc feasting, however, could pose a problem for vegetarians or vegans. Since this day also marks the time when the ewe's give milk, dairy products and roast lamb are traditional food fare for the holiday. To my mind, since the theme we are working with is that of sustenance, I feel that these foods can be substituted while still remaining ritually appropriate. These days, there are plenty of vegan and vegetarian meat and dairy alternatives that can easily replace lamb and milk products. As a different option, spicy foods can be eaten (in honor of increasing sunlight) for the meal, as cayenne pepper is aligned with the sun, and cinnamon is as well (which could provide an option for spicing up dessert).

The last traditional task is the creation of a protective amulet. One of the reasons for this is that the late winter is such a fragile, vulnerable time and it makes sense to protect what we've been able to preserve through the cold so that we may begin the spring season with as much of a solid foundation as possible. Another practical reason for use of protective charms at Imbolc is for them to be a special ward against fire. Between the "re-lighting of the hearth fire" and/or using lots of candles, it's a good idea to have that bit of extra magical reassurance, although it is still advised to keep a close watch on any open flames. Aside from the indoor fire concerns, so too are there potential dangers outside the home, such as lightning or, in modern times, faulty electrical fixtures or equipment. While it may seem overly cautious to worry so much about fire dangers this deep into winter, it is a traditional holiday practice and demonstrates not only a healthy respect for the power of fire but also an awareness of its full nature—life-giving and destructive.

Once we have readied ourselves and our living environment, we are then prepared to conduct an Imbolc ritual. Through the ritual we can then call upon the power we seek and utilize it to help manifest its qualities in our lives. If each of the five tasks that have been presented are completed, either as part of the Imbolc ritual or prior to it, an energetic path is paved that connects the celebrants to the power of Imbolc. But what do we do with this power?

The delicate energy that is present during Imbolc is excellent for creative workings. The magic of beginning new projects, expansion, success, and nurturing long-term goals all fit perfectly into the rhythm of this sabbat. Another aspect of the power dynamic available now is one of blessings and initiations. This time of year is ideal for any type of new beginning. Imbolc is really the threshold to the springtime and all the growth and eventual abundance that can bring, but as with any type of cultivation, the correct preliminary steps must be completed to create the conditions that will support future prosperity. In other words, if no seeds have been planted, how could anyone expect flowers to bloom? Continuing with the gardening metaphor, the seeds are planted at Imbolc, they sprout around the vernal equinox and, provided that they have been watered and cared for, begin to bloom and/or bear fruit at Beltane and throughout the summer season before the waning time occurs. Whether it is the blessing of new candles, initiations into a coven, long-term prosperity magic, cleansing and protection for the body and spirit, divination to determine the upcoming weather, or any creative pursuits we may wish to begin, the energy of the Imbolc sabbat can be called upon to amplify our own magic so that our intentions are carried forth into the world to manifest spectacular results. This work can be done solitarily or within a coven, and it may be completed purely as an act of personal power coupled with the energy of the day or could be worked as part of more specifically devotional sabbat ritual with the help of one or more deities.

You may have noticed that other than the reference to the cross amulet named in her honor, I have not focused on the goddess that is most often linked with this sabbat: Brigid of the Tuatha Dé Danann. The main reason for this is that I am trying to concentrate on the unique energetic pattern expressed through the holiday, which can be accessed regardless of specific tradition.

Brigid, one of the daughters of the powerful deity Dagda, has been revered for thousands of years and is so beloved, particularly in Ireland, that her Pagan veneration could not be stamped out. Even though Christianity had a very strong hold on the nation, the love held in the hearts of the people for the goddess Brigid could not be extinguished. The Christians decided to canonize her as Saint Brigid, wherein her story was altered to include the idea that she was born of mortal parents ("coincidentally" on the first of February) and performed her healing and charitable works as a Christian and friend of St. Patrick. In fact, the two of them were termed "The Pillars of Ireland."

As the Tuatha goddess Brigid, she is known to be a powerful deity with dominion over smithcraft, healing and healing wells, wisdom, inspiration, creativity, childbirth, and, most notably, flame. Brigid fully embodies the power and mystery of the Imbolc sabbat. She has been called the goddess of the eternal flame, and her Pagan shrine in Kildare, Ireland, had a flame that was kept continuously burning and was guarded by her priestesses. Once Christianized, her shrine became dedicated to Saint Brigid and a flame was still kept, though it's now tended to by nuns. Her worship is not limited to Ireland; she has been revered in many parts of western Europe and also very strongly in Scotland where she is known as Bride, a goddess of the light half of the year, who is seasonally imprisoned by Cailleach, an ever-ancient hag that in this sense personifies winter. In time, Bride is able to escape her captivity and thus spring is allowed to return. Devotees of Brigid can certainly merge their personal practice with the concept that I am outlining, if desired, but I primarily wished to explore the essence of Imbolc as a magical day in its own right, free from specific denominational constraints.

It is my belief that as human beings, each of us has a claim to the energies found on the sabbats, regardless of our individual religious practices. At its core, this special day, this sabbat, is a powerful nexus (a point of connection) between the realms, and much like each of the traditional witch holidays, is considered to bridge the gaps that separate the physical, mental, and astral planes, giving us the opportunity to fully engage our whole being to potentially stretch beyond our everyday limitations and reach the essence of creation.

Cosmic Sway

Daniel Pharr

IMBOLC IS THE FIRST day of spring on the Celtic wheel. The seasonal shift begins on this day, and planetary energies begin the battle of transition from cold to warm. Coming out of the cold and darkness of winter and into the warmth and rejuvenating life cycle of spring is the perfect time to assess last year's accomplishments and set this year's goals.

Taurus Moon

The night of February 1 is partially illuminated by the first quarter Moon in Taurus. Patience, diligence, perseverance, and practicality are on the rise. The Taurus Moon is a positive influence on the tenacious workers of protracted activities and demanding occupations, but coupled with the first quarter Moon, will create a need to complete, accomplish, and see the effect of a long effort. Don't overestimate the ability to push through every obstacle, remembering some obstacles are best routed around.

The Taurus Moon can often be a time to indulge in comfort. However, this particular Taurus Moon may illuminate hidden hindrances. Unless plans for a break in the stress were made in advance, it's best to acknowledge the impediments blocking that path, sharpen the broadsword, and keep slaying. The quick-witted and the quick-acting are at a disadvantage right now, with energies bowing to the steadfast and resilient.

Gardening

There are a few opportunities to get a jump on the growing cycle. Planting days are rare on the current lunar-zodiac path, as the moon is often waning or has only recently begun waxing when in the water signs. February 6, and March 4 and 5, with a waxing Cancer Moon, will be good for planting under glass. Lettuce, endive, artichoke, spinach, leek, scallion, onion, cauliflower, broccoli, cabbage, brussels sprouts, peas, celery, and tomatoes will all start well when sown under glass. Save sowing the parsnip, radish, and carrot for March 8 when the waxing Moon is in Virgo.

Full Moon

The Leo Moon will bring out the inner desire to be noticeable. Applause and signs of appreciation will be in high demand. Everyone, to a certain degree, will want to be seen, and more so, will want to be admired. The tiniest bit of praise this day will go a long way. Tell someone they look nice and compliment their appearance—their shoes, tie, a new haircut, their smile. Begin something new like a diet, or set a bold goal and announce it to your clan. Finish the announcement with a rousing "Who's with me?!" to drum up support. The Full Leo Moon is on February 9 at 2:33 in the wee morning hours. The Moon will begin a quick move out of Leo and into Virgo by going void of course at 11:08 a.m. and then into Virgo at 6:38 p.m. Work the Full Moon ritual the night before, culminating the magical activities to coincide with the moment of the Full Moon to garner all of its influence. The painstaking efforts required by Virgo will completely change the event if the Full Moon celebration is delayed until the evening of March 9.

Dark Moon

The dark Moon will be in Pisces at 10:31 a.m. on February 23, having only entered Pisces nine hours earlier at 1:37 a.m. Any ritualistic activity before then will be under a capricious void of course Aquarius Moon. The energies will be those of discipline, submission, and subordination, and when void-of-course, spontaneity is always a factor. These traits could fit nicely into a ritual exploring the shadow side of emotion, the dark passenger of the conscious and unconscious minds, and the underworld and its secrets.

In the early hours of the morning with the Pisces moon, the energies will shift from understanding, study, and reasoning into the Piscean energy of openness and receptiveness. Emotions will take the lead over intellect. Empathy will trump apathy. Feelings will dominate logic. This will be the time to rely on the sight, the knowing. Six senses will be scanning for inspiration.

Planting the Seed

The best timing for this ritual is on or before the Full Moon. Find a place in nature, preferably near water, and have a fire if this is being done on the high holiday. Think about the accomplishments to be made in the coming year. Make a list of every desired undertaking. For most folks, once the list is written, there will likely be several years of effort required to fully realize all of the listed endeavors. Reduce the list to the few deeds that can be completed in this year's growing season.

Like any plant, an idea or a project starts by planting the seed and then tending to the growth until winter arrives and the plant dies. For self-motivation and a reminder to get to work, name some of the plants being sown under glass for the goals being set. An example might be sowing broccoli indoors or under glass and naming the broccoli "my new job" and writing the name on the container; or planting tomatoes and naming the plant "my Ireland vacation." The idea here is that every time the plant is watered or cared for, when the plant is transplanted to dirt in the spring, and every time a bunch of broccoli or a tomato is harvested, the plant is a reminder of the goal set and the work that needs still to be done.

Valentine's Day

Valentine's Day, February 14, is on a Friday, with a waning Moon in Scorpio. Emotions will be hot in the family. Relationships may pose difficulties. The Scorpio Moon will often fuel sexual relations, but this particular moon will burn rather than sensualize. Working late might prove the best course. Consider postponing the celebration of love until the waxing Taurus Moon on February 28 and 29, or wait until March 8 under the Virgo Full Moon. Blame the delay on the Moon. Send flowers, chocolate, gifts, and apologies. Virgo will help with the details, and both days are excellent for romance. If Valentine's dinner and drinks are a must on the fourteenth, dine somewhere familiar—this is not a Moon that favors trying new foods. Eat lightly, drink lightly. If the conversation or circumstances turn dark, be prepared to duck and cover, as this is a drink-in-the-face sort of Moon.

Full Moon

The Full Moon preceding Ostara will be on March 9 at 1:47 p.m. in Virgo. If the esbat celebration includes the building of energy, the evening of March 8 might be a better choice than the evening of the ninth. Attention to detail during this Full Moon will bring the most joy to the participants, and happy people ignore the little things. The precision of this Virgo Moon will illuminate culpabilities that would otherwise go unnoticed or be disregarded.

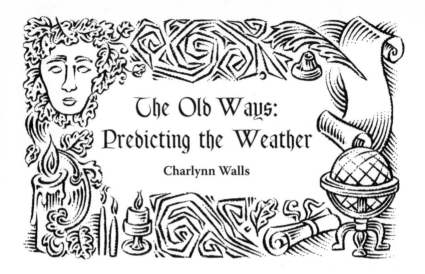

The Old Ways: Predicting the Weather

Charlynn Walls

GROUNDHOG DAY IS SOMETHING that used to be a big deal where I lived. I remember watching the local news station as a kid in school. They would do their report and then they brought on Punxsutawney Phil. He, of course, was the groundhog that would tell us if spring was near or if we were still in the icy grip of winter for the next six weeks. We waited with baited breath as we tried to tell if Phil had seen his shadow or not. Only after Phil had had a lengthy conversation with an oddly dressed man presiding over the festivities did we find out what occurred.

Imbolc is the first festival after the longest night of the year. The days are slowly getting longer and the impatient wait for spring is in full swing. Imbolc heralds the return of the sun, a time when the Goddess returns to speed the way for spring.

When Will Winter End?

There are several traditions from Europe that gave rise to the observance of Groundhog Day in the United States. For those that put plough to field, the festivities were a welcome diversion to the monotony of winter. To brighten the spirits of their congregations the clergy would pass out candles. The correlation between that act and the weather seems to extend to the sayings that were used to help predict winter's end.

According to an old English song:
If Candlemas be fair and bright,
Come, Winter, have another flight;
If Candlemas brings clouds and rain,
Go Winter, and come not again.

According to an old Scottish couplet:
If Candlemas Day is bright and clear,
There'll be twa (two) winters in the year.

Another variation of the Scottish rhyme:
If Candlemas day be dry and fair,
The half o' winter to come and mair,
If Candlemas day be wet and foul,
The half of winter's gone at Yule.
(Previously published on Groundhog.org)

The implication of these rhymes is that if the day is bright and clear then winter will continue, and if the day is cloudy then spring is near.

Animals as Predictors of Weather

If looking outside to get a feel for the weather seems to be a little unfair, we can always turn toward our animal brethren to help us make the call. Here are a few other predictors of weather that we still see supported in the *Old Farmer's Almanac*:

"Expect rain when dogs eat grass, cats purr and wash, sheep turn into the wind, oxen sniff the air, and swine are restless."

"If the groundhog sees its shadow on Candlemas Day (February 2), six more weeks of winter remain."

"When horses and cattle stretch out their necks and sniff the air, it will rain."

"When rabbits are fat in October and November, expect a long, cold winter." (*Old Farmer's Almanac*)

Animals are more connected to the land than we as humans tend to be. They have heightened senses that increase their ability to survive. By observing what is going on in the natural world we can connect to the land and its cycles, and utilize their behavior to make predictions about the weather.

Meet Phil

So, how did a groundhog become a predictor of the weather? Some of the settlers in Pennsylvania were from regions in and around Germany. They would often watch animal behavior to predict the weather. They would watch the hedgehogs near their homes to see what they would do on Imbolc. It seems that this tradition found its way across the Atlantic to their new home.

In 1887, the first Groundhog's Day was observed in the United States. This holiday began when the Punxsutawney Groundhog Club became involved. They reported that Phil could predict the weather. He has been making predictions about winter's end for over 130 years now. People come from all over to partake in the festivities, and those who cannot arrive in person can tune in via television or webcast.

Celebrating Imbolc: Making Your Own Predictions

During February, when we are in the middle of winter, you can watch the world from your window. In doing so, you can incorporate your own take on weather predictions into your Imbolc festivities.

Watching Nature on Your Own

If you are on your own during the morning hours of Imbolc, turn to a window that looks out on your yard, a field, or the woods. Watch for animals that may emerge during that time and watch their behaviors. Do the birds sing? Do the animals seem full of purpose, diligently foraging for food? Tune in to the energies of the animals and the land and draw your own conclusions as to when you think winter will end. Write down your prediction. Once the earth begins to thaw, take a look and see if you were right.

Share the Fun with a Group

If you are a part of a group, plan to gather together to watch Punxsutawney Phil look for his shadow. Have everyone put their predictions onto a slip of paper and collect them. Tally up the answers and then watch the results. Did you all agree that he saw his shadow or not? Share other observations and interpretations from what you viewed.

References

"History." Groundhog.org. 2018. http://www.groundhog.org/about/history/.

K, Amber and Azreal Arynn K. *Candlemas: Feast of Flames*. St. Paul, MN: Lewellyn Publications, 2003.

McCoy, Edain. *The Sabbats: A New Approach to Living the Old Ways*. St. Paul, MN: Lewellyn Publications, 1994.

Morgan, Sheena. *The Wicca Book of Days*. London: Vega, 2003.

Neal, Carl F. *Imbolc: Rituals, Recipes & Lore for Brigid's Day*. Woodbury, MN: Lewellyn Publications, 2015.

Nichols, Mike. *The Witches' Sabbats*. Albany, CA: Acorn Guild Press, 2005.

Old Farmer's Almanac. "Can Animals Predict Weather? Animal Proverbs." https://www.almanac.com/content/can-animals-predict-weather-animal-proverbs.

Feasts and Treats

Mickie Mueller

IMBOLC IS A CELEBRATION of the time of the year when the snow and ice begins to give way to the slowly growing sun. It's also the feast day of the Goddess Brigid; she's honored among kitchen witches far and wide for her aspect as a goddess of the hearth and home. We always light a candle in each room at sunset to bless our home at this time, and usually serve something warming and creamy. This is tradition because this is the time of the year when the ewes are in milk, reason to celebrate at the end of a long, cold winter. I always serve a dessert that uses blackberries since it's a lovely treat and a sacred plant of Brigid. Don't worry if you don't eat dairy; we have so many good substitutions available today that it's not hard to alter a dish, so I've added those options.

Yogurt Drop Biscuits with Honey Butter

This is such an easy biscuit recipe that even people who don't do much baking can easily re-create it. Using self-rising flour makes these lovely little drop biscuits light and fluffy and about as simple as using a mix. With a couple substitutions you can make this a gluten-free and/or dairy-free recipe. I use herbs de Provence from time to time in my kitchen witch magic for blessing and good vibes.

Prep time: 10 minutes
Cooking time: 15–20 minutes
Servings: 9 biscuits

Honey Butter

½ cup softened butter (1 stick) or coconut butter
2 tablespoons honey

Mix in a small dish with a fork until completely blended

Biscuits

1½ cups self-rising flour (or 1½ cups all-purpose or gluten-free
flour, 2 ¼ teaspoons baking powder, ¼ teaspoon salt)
1½ cups Greek yogurt or dairy-free Greek yogurt
1 tablespoon herbs de Provence

Preheat oven to 400° F (200° C). Mix all ingredients with a wooden spoon in a mixing bowl. You may need to add a bit more yogurt to make it a soft, moist dough. Drop spoonfuls of approximately ¼ cup onto a parchment-lined baking sheet. Bake for 15–20 minutes. Serve warm with honey butter.

Clam and Mushroom Bisque

This isn't your grandma's clam chowder; it's a lovely, creamy bisque soup that's warming, comforting, and quick to make for those chilly and early Imbolc evenings when the sun is still going down fairly early. Most of the alcohol from the wine will cook away, but if you prefer, you can use a light broth instead, although the wine gives it a wonderful flavor.

Prep time: 10 minutes
Cooking time: 20 minutes
Servings: 4

6 tablespoons butter, divided
8 ounces fresh sliced mushrooms, white button or cremini
2–3 garlic cloves, minced

1 teaspoon salt

1 teaspoon white pepper (or black pepper)

6 tablespoons all-purpose flour (or gluten-free flour mix)

4 cups milk (or substitute coconut milk, unsweetened soy milk, or almond milk)

½ cup white wine

1 (6.5-ounce) can minced clams

Melt 2 tablespoons of butter in a soup pot and sauté mushrooms until lightly browned, about 5 minutes. Add the garlic, salt, and pepper in the last 2 minutes of cooking. Add the rest of the butter to the pan and melt, then mix in the flour and cook for about 2 minutes. Pour in the milk and mix with a wire whisk until smooth. Add the can of clams (undrained) and the white wine. Adjust heat to medium/low and stir with a spoon continuously until thickened. Serve hot.

Gourmet Grilled Cheese

Soup and sandwiches seem like simple fare, but with a few additions and thoughtful choices for bread and cheese, this comfort food can be elevated. This isn't a complete ingredient list, but a list of ideas of what you can add to create a high-end grilled cheese sandwich. Pick and choose, mix and match, and be inspired this Imbolc to create something crispy on the outside and creamy and delicious on the inside.

Prep time: 5 minutes

Cooking time: 15 minutes

Servings: 4–6

8–12 slices of bread: sourdough, rye, Italian, or any artisan bread of your choice

Cheese: cheddar, muenster, swiss, pepper jack, gouda, vegan cheese; grab some of your favorite cheeses or try something new

Butter or coconut oil

Other topping options:

Fresh, sliced, sautéed mushrooms

Sliced, sautéed white onions

Sliced, sautéed bell pepper

Cooked bacon, turkey bacon, or veggie bacon

Sliced raw avocado

Thinly sliced apple or pear

Tip: Great combos include tomato and basil with mozzarella, thinly sliced apple and gouda, mushrooms and onions with swiss.

Set out the dishes with cheese choices and any other toppings you've opted for. Allow everyone to choose their own breads, cheeses, and other additions.

For each sandwich, butter one side each of two slices of bread and place one slice in a heated skillet on medium-low to medium heat, butter-side down. Stack cheeses and other toppings on the bread slice and top with the other piece of bread, butter-side up. If you cover the skillet while the first side cooks, it helps the cheese to melt. Flip the sandwich to cook both sides to a golden brown. Slice if you wish; serve hot.

Cast-Iron Blackberry Crumble

You don't have to use a cast-iron skillet for this one, but it's a lovely way to make it and it keeps the crumble hot a bit longer. If you don't own a cast-iron skillet, you can make this in any oven-proof skillet or a pie pan. I usually make some kind of blackberry dessert on Imbolc because blackberries are sacred to Brigid. Blackberries consumed on Imbolc are usually preserves or frozen, because even though they're associated with the goddess whose feast day is Imbolc, they're not in season this time of the year.

Prep time: 10 minutes

Cooking time: 35 minutes

Servings: 6

Filling

4 cups frozen blackberries

2 tablespoons of sugar or alternative sweeter like honey, stevia, or agave

1 tablespoon flour or gluten-free flour blend

1 teaspoon cinnamon

Topping

½ cup old fashioned oats

½ cup crushed rice squares cereal, like Rice Chex or other brands

2 tablespoons flour or gluten-free flour blend

3 tablespoons honey

½ teaspoon cinnamon

¼ teaspoon cardamom

3 tablespoons butter or solid coconut oil

Preheat oven to 350° F (177° C). Place berries in skillet and toss with flour, cinnamon, and 2 tablespoons of sweetener of your choice. Cook over medium heat for about 3–5 minutes, stirring occasionally to allow the berries to thaw, releasing their flavor and forming a light sauce. Adjust sweetener to taste. In a separate bowl, mix oats, crushed rice square cereal, flour, honey, cinnamon, and cardamom. Add butter or coconut oil and blend with fingertips or a fork, cutting in the butter or coconut oil. Sprinkle topping mixture all over the berries. Bake at 350 degrees for 30 minutes or until topping is golden brown and berries are bubbly. It is delicious served with vanilla bean ice cream or whipped cream.

Crafty Crafts

Ember Grant

WE HAVE NO HARD evidence about how Pagans actually celebrated the festival of Imbolc, but we do know that it came to be associated with St. Brigid, a figure believed by many to be a remnant of worship of an ancient Celtic goddess—also known by other names, including Brigit and Bride.

By the early eighteenth century, and probably somewhat earlier, there are some specific accounts of rituals. In particular, in his book *Stations of the Sun*, historian Ronald Hutton mentions one from the Outer Hebrides, off the west coast of Scotland, as described by Alexander Carmichael. On St. Brigid's Eve, "Adult females spent the eve making an oblong basket in the shape of a cradle, *leaba Bride*, 'the bed of Bride.'" An icon of Bride (Brigid) was decorated and placed into it; the goal was to welcome Bride to visit for the night so she would bestow good fortune on the home (Hutton 1996).

Bride's Basket

This description of the Bride's Bed ritual inspired me to make my own version: a Bride's Basket. This basket can be used to welcome Brigid into your home and ask for her blessings.

Materials

Dish to use as a mold—a plastic or glass bowl. (To achieve the cradle shape, use an oblong dish or ovular bowl; round is perfectly fine if that's all you have. I used an oval-shaped ramekin.)

Cling wrap ($2)

Tacky craft glue that dries clear, such as Elmer's Craft Bond ($3)

1 package of raffia (around $5, depending on package size)

Scissors

> *Cost:* $10
>
> *Time spent:* 30 minutes to 1 hour, not including drying time

First, wrap the bowl with cling wrap and secure the ends of the wrap inside the container. Use plenty of wrap. The entire dish should be covered, with the ends of the plastic wrap on the inside of the dish. Pour some glue into a container and submerge the raffia strands into the glue. Be sure they're well-coated. Smooth glue over each strand of raffia. If you dislike the dunking method, you can apply the glue with your fingertips. Either way, you need to be sure the entire strand of raffia is coated with the glue.

Working quickly, wrap the raffia all around the outside of the bowl. Your hands will get messy, but bare hands are easier than trying to wear gloves. You'll need to wrap in two ways: first, in circles around the dish horizontally, keeping the strands tight against each other. Then, you will also need to wrap the raffia vertically over the top and bottom of the bowl (you will simply cut away any unnecessary pieces from the top when the bowl is dry). Wind the raffia around and stick the ends to the bottom of the bowl. After you wrap the sides, wrap across the top and bottom (remember, the top will be cut off). Criss-crossing the strands in many directions will make a stronger bottom for the basket. If desired, wrap one final strand or two around the top to finish it and create a header.

It's fine if there are gaps in your basket; it doesn't have to be perfect. When you're done, be sure to smooth down any pieces that are sticking up before leaving it to dry. You can still slide the raffia around during the drying process, if you choose, to even out the

strands and close up any large gaps. When you've covered the entire bowl, allow the glue to dry—overnight is best. Leave it to dry bottom-up on a cookie sheet or baking rack.

When the glue is dry, or dry enough that you feel comfortable working with it, it's time to remove the raffia from the mold. Begin by cutting away the top. Don't worry about the edges yet; you'll trim those last. For now, you just need to create an opening. Next, carefully peel away the raffia "bowl" from the mold. The cling wrap should prevent it from sticking. Work slowly, releasing a section at a time. Peel off the cling wrap and discard it. Finally, trim away the rough top edges with scissors. You now have a basket to use for Bride's Bed.

Here are some tips for success:

1. Lay out cut raffia strands beforehand so you can grab them easily. You can alternate between long and short strands (which may be helpful if you have a dish that is longer than it is tall).

2. I stopped about four times during the process to wash my hands. This will happen.

3. The "tacky" craft glue may be stickier than simple "school" glue, but it's still easy to clean up and may give your basket a tighter hold. The school glue is thinner and takes longer to dry. Just be sure to clean your work surface quickly—it will be easier. If the glue does dry on your counter or hands, a mesh sponge works great to scrub it off.

To use your Bride's Basket in your Imbolc celebration, you can follow the traditional ritual and place a corn dolly or wheat sheaf inside it to symbolize the goddess. You can also place symbolic offerings in it, such as small crystals or something else of importance to you for this time of year, or decorate it with three battery-powered tea lights to represent Brigid's triple aspects of poetry, smith-craft, and healing. Place the basket on your altar or other special place overnight and ask the goddess Brigid to bless your home.

If you want to use your basket later for practical or decorative purposes, you can line it with extra loose raffia or other filler material, such as decorative fabric or even moss. Or you can save it and use it for Imbolc each year.

Salted "Ice" Candle

Candles are often the centerpiece of Imbolc celebrations. Here's a fun way to "dress up" candles to evoke the season.

Materials

Epsom salts ($2–$5 depending on size of package)
Mod Podge, or other craft glue that dries clear ($2–$7)
Pillar candle ($5–$10)
Paint brush or sponge to apply the glue
Tray or cookie sheet
  Cost: $9–$22
  Time spent: About 10 minutes

Pour a layer of Epsom salts onto a cookie sheet or tray. "Paint" the glue onto the candle—you can cover the entire candle at once, if you like, or work in sections. While the glue is still wet, roll the candle in the salt.

At first, the salt will look like ice crystals. As the glue sets and the ice crystals absorb the moisture, they will turn white and look like bits of sleet. The candle will still be pretty, but won't have the same ice crystal appearance. You can go ahead and use the candle, though, even before the glue is completely dry. In addition, consider placing the candle in a dish of Epsom salt while it's burning. You can add the leftover salt to your bath for a relaxing soak. Either way, never leave a burning candle unattended.

Reference

Hutton, Ronald. *Stations of the Sun: A History of the Ritual Year in Britain.* Oxford: Oxford University Press, 1996.

A Crystal for Every Season: Selenite

Charlie Rainbow Wolf

IMBOLC—ALSO SOMETIMES CALLED CANDLEMASS—is the initial festival of the calendar year, and the first of the spring festivals. It is at this time that the northern hemisphere starts to celebrate the end of winter and the promise of spring. Imbolc honors the goddess Brigid, who was later adopted into Christianity as St. Brigid. Both the goddess and the saint are associated with milk and fire.

Popular Imbolc crystals include—but aren't limited to—agate, amethyst, milky quartz, moonstone, onyx, peridot, selenite, and sunstone. Look for stones that show light breaking through the darkness. This is a time of evolution, and of removing what's holding you back, so that you can grow into your authentic self. Stones that are veined with lighter colors piercing darker backgrounds represent this so well.

Selenite

Of all the stones affiliated with Imbolc, my favorite has to be selenite. There's just something rich and ethereal about it, with its pearly white color and tubular formati2n. Selenite polished into a sphere seems soothing and relaxing, while the natural column shape, with its often-jagged formations, makes me think of castles and towers from other realms.

Selenite has its unique appearance because of the tabular way in which it forms. It's a type of gypsum, the same mineral associated with alabaster, satin spar, the desert rose, and gypsum flowers. It's translucent and predominantly white, although other hues are often represented if the stone has inclusions.

Selenite is a compound composition of calcium sulfate dehydrate. You might think that there is selenium in selenite, but there isn't. Like selenium, selenite gets its name from a reference to a Greek word for the moon. The largest crystals have been found in the Cueva de los Cristales, in the Naica Mine in Chihuahua, Mexico. This cave was discovered in 2000, and many healers believe that the timing of this—the discovery of these huge healing stones at the dawn of the new millennium—was no coincidence.

Selenite is quite fragile—only a 2 on the Mohs scale—so handle it carefully. It's also water soluble, so care must be taken not to get it wet. Clean it with only a slightly moist cloth—or better yet, a soft brush—and never immerse it in water.

I first discovered selenite back in the 1990s, when it was just starting to gain popularity. The shop owner introduced me to a large selenite tower and placed it on a light box. I was mesmerized by the way the stone channeled the light, and I knew that I had to explore its potential.

Healing Properties

Even though I've listed selenite as my favorite stone for Imbolc, please don't limit yourself to only working with it during this time of year. According to Katrina Raphael, selenite is one of the stones that can help to create newness by lifting awareness and enabling you to resonate on a higher vibration (Raphaell 1990). This is profound when doing magical ceremony and ritual, but it's also something to strive for on a daily and personal basis, too.

Selenite's milky white color and its ability to channel light make it an excellent crown chakra stone. If you work with spirit guides, this is a mighty ally when it comes to communicating and connecting with them. It's naturally gentle, yet also efficient in conducting energy and messages between you. Try holding the stone over your heart chakra while you meditate, and open yourself to what the universe wants you to hear.

As a healing stone, selenite has a reputation for calming the emotions and helping you to find inner peace and balance. Even though this is a gentle stone, it's not one to be trifled with. There's power in grace, and strength in compassion and understanding. Remember, selenite is considered one of the stones that was discovered at the dawn of the new century in order to birth us into a higher plane of consciousness. If you believe this then you must take it seriously and allow yourself to grow and develop. Be open to any spiritual changes you want to invite into your life when working with selenite, and remember that—like all growth and change—some of these may be uncomfortable until you have fully adjusted to them.

Selenite lends itself very nicely as a stone for Imbolc, for just as this is the festival of milk, selenite is a stone that is feminine in nature. It's believed to be an uplifting stone, and including it in ceremony or ritual not only raises the vibration in a positive way, but also helps protect from outside influences and unwanted or negative energy. It's linked to fertility and the Moon, too, so it's an influential tool for Moon magic, and for any rituals or ceremonies that deal with conception, inception, and new beginnings.

Selenite wands are neither expensive nor hard to obtain, although they are more fragile than other healing wands. They are considered by some vibrational workers to be the best conduit for healing energy because of their tubular formation and ability to carry light. It's possible to use a companion crystal along with a selenite wand so that you get the energy of both stones in rituals or healing practices. Place a selenite tower on a light box to bring a healing ambience into a room, or on your altar to enhance your devotions.

A Selenite Meditation

Here's a very simple yet remarkably effective meditation to do when working with selenite. You can use a selenite sphere, a wand, or a small tower for this. Quiet your environment by turning off all distractions such as phones or televisions. Relax your body and your spirit by taking three deep breaths, in through your nose and out through your mouth. Make sure that your arms and legs are not crossed, and that you're sitting comfortably.

Place the selenite on your heart, and focus on your heartbeat. With every beat, envision the crystal getting larger and yourself getting smaller, so in your mind's eye you are able to enter into the stone. Find the brightest shaft of light running through the crystal's structure and see yourself traveling up it.

Now, focus on what you need. Perhaps you're stressed or worried about something. Maybe you feel lonely or alone. You might just want a closer connection with your guides, or nature, or your environment. Whatever it is, the light in which you're traveling will bring that into your heart and into your life if you just let it.

When you feel at peace and at one with the light, focus once again on your heartbeat. Picture the stone getting smaller, until you can step out of it, where you're once again sitting holding the stone. Take three deep, grounding breaths, in through your nose and out through your mouth, and open your eyes. Get something to eat or drink—nothing alcoholic, please—to help you return to this reality.

References

Barthelmy, Dave. "Gypsum Mineral Data." Flame Tests. http://webmineral.com/data/Gypsum.shtml#.W2hlq9JKhQA.

"Cave of Crystals 'Giant Crystal Cave." Geology Page. 2016. http://www.geologypage.com/2016/06/cave-of-crystals-giant-crystal-cave.html.

Raphaell, Katrina. *The Crystalline Transmission: A Synthesis of Light*. Santa Fe, NM: Aurora Press, 1990.

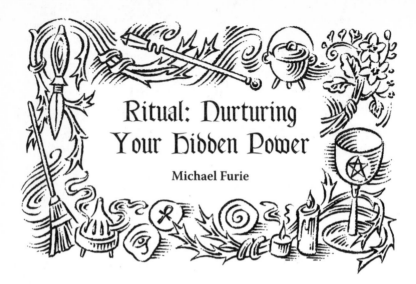

Ritual: Nurturing Your Hidden Power

Michael Furie

THIS RITUAL ACKNOWLEDGES THE different themes found in Imbolc, utilizing them in the creation of a spell pouch that is similar in nature to a mojo or medicine bag. The intention of this spell pouch is to enhance one's personal power and any abilities they wish to encourage. Before this ritual can be worked, all of the items needed must be assembled and properly prepared.

Items Needed

1 square of natural cloth or leather (in your favorite color) between 3 and 5 inches in diameter

Red, white, and black cords or yarn (about one foot in length, braided together)

Personal item (lock of hair, nail clipping, etc.)

Small tokens or pictures of qualities you wish to enhance

1 square of fresh paper (a 3-inch square should be sufficient)

Pen with ink in a favorite color (or red)

1 teaspoon sunflower seeds in shells, dried (for luck, strength, and energy renewal)

1 tablespoon dried sage (for prosperity and wishes granted)

1 pebble, gathered near the home (to connect to the land)

Imbolc incense mixture (basil, cinnamon, peppermint—dried, 1
    teaspoon each)
Censer and self-lighting incense charcoal
Cup (with water)
2 small bowls of salt
Cauldron (or fireproof bowl)
Wand
Pentacle (or small platter)
3 red candles
1 white candle

Prior to beginning the ritual, set up the altar facing the north
with the cauldron in the center and the white candle within it. The
cup of water should be set directly to the left of the cauldron and
the wand placed on the right. Above the cauldron at the back of the
altar, set the three red candles in a row from left to right and put
the censer between the middle candle and the cauldron. Place one
of the bowls of salt on the right between the cauldron and the wand
with the pentacle in front of the cauldron to the south. The pentacle
will be the working area so all of the ingredients of the spell pouch
(the first nine items listed) should be placed around it. If the incense
mixture or self-lighting incense charcoal are not available or desired, premade stick or cone incense in any of the individual scents
(mint, cinnamon, or sage) could be used as a reasonable substitute.

Once the altar has been arranged, run a bath or take a shower
and bring the other container of salt. Hold the salt in your weak
hand (the one you don't write with) and hold your strong hand over
it. Mentally envision pure white light being sent from your domi-
nant hand into the salt in order to bless it with the intent that it will
purify all that it touches. If you are taking a bath, pour the salt into
the tub of water. If you are taking a shower, wet the salt with a small
amount of water and use it as a salt scrub on your skin and wash it
off with the shower. While you are bathing, make a special point
of washing your head, hands, and feet, as this is a traditional focus
for cleansing during Imbolc. As you bathe or shower, think about

which qualities and abilities of yours you would like to advance, and also try to brainstorm a symbol or set of symbols that would signify a personal emblem for you. Once cleansed, step out of the bathtub and get dressed according to your personal preference before returning to the altar area.

At the altar, light the three red candles and pick up the wand. Use the wand to cast a circle; beginning in the north and moving clockwise, mentally send energy through the wand, forming a magical orb containing the entire altar area. Once the circle is complete, stand at the center in front of the altar, facing north, and call to the energies of earth with these words: "Power of earth, hear my plea, attend this rite, come to me."

Turn to the east (air), then south (fire), then west (water), calling in each element to its direction. Finally, face the altar once more, lighting the white candle with these words: "I kindle this fire as a beacon to the power of Imbolc. From each corner of the earth, I call you now, take heed, and come forth."

Pick up the second bowl of salt and bless it in the same manner as before. Pick up the cup of water and, holding it with both hands, mentally send white light into the water, cleansing it of any energies not in harmony with your rite. Once finished, pour the salt into the water. With your fingers, sprinkle a bit of saltwater around the circle in a clockwise motion, neutralizing any disharmonious energy that may still linger. Light the incense and, if safe, carry the incense in a clockwise motion to charge the energy of the circle with the correct intentions. The circle is complete. If you're choosing to work with deities, now is the time to call upon them in your own words.

Once you're ready, take up the pen and paper and create a personal symbol for yourself that only you will know. You can add astrological information or personal details as you see fit and also add a list of attributes that you wish enhanced through this work. When you are finished, fold the paper, making each fold toward you, and place it on top of the fabric square that'll become the pouch. Going through each in turn, pick up the items that will be going into the pouch, blessing them in a similar fashion as the salt and water, substituting the specific intentions depending on which item is being blessed. For example, each of the tokens should be charged with the idea that they will enhance the abilities of that which they symbolize, and the herbs and seeds should be blessed with the intention given in parentheses. After all the items have been prepared, they should be bundled together in the fabric, using the braided cords to tie the corners together, creating the spell pouch. Wrap the cords around it and tie nine knots in the tail, giving it a knotted handle and sealing in the magic.

Once tied, sprinkle a bit of the saltwater on the pouch to bless it with the powers of water and earth, then hold it briefly over the white candle's flame (high enough above that it won't ignite), and over the incense smoke, to charge it with the power of fire and air, respectively. Now, holding the bundle in both hands, close your eyes and go into a meditation.

In your mind's eye, see a mystical portal appear before you. Envision yourself standing up and entering this portal. Allow it to transport you to a magical meadow. In this meadow, see the snow-covered trees and ground. Feel a crisp chill in the air, sense an eerie stillness. Look into the meadow and notice that there is an old well in the center. Walk over to the well and look inside. Observe how incredibly dark it is inside; it is so dark that there's almost a vacuum-like quality to it, as if it were trying to pull you inside. Resist the pull and see a large rope dangling out of the well. Place your spell pouch into your pocket and, using both hands, pull on the rope to free whatever is down inside this well.

After an immeasurable time, you begin to see a light growing steadily stronger from the depths of the well. Pulling on the rope faster, the light gets stronger and stronger until, at long last, you pull up a cauldron filled with shimmering light; the light of Imbolc. As you free the cauldron of light, the meadow is instantly transformed; the snow has vanished and lush green grass on the ground and vibrant leaves in the trees fill the area with warmth and life.

Instinctively, you touch your spell pouch to the light; some of its power is absorbed into the bundle, further charging it with power. You can now carry this power with you to shine like a beacon of light in the everyday world. Return to the portal and be transported back to your physical form. Once rejoined, open your eyes.

It is now time to conclude the rite and open the circle. Thank and release each element in turn, moving counterclockwise: west, south, east, and finally north, saying, "Power of (name correct element), thank you for your help this hour. I release you now; go in power."

Thank any deities you have called and extinguish the candles in reverse order of lighting. Lastly, take up the wand and use it to open the circle by walking counterclockwise, having the wand absorb the power. The spell pouch is now ready. You can carry it with you where it will not be seen or store it in a place where you will be able to see it often, but where others will not find it.

Notes

Notes

Ostara

Prayer Tree Magic

Blake Octavian Blair

IT IS THE TIME of the Spring Equinox! Anticipated by many, this sabbat marks the official beginning of spring. Whether we are still in a snowy wonderland of bare-branched trees that form lace against the sky or we are starting to see a green tinge in the tree-tops signifying the peppering of emerging buds, spring approaches. Trees are there for us, providing their stoic presence and connection to the sacred year-round. It's really no wonder that cultures throughout time and the world over have used them as sites and even conduits for prayer.

Many people's minds only turn toward actually contemplating and communing with trees during their times of shift and transformation. Everyone takes note when the leaves change color in the fall, creating a gorgeous, fiery, autumnal canopy, and when the bare branches reach to the sky in winter. Of course, now we look for or notice the buds as a sign of the coming green in spring. However, in between these times of transition lies the majority of the year. The Spring Equinox is a great time to ride the energy of growth, new life, and new beginnings to commit to growing our understanding of the sacred relationships we can have with trees. When a tree is used as a focal point and partner in prayer, it can be communed with throughout the entire year and a relationship can be built. Many cultures have maintained this practice from ancient times to the present day.

Shamanic peoples from Mongolia and regions of Siberia use a form of prayer tree called a *barisaa*. The barisaa represents the World Tree. For the practitioner performing a ceremony at the barisaa, it mirrors and becomes their axis mundi. The spirit of the tree itself is communed with and honored, but the tree also serves as a conduit to the Otherworlds, filled with a plethora of spirits to be honored and worked with. Drumming and dancing during ceremonies is extremely common, as the drumming acts as a sonic driving technique to assist in carrying the trance state as the shaman travels to the Otherworlds and merges with spirits. During the ceremonies, offerings of food and drink are made. Traditional offerings include vodka, milk, honey, and prayer ties or flags. The prayer flags tied to the Siberian and Mongolia barisaas often take the form of *khadags*. Khadags are ceremonial scarves of various colors (each for various purposes) used in Tibetan Buddhism. Shamanism in these regions is often very heavily influenced by and incorporating elements of Tibetan Buddhism. The barisaa becomes a place of power, as it is used over time, ceremony after ceremony. The shamans from the Buryatia region in eastern Siberia also similarly use prayer trees; however, they specifically hold the birch tree sacred for this purpose, even planting entire sacred groves of birch for their use.

The connection of sacred trees with Buddhism doesn't end with the shared ground of Buddhism and shamanism. In fact, the Buddhist tradition itself holds trees in a sacred place. The sacred bodhi tree plays a pivotal role in the story of the Buddha Guatama Siddhartha's enlightenment. There is a Buddhist temple at Bodh Gaya, India, at the site said to be where Siddhartha obtained enlightenment while seated under a bodhi tree. This bodhi is also known as a sacred fig (*Ficus religiosia*). The temple, Mahabodhi Temple, has a sacred fig on its grounds said to be descended from the tree that the Buddha sat under. For this reason, this temple is one of the major sacred pilgrimage sites for the past couple thousand years.

Of course, throughout regions practicing Tibetan Buddhism, prayer flags with different printed designs, colored to represent the five elements, can be found hung in trees among other locations, to carry prayers on the wind. The sacrality of trees is inherently displayed in their being chosen as the sentry to hold such vessels of prayer.

As we continue looking at just a few of the cultures that engage in their own versions of prayer tree magick, we of course will start to notice patterns of parallel practices with obvious similarities. One such practice is that of the Celts and the use of prayer ties called clooties or cloughties. This practice carries along the elements of tying prayer ties and flags to trees, as well as the practice of sacred pilgrimage. It is still a fairly popular practice throughout the British Isles and Brittany. Strips of cloth, colors chosen carefully for intention, are tied to the branches of sacred trees. Imbued with intention, they are to carry prayers to and petition the nature spirits, spirits of place, and various saints and deities for their assistance. Though not a requirement, the trees are often situated near healing wells, springs, or bodies of water. In these cases, the clooties are often dipped in the healing waters, and if the petitioner has an ailment they're praying for healing for, they may rub the affected area with it before tying it to a limb or branch of the tree. Though healing prayers are a common intention for clooties, the range of different intentions for clooties are as numerous as any other type of spellwork. Many species of tree are used as clootie trees; however, oak and hawthorn trees are particularly popular. Also, any tree known to be a "fairy tree" is a popular candidate for a clootie tree; it never hurts to have the Good Folk on your side. Thusly, the traditional triad of fairy trees—oak, ash, and thorn (hawthorn)—are often used as prayer trees and found bedecked in a finery of clooties and offerings.

Another type of tree that holds particular sacredness for the Celts is the apple tree. There is something of course inherently magical about a fruiting tree. A grove of apple trees tended with love and care will produce a crop of fruit to then nourish us, as we have so nourished them. The lore of the sacredness and magick of the apple tree and its fruit goes far deeper into the mystical with its connections to Avalon. In fact, Avalon literally means "Isle of Apples." It is said that apple trees grow in abundance in the forests of Avalon. Glastonbury Tor, which lies in the county of Somerset, is said to be the location of Avalon, and perhaps its entrance in the apparent world. Interestingly, those who hold the stories of the Avalonian otherworld sacred will surely let you know that the county of Somerset is also indeed home to a large number of apple orchards. Coincidence? I'll let you decide.

In the Japanese tradition of Shinto, trees often serve as *yorishiro*. Yorishiro are objects capable of housing spirits, serving as vessels. The spirits they house are called *kami*. While kami spirits are hard to describe in a brief description, it can be said that they are the elements of nature and the essences they possess, all at once. Some even believe ancestors can become kami after death. Kami are also considered manifestation of the power of the universe or the life force energy, similar to the concept of mana in Maori belief or prana in Indic religions. These trees housing the kami have become sacred themselves over time, increasing their power as sacred sites, due to the combined powers of the tree as a sacred being and spirit itself, as well as that of the kami housed within. These yorishiro trees become sacred shrines themselves, attracting regular worship and pilgrimage. They are often marked with the tying of ornamental ropes around their trunks. Again, we see many cross-cultural similarities in practice with some of the cultural traditions previously discussed.

Sacred trees have even had their role in creating and maintaining communal peace. The Iroquois legend of the eastern white pine is exemplary of this. There are five nations whose lands abutted to each other in the area we now know as New York state: the Mohawk, the Oneida, the Onondaga, the Cayuga, and the Seneca. The legend goes that a man named Dekanawidah wanted to bring peace among the five nations who were constantly at war with each other.

So, Dekanawidah decided to travel throughout the five nations and attempt to create peace and unity through dialogue and understanding. Unfortunately, as is often the case, he was not always met with a kind listening ear or people understanding of his mission. However, Dekanawidah decided to plant an eastern white pine on the land of the Onodaga nation, which was situated geographically in the center of the five nations. Symbolically, this tree is said to have four roots, dubbed "the Great White Roots of Peace," which extend out to the four cardinal directions. The eastern white pine also features five needles per branch, and thusly symbolized the five involved nations. Dekanawidah, according to legend, was able to get leaders of the five nations to gather under this sacred tree to discuss important matters and bring peace among their nations. Anthropologist AC Parker even posits that Iroquois and Westerners might have buried weapons under trees or planted trees on top of buried weapons as part of peace treaties.

Of course, the act of planting a tree in and of itself can be a form of prayer that can cross over the bounds of specific religions. Trees are often planted in memorial to people who have passed away. It is becoming popular even to plant trees as part of wedding celebrations, with the newly planted tree growing from love and care along with those getting married, whose relationship also grows with love and care. Planting a tree is also a fantastic addition to a house blessing. The planting of a new tree in a new home signifies the putting down of roots and creating stability as the new occupants grow and create a life in their new home. My husband and I included the planting of an apple tree as part of our house blessing that was performed by our grove. (We already had another apple tree to be a pollination partner for the new one!)

As spring settles in around us, bursting with budding new life, think about renewing your relationship with the sacred tree spirits that exist around you. Tending to trees helps leave a legacy that will outlive us in our current human incarnations. When we invest in trees, we invest in ecosystems and all life on this grand planet, both present and future. In closing, I'll present you with an old Greek proverb: "A society grows great when old men plant trees whose shade they know they shall never sit in."

References

Rogers, S. A. "Tree of Peace: The Iroquois Legend of the Eastern White Pine." 2017. http://easternwhitepine.org/tree-of-peace-the-iroquois-legend-of-the-eastern-white-pine/.

Mueller, Mickie. *Voice of the Trees: A Celtic Divination Oracle.* Woodbury, MN: Llewellyn Publications, 2011.

Tkacz, Virlana, Sayan Zhambalov, and Wanda Phipps. *Siberian Shamanism: The Shanar Ritual of the Buryats.* Rochester, VT: Inner Traditions, 2015.

Cosmic Sway

Daniel Pharr

OSTARA, THE SPRING EQUINOX, the day of equilibrium, is a solar holiday on March 19 at 11:49 a.m. under a waning Aquarius Moon. The high holiday comes a few days early this year, and is the earliest Spring Equinox since 1896. Interestingly, since 2000, Ostara arrives every Leap Year earlier than the Leap Year before and will continue to do so until the end of this century.

Ostara

This day at the exact time, the dark and light energies stand as equals, night and day are of equal length. A favorite practice to celebrate Ostara is to stand eggs on their ends. Remove the eggs from the refrigerator and let the eggs warm to room temperature on the counter. When nearing the moment of equilibrium (the timing does not need to be exact) move the eggs to a surface that will not be affected by vibration or disturbance. Hold an egg gently between the fingers of both hands on its larger rounded end. Find the balance point and slowly let go. This may take several tries and several minutes, but eventually an egg will stand on its own. Stand eggs everywhere, like stones on the Celtic landscape. Take a photo.

This waning Aquarius Moon will provide an opportunity to draw on the inner darkness for strength and inspiration. Ostara being the time of the quickening, the time the earth begins to burst forth with new life, it is a favorable phase to begin a major effort or significant project. New affairs requiring forethought and analysis are particularly supported in this lunar arrangement. Look inward at previous losses and lessons learned, extract the wisdom from each, and bring this knowledge forward into the new venture rather than holding on to defeat and thinking of retribution.

Dark Moon

The dark Aries Moon on March 24 at 5:28 a.m. is also the calculated stint of lunar energies to coincide with the Ostara celebration. This is a time of coming out of the darkness and into the light, from dark Moon to waxing Moon, and Aries will add the fire to push new plans into full form and set the schemes in motion. Use this Moon and the coming Taurus Moon to drive plans forward, making significant progress by the Full Libra Moon in two weeks.

Gardening

Planting will be ideal on March 26 and 27, as well as the daylight hours of March 28, and especially under the light of the waxing Taurus Moon during those days. The waxing Cancer Moon, beginning an hour after sunrise on March 31, and continuing on April 1 and the morning of April 2, will likewise be an excellent period for sowing, and the dark hours under the shining Cancer Moon will be even better. If the soil is still cold and nights are still approaching freezing, sowing under glass is best, and rather than providing a list of suitable food plants for sowing, I recommend that you sow them all. Once April sun has warmed the soil, save for the fruit plants, sow all seeds directly in the ground, although check the weather forecasts, as this year could see late snows, which would push direct planting into May.

Great Conjunction

A new thirty-year cycle started on January 12, 2020, with Saturn conjunct Pluto. Jupiter joins the fray on December 21, 2020. The Great Conjunction, as it is named, is associated with huge shake-ups, politically and planetarily, literally and metaphorically. Nine US presidents have been killed, died of illness, or experienced an assasination attempt during a Great Conjunction. Volcanic eruptions and earthquakes are also more common. The Great Conjunction is all about destruction. To add more misery, the weather predictions for the winter this year are heavy snows brought on by a strong La Niña depression off the coast of Central and South Americas. The time for preparation is in the spring and summer. Prepare for a lack of food, water, and electricity during the winter months. Sow heavily in the garden this year, and sow often, taking advantage of the planting days. Can and dry and pickle and ferment; save all of the food possible in case of a long, difficult winter. Stock up on firewood if that is an option, otherwise prepare for long power outages and lack of heat. Water is always the most important emergency provision, so store water, as well as gasoline for a generator. Don't forget blankets, candles, and matches.

Full Moon

A Full Libra Moon will shine upon esbat celebrations on April 7 at 10:34 p.m. This fine Libra Moon is all about balance, fairness, and justice. Libra, a masculine air sign ruled by the feminine Venus, exhibits balance in all its energies and influences. The celebration of this Full Moon should include ritualistic aspects positively enhanced by charm and cheerfulness, romance and diplomacy, as the Libra Full Moon will shine joyfully on relationships of all varieties.

Easter

Easter is on Sunday, April 12. This mundane lunar holiday falls annually on the first Sunday after the first Full Moon after Ostara. The whole of the daylight hours will be experienced in a void-of-course

Sagittarius Moon, which will go void at 7:45 a.m. and move into Capricorn at 8:05 p.m. The inspiration, encouragement, and idealism of the Sagittarian Moon that have dominated for the last couple of days will, over the course of the day, slowly lose the struggle against the practical, organized, process-driven motivations of the Capricorn Moon. If family time is contemplated, be aware of the shifting lunar influences and be prepared to check Sagittarianism at the door. Be practical.

Dark Moon

April 22 at 10:25 p.m. will mark the arrival of the Taurus dark Moon. Taurus naturally brings forth vim and vigor in a stubborn, never quit, no stop, moving mountains way. In opposition to being pushed or cornered are the exact same qualities focused on never giving in, never moving from that spot, and not moving until asked nicely. The grounded nature of Taurus soothes even the most savage. Taurus is a feminine earth sign and is ruled by the feminine Venus. The dark Moon will bring out the hidden strength behind the Taurus qualities. The evening's esbat would do well to focus on the realization of the inner immoveable stability and motivating willpower, bringing these into the light of day to be embodied and benevolently called upon at all times, not just the times of stress and pressure.

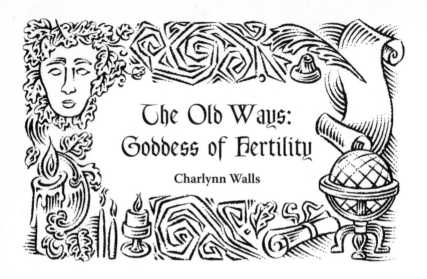

The Old Ways: Goddess of Fertility

Charlynn Walls

GROWING UP, MY SPRINGTIME traditions centered on the dyeing and hunting of Easter eggs. All the cousins in our family would gather together at my grandparents' house the night before Easter. We would spend the day dyeing eggs in preparation for the hunt. Not to mention the hunt for candy and the elusive chocolate bunny.

Many members of my family came from a Christian background and they were very fond of Easter. As a young adult I had difficulty understanding what eggs and rabbits had to do with the religious holiday. As I grew older and started my exploration into Paganism, I came to understand and appreciate how these symbols worked into the mythos and were central components in the celebration of Ostara.

Ostara, or the vernal equinox, is observed between March 20 and March 23 in the northern hemisphere. It is traditionally a time when the greening of the earth takes place and seeds are sown into fertile soil. Grass and flowers begin their journey to the surface. Animals begin to give birth after the harshness of winter has passed, and the earth begins to soften.

The Goddess

The goddess Ostara, or Eostre, was popular among the Anglo-Saxon people of Northern and Central Europe. She was often referred to by both names. The goddess presided over springtime and all its components, including that of fertility. It is through her sacred fertility symbols of the rabbit and the egg that she is still recognized by the masses. The Venerable Bede noted that her name was taken directly to the Christian holiday of Easter, as she was so loved.

The Egg

The egg is a small but powerful representation of fertility. It expresses the fragility and infinite possibilities of life. From the egg comes the origins of new life and creation. For such a small package, it represents quite a lot. The egg has been used as a fertility amulet and given as a gift.

According to McCoy, the Easter egg as we now know it resulted as a gift from the rabbit to the goddess Ostara. The rabbit dyed her egg in swaths of color to win her favor. The rabbit then delivered the gift to the goddess. Ostara was said to be pleased and it soon caught on with children in the area. The idea of decorating eggs has continued throughout the years.

Eggs like those created by Fabergé were opulent and ornate works of decorative art. Children in the United States continue to spend time hunting the eggs that they worked so hard to decorate, thanks in part to the first presidential egg roll in 1878 under Rutherford B. Hayes. The tradition continues today over 140 years later.

The Rabbit

The Easter Bunny is another symbol that is associated with this turning of the seasons. Ostara was a goddess of spring, and the hare was thought to be sacred to her. The rabbit is the one who presented her gift of the egg to the goddess and is the one who continues to hide them throughout the world.

Since they seem to multiply seemingly overnight due to the short gestation period of the rabbit, it is no wonder that they have become synonymous with fertility. However, they also are harbingers of abundance and balance, which is perfect for this sabbat.

Celebrating Ostara

There are many ways that you can celebrate the coming of the spring and the fertility of the earth. Consider using the symbols of Ostara to build your rituals. Creativity is key.

Decorating Eggs

Eggs can be decorated in a variety of ways. One way that you can incorporate this tradition into your Ostara rituals would be to draw sigils that will help to birth new ideas on the shells prior to dyeing. An easy way to achieve this is by taking a wax pencil or white crayon and drawing the desired sigils on the eggs and then dyeing them. The dye could be a commercial one you can find in the store or you could create natural dyes. Natural dyes can be made with turmeric, red or yellow onion skins, grape juice, and beet juice, to name a few.

New Beginnings

This is the perfect time of year for new beginnings. Instead of fortune cookies, use the plastic eggs you find at the supermarket. You can insert inspirational phrases and ideas inside of the shells. These eggs can then be hidden, and those who find the eggs are blessed during the next phase of the year.

One could also extend this to placing the pieces of paper into the hollow chocolate rabbits you find at the grocery during this time of year. In order to add the paper, you will need to create a small incision or hole in the rabbit. Once you place the paper inside you must close the hole. You can achieve this by taking chocolate chips and melting them over a double boiler. Spread the chocolate across the opening and wait for it to harden. These can be distributed during cakes and ale of the sabbat rites. These rabbits will be sure to bring an element of fun to any ritual.

References

McCoy, Edain. *Ostara: Customs, Spells & Rituals for the Rites of Spring*. St. Paul, MN: Lewellyn Publications, 2003.

———. *The Sabbats: A New Approach to Living the Old Ways*. St. Paul, MN: Lewellyn Publications, 1994.

Morgan, Sheena. *The Wicca Book of Days*. London: Vega, 2002.

Nichols, Mike. *The Witches' Sabbats*. Albany, CA: Acorn Guild Press., 2005

"The Power of Rabbits." The Pagan Grove. 2010. https://pagangrove.wordpress.com/2010/02/13/137/.

"The White House Easter Egg Roll." The White House. https://www.whitehouse.gov/eastereggroll/.

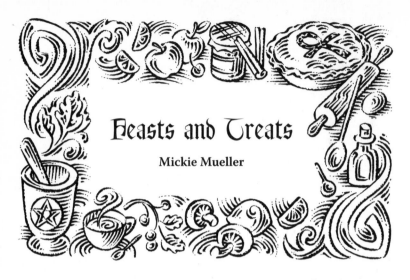

Feasts and Treats

Mickie Mueller

I BET YOU'RE NOTICING that spring is in the air, and you're probably seeing the signs in the produce aisle, as spring veggies and fruit become more abundant. Of course, eggs are traditional for Ostara as a symbol of inception and fertility. I've included two egg dishes because both are delicious, and I just couldn't decide. Many magic users choose Ostara as a day to bless the seeds they will sow this year, so I added a dessert that includes magical seeds that function in the recipe as eggs; what could be more Ostara than that?

Spinach and Artichoke Brunch Soufflés

The recipe comes from my daughter Brittany, who is a vintage fashion blogger and a great cook. She and her family used to get similar ones when they went out for brunch, but decided to attempt making them at home for a thriftier treat. She's since made these for many family gatherings and they're always a hit for Ostara. She generously gave me permission to share it with you. (Find Brittany's vintage life at VavoomVintage.net.)

Prep time: 20 minutes
Baking time: 10–15 minutes
Servings: 16 muffin cups

6 tablespoons butter or margarine

2 cups milk or milk substitute

2½ tablespoons all-purpose flour or gluten-free flour mix

6 eggs or egg substitute

½ cup fresh, chopped spinach

½ cup chopped artichoke hearts

2 green onions (scallions) thinly sliced (both the white and green parts)

2 rolls of refrigerator crescent rolls, any brand (they make gluten-free ones if you prefer)

¼ cup shredded Asiago cheese or cheese of your choice

Optional: ¼ cup crumbled bacon, veggie bacon, or prosciutto

Preheat the oven to 350° F (177° C). First, you'll make a béchamel sauce. I know that sounds intimidating, but it's actually really simple. Melt butter over medium heat in a medium-size sauce pan. Then stir in the flour and cook it for about 5 minutes, stirring until it turns thicker and golden. Pour in about ¼ cup of milk and mix constantly for about a minute, then add the rest of the milk and whisk it with a wire whisk continuously until smooth. Cook until thickened, stirring with a wooden spoon. Once thickened, adjust heat to low.

Beat eggs in a bowl, then whisk them into your béchamel sauce and cook on low until the mix gets much thicker. Mix in spinach, artichoke hearts, and scallions. You can also add optional crumbled bacon, veggie bacon, or prosciutto now.

Spray 16 muffin tins with non-stick spray. Lay one triangle-shaped piece of crescent dough in each muffin tin. Fill each tin about halfway with the filling and fold the ends of the dough over the top. Bake for 10–15 minutes until dough is golden brown and filling is firm. As soon as you remove them from the oven, sprinkle tops with shredded cheese. Serve hot, but they're also delish after they cool.

Spring Fritatta

Fritatta is a dish that works for breakfast, brunch, or brinner (breakfast for dinner). It sounds really fancy, but is really quite easy to make and can use a variety of ingredients. It's traditionally made with whatever you have around, so if you want to substitute ingredients, feel free to be creative. I love this spring combination of veggies; it's a celebration of growth and abundance to come. I use my trusty witchy cast-iron skillet for this recipe, but any large, flat pan that you can use on the stovetop and in the oven will work.

Prep time: 10 minutes
Cooking time: 15 minutes
Servings: 4

½ cup diced onion
2 cups asparagus, cut into 1-inch pieces
1 carrot, grated
¼ cup peas, fresh or frozen
2 cup spinach, chopped
8 eggs or egg substitute
⅓ cup milk (or substitute cream for an extra creamy fritatta)
3 tablespoons olive oil
Salt and pepper to taste
½ cup crumbled feta cheese or other cheese of your preference
Your choice of ½ cup browned sausage, bacon, vegan bacon, chickpeas, or veggie sausage (or ¼ cup chopped smoked salmon)

Preheat oven to 350° F (177° C). Sauté diced onion and asparagus in olive oil on medium heat. Once they're tender, add shredded carrots and peas and cook for a couple minutes. Then add spinach and cook until wilted.

Beat eggs and milk in a large bowl; resist the urge to overmix, just beat until the yolks and whites are blended together. Add your choice of meat or meat substitute and cheese, salt, and pepper to the bowl, then pour the egg mixture into the hot pan over the other ingredients. Cook it while stirring, over medium heat, about 4–5 minutes until the bottom sets and sides pull away from the pan a bit. Place the skillet in the oven and bake an additional 3–4 minutes minutes. Serve it in pie slices.

Spring Greens Salad

If you're serving breakfast, a fruit salad pairs well with these dishes, but for brunch or a later meal, a spring salad is a lovely side dish. This salad has both fresh seasonal greens representing new life and the dried fruit and nuts that were traditional mainstays of winter and welcoming spring.

Prep time: 10 minutes
Servings: 6

5 cups of spring greens, including arugula, baby spinach, and romaine
4 green onions, thinly sliced on the bias
½ cup dried cranberries
½ cup walnuts
½ cup feta (or sub cheese of your choice)

Honey Balsamic Vinaigrette Dressing
⅓ cup balsamic vinegar
¼ cup olive oil
3 tablespoons honey
1 tablespoons Dijon mustard
½ teaspoon pepper
½ teaspoon salt

Toss all salad ingredients in a large salad bowl. Add all the ingredients for the dressing to a small bowl and whisk while drizzling in the olive oil. Toss the salad with the dressing and serve.

Ostara Seed Cakes

I've made several variations of this dessert over the years. This is basically a cake mix hack; you can use any yellow cake mix, or do what I do and grab a gluten-free cake mix for these charming cupcakes. These sweet treats celebrate the seeds that we plant in the spring and the blossoms that they will become.

Prep time: 20 minutes
Baking time: 15–20 minutes
Servings: 24 cupcakes

1 white or yellow cake mix of your choice (instead of eggs, this recipe uses the magic of healthy chia seeds)
1 tablespoon black chia seeds for each egg the mix calls for
3 tablespoons water for each egg the mix calls for
Melted butter or coconut oil, to substitute for oil in mix
Whipped cream or vegan whipped cream
2 tablespoons shelled unsalted sunflower seeds
1 teaspoon dried or fresh lavender buds
2 tablespoons chopped dry or fresh rose petals
Edible flowers and herb leaves (try petals of roses, carnations, marigolds, pansies, lilacs, violets, or leaves of thyme, sage, and rosemary. Rinse and allow to dry on paper towel.)

Add the chia seeds to the water and set aside for 15 minutes; the mixture will become a gel-like consistency.

Follow the instructions on the box mix, but add the chia seed mixture instead of eggs and the butter or oil of your choice. If the instructions call for water, add accordingly. Mix according to directions and once the batter is ready, stir in the lavender buds, chopped rose petals, and sunflower seeds. Pour into cupcake tins with paper liners. Bake according to the cupcake directions on your mix box.

Now you can make the sugared flower petals and herbs while your cupcakes are in the oven. Simply brush a very thin coating of the gel left in the bowl that your chia seeds were in onto the petals and leaves and then sprinkle sugar over them. Let them dry on waxed paper. Once the cupcakes are baked and cooled completely, top with whipped cream or vegan whipped cream and decorate each with a sugared flower or flower petal.

Crafty Crafts

Ember Grant

AT THE SPRING EQUINOX, day and night are equal in length, but the light continues to dominate, bringing new life to the land. Eggs are a classic symbol of rebirth and new beginnings. These two crafts can be combined into one project, or done separately

Artistic Eggs

You can have decorative eggs that last forever by drying out real eggs and painting them. You can use any kind of eggs for this project, but white ones may be best for painting purposes. If you don't want to decorate an entire dozen, many stores sell eggs by the half-dozen.

Materials
Real eggs ($2–$6)
Acrylic paint ($2–$10, depending on how many colors you use)
Push pin or tack
Paint brushes
Optional: assorted ribbons, glitter, rhinestones, etc.
   Cost: $5+ (depending on your choice of supplies)
   Time Spent: including preparation and drying, several hours to a day

First you need to empty and dry the eggs. It's fairly easy to hollow out an egg, and there are variations of the method, depending on personal preference. Basically, you need to poke a hole in each end of the egg; you can do this with a push pin or tack. Some people put a piece of tape on the each end of the egg in order to reduce the risk of creating cracks. I've had success both ways.

After you carefully poke a hole in each end of the egg, you'll need to gently blow air through the egg in order to push out the insides. You can use a straw if you wish, but you don't have to. If you don't want to waste the egg, empty the contents into a bowl—then you can use the eggs in baking or scramble them.

Once the egg is empty, run water through it; you can simply hold it under water running from the faucet. Then let the egg dry several hours or overnight.

Now it's time to decorate it. Of course, it's thin and fragile, so you may want to arrange a holder for the egg so it doesn't roll around. You can cut an empty cardboard paper towel or bath tissue holder and make a ring for the egg to sit in. You can push a wooden or metal skewer through it, too, but that may risk breakage—it depends on the size of the holes in the egg. Don't worry about the holes for now; we'll address how to conceal those later.

There are endless ways to decorate these eggs! For an easy and vibrant look, use acrylic paint and add glitter. Try using a solid color, then add glitter while the paint is still wet. One of my favorite techniques is to use light blue paint, like the color of a robin's egg, and glitter in blue, silver, or iridescent shades to make it sparkle. When the paint is dry, you can glue ribbon onto it as well.

Another idea is to draw on your egg with markers and add magical symbols. If you're feeling ambitious, try to re-create the look of a Fabergé egg design. You can display your eggs in egg-cup holders, if you have them, or make ring stands out of cardboard.

If you want to hang your egg, thread a ribbon through it and tie a knot at the bottom. One way to accomplish this is to thread the

string or ribbon all the way through the egg using a long needle or large paper clip.

To cover up the holes in the egg, you can put some masking tape over them before you paint, or affix decorative rhinestones or stickers in those places. Or, you can simply strategically place the egg in an arrangement so the holes don't show. You can use the basket you made at Imbolc—just add some moss and convert it into a nest to display your eggs; this makes a lovely altar decoration. You can also give these eggs as gifts. One lovely way to display your egg is by adding it to a spring floral arrangement in a decorative flower pot.

Decoupage Flower Pot

Prepare for the upcoming planting season by making a special flower pot. You can use it to start your first seeds of spring, or use it to create a silk or dried arrangement. These also make wonderful spring gifts, centerpieces, or altar decorations. Since we're going to apply paper to the pot, use caution if putting it outside. There are ways to make decoupage items waterproof, so you can take that extra step if you wish.

Materials

Terra-cotta planter, approximately 4–6 inches tall ($2–$10)
Assorted decorative scrapbook paper ($3–$10)
Mod Podge Hard Coat ($7)
Brush or sponge (price varies)
Optional: seeds, potting soil, silk floral supplies, etc.

Cost: $12+ (depending on choice of supplies)

Time Spent: several hours to several days (allowing for drying time)

Choose paper that features designs and colors for the season, and tear the paper into pieces and strips in a variety of sizes. Make a few long strips for the top part of the planter, and make larger ones for the rest of the pot. Tearing the paper rather than cutting it gives the edges a more interesting and rustic appearance. If you've never created a decoupage project before, it's really easy—just don't overthink it! You're going to glue the paper in patches onto the pot, overlapping them somewhat. It's okay to have a few bare places where the terra cotta shows through. Scrapbook paper works well for this project because it's thick enough to work with, but not too thick that it's hard to adhere to the surface.

First, make sure your pot is clean and dry. Review the specific directions on the Mod Podge container before you begin; you need to be sure to have the hard coat type. You're going to decoupage a section at a time.

Begin by brushing on a thin layer of the glue, then add the paper and press it down, followed by another layer of glue over that. Then proceed with another piece of paper, and so on. Allow each coat of glue to dry (about twenty minutes) before adding a second and third coat of the glue.

The finished product will have a "patchwork" look, unless you decide to cover the entire pot. You can glue a ribbon onto the pot as well, or add other decorative features. Once the project has cured over several days, you're ready to fill it!

Use it as a traditional planter if you'd like, or combine this project with the Artistic Eggs project and make a lovely floral arrangement that features one of your decorated eggs. To do that, place a small piece of floral foam in the bottom of the pot and add some silk or dried leaves and flowers of your choice. Stuff some decorative moss around the base of the flowers. You can attach a decorated egg to a wooden skewer and stick it into the foam if you like, but I prefer to just nestle the egg in the moss at the base of the flowers (this is also a good way to disguise the holes in each end of the egg). You will end up with a simple yet elegant seasonal centerpiece for your dinner table or altar.

I used soft, muted shades of pale green, gray, blue, and mauve that matched the paper I used on the flower pot, and let my bright "robin's egg blue" glittering egg give the arrangement a pop of color.

A Crystal for Every Season: Fluorite

Charlie Rainbow Wolf

OSTARA IS THE SECOND festival of the spring, and occurs at the Spring Equinox, when the days and nights are of equal length. It's a time of balance and focus, of new beginnings and fertility. Many different traditions have a sacred festival at this time of year, including—but not limited to—Pagan, Christian, Wiccan, Hindu, Sikh, and Jewish traditions. It's named after the goddess Ostara, who represents the dawn light. It stands to reason, then, that the crystals associated with this festival reflect the light, balance, and fertility that it brings.

Some of the more popular and easily obtainable stones include amazonite, chrysoprase, fluorite, garnet, jasper, lapis, and rose quartz. You could also include agate in this, provided that you chose it carefully. Both agate and quartz come in such a wide variety that it's usually easy and fairly inexpensive to choose a suitable stone from these categories.

Fluorite

My top choice for an Ostara stone has to be fluorite. With its myriad of translucent hues and frequent bands of color, it always seems such a positive stone, oozing with potential. Fluorite is predominantly four colors—blue, purple, gold, and white—although pink, green, and even black are not uncommon. They're all translucent, and sometimes the different shades are found blended together in the same stone.

The molecular structure of fluorite is one of a nearly equal balance of calcium and fluorine. With a hardness of only four, it's not a particularly robust stone. It scratches easily, so care must be taken—particularly if you've got it in a bowl of tumbled stones—that you don't mar the surface. Fluorite is cut and polished into many different shapes, including spheres, merkabas, pyramids, and more. Polishing brings out the color and depth in the stone, although raw crystals may also be used in meditation, healing, and ceremony.

It doesn't matter what hue you choose for your Ostara festivities. All fluorites are said to be protective and useful when it comes to grounding energy and stabilizing the spirit. They're cleansing and creative in nature, and many healers use them for clearing out negative energy and restoring balance. It's believed by those who work with this stone that it has the potential to increase intuition, promote inspiration and new ideas, and assist in connecting with spirit guides or the higher self. The different shades add subtle nuances to these qualities, so choose the appropriate color to go with the theme of your ritual or celebration. Fluorite is of particular use if you're conducting your ceremony or connecting with others online, as it is said to benefit those who work with technology.

Blue

Blue fluorite comes in many shades, from the palest of ice blues to a faded denim hue, to almost turquoise, into a lilac that's nearly purple. It's a throat chakra stone, said to promote honesty and clarity, and to help you to release any karmic residue that may be holding you back from being everything you have the potential to be. Choose this stone when your main concerns are communicating, visualizing what you want, or calming nervous energy. If you're trying to break a habit or let go of an attachment from the past, or if you desire to commune with any of your guides and spirit helpers, blue fluorite is your friend.

Gold or Yellow

Select this stone when you need to focus and clear your mind. If you have an idea you're hoping to execute, gold fluorite will assist the logical and reasoning side of your brain to align your actions with your intent so that your plans are successful. It's a solar plexus chakra stone, and resonates with your willpower and integrity. If you practice any form of divination, this stone might help you find a lost or missing object, or at least bring you the clarity to get some idea where it could be. If your emotions are jangled, working with yellow or gold fluorite has the potential to calm your nerves and bring a sense of peace. It also helps you to see things from a different angle, which is always a good thing.

Purple

Many healers believe this to be the most soothing of all the fluorites, and there's a part of me that agrees. I've got a beautiful fluorite necklace made of irregularly shaped tumbled stones, striped with shades of purple and cyan. It may be mind over matter, but when I wear it, I feel less stressed somehow. It's a third eye chakra stone that helps you not just see new ideas clearly, but also assists you when it comes to cutting through the illusions to find the truth in what you experience. If you're seeking to heighten your intuition or unlock latent psychic talents, this is the stone to use.

White

White fluorite ranges from nearly clear to nearly opaque. It's a crown chakra stone, and if you work with spirit helpers it will help you to contact their purity and wisdom. Its energy is gentle yet strong, and works with you when you need to nurture compassion and understanding without turning into an enabler or a doormat. If your goal is to bring clarity, purity, and focus into things, then white fluorite is an excellent ally to have with you. Crystal healers believe that wearing white fluorite will repel electromagnetic energy, as well as help to prevent you from psychic attack or other maliciousness.

Other Fluorites

This stone is also found in shades of black, green, and pink, sometimes found together in the same stone. The green echoes growth and progress, bringing a new and fresh energy with it. Green is the color of the heart chakra, and helps you to work through past hurts, attachment issues, or addiction. Pink is also a heart chakra color, with a positive and soothing energy. It is the color of universal love, not the love that is borne of ego, but the unconditional love that comes with compassion, understanding, and acceptance. Fluorite is also found in the darkest of colors, so dark that it looks translucent black. Black is grounding, a root chakra color, and this stone helps with those things too. Healers use it to cleanse the aura and balance energy.

Reference

Barthelmy, Dave. "Fluorite Mineral Data." Flame Tests. http://webmineral.com/data/Fluorite.shtml#.W2hpGtJKhQA.

Ostara Tree Blessing Ritual

Blake Octavian Blair

TREES ARE POWERFUL MAGICKAL ALLIES, and we often look to them as our way of tracking the seasons since we watch the cycle of life through the foliage on their branches. Perhaps you'd like a prayer tree of your own to perform ritual at, work with, and develop a relationship with. This ritual will aid you in blessing and consecrating your own prayer tree and even provide you an option to plant one, if you so choose.

The vernal equinox is associated magickally with a time of new beginnings, making this the perfect time to begin your relationship with a new tree friend. You can of course perform this ritual directly on the vernal equinox proper; however, this is not essential. In fact, depending on where you live, and if you're choosing to plant a tree or simply bless an existing one, you may need to slightly adjust the timing of this ritual for when the weather will allow you to accomplish your goals. This is quite fine, as we can celebrate both the "official" coming of spring at the vernal equinox, and/or when spring weather actually arrives. When planting a tree, always remember to do what's best for the health of the tree! Your local nursery, which is a great place to purchase your tree, can provide you guidance for your specific type of tree.

You can perform this ritual alone or with just a few loved ones, or you can have your entire coven, circle, or grove participate. Parts can be carried out by all one person or divided up among a group. While the ritual can be done solo, it is admittedly far easier to plant a tree with at least two people. If you do belong to a group, I find it's especially meaningful and powerful to have them participate. Feel free to adjust and adapt the ritual as you need!

If you are planting a tree, I suggest pre-digging the hole for the tree, as well as preparing the dirt and compost mixture that will go back into the hole during the ceremony prior to beginning the ritual. A common rule of thumb for the size of the hole is twice as wide and twice as deep as the root ball. However, please consult the nursery you purchased the tree from on how large you should dig the hole for your specific tree, and for detailed planting instructions. You should also be able to purchase compost from the nursery.

Supplies and Tools

If planting:
Tree
Shovel
50/50 dirt and compost mixture
Gardening gloves
Plenty of water (a hose hooked up to a water connection is ideal)

For the Blessing:
Offerings such as small crystals or stones, herbs, etc.
Incense and/or smudge of choice and a safe fireproof vessel
   to burn it in
Matches or lighter
Chalice or drinking horn
Libation of choice (also, corkscrew if needed!)
Bell, drum, or rattle

Preparation

The ritual space will be the site of the tree planting or blessing the existing tree. If you are planting, have the tree already near the dug hole, and the dirt compost mixture (50 percent dirt from the hole and 50 percent compost) just to the side of the hole. I find that for a planting, it's best to work sans altar and simply have your ritual tools and supplies in a basket and pull them out as needed for use.

Ritual

Gather just outside the perimeter or the ritual area. Smudge each participant. After a participant has been smudged, they process into the ritual space and circle three times around the tree or dug hole and choose a place in the circle. When all are present, the ritual leader can proceed.

Create sacred space by following the protocols of your tradition. This can include circlecasting, calling the spirits of the directions, spirits the land, deities, and so on. Due to the nature of this ritual, I highly suggest calling in the spirits of the land, both of nature and the ancestors who preceded you on the land. Also, invoke the spirit of the individual tree you are working with—the greater spirit of the species of the tree. Ask them all for assistance in your ritual intention.

Officially welcome everybody and announce your intentions for this tree, and what it means and symbolizes to you. Speak of your intentions to begin a new relationship with this tree as new life begins to bud throughout nature this spring. Tell the gathered participants what it means to you for them to participate and play a role in this ritual dedication with you.

Planting

(Note: If you are blessing an existing tree instead of planting a new one, skip ahead to the "Blessing: For an Existing Tree" section.)

You'll want to follow the specific advice of your nursery in planting your tree. However, general guidelines are as follows. Place a few shovelfulls of dirt mixture into the hole until the tree is at the appropriate depth when the rootball is gently placed into the hole. It is helpful to have a person to assist you in handling and holding the tree, while you also manage the shovel. When appropriate depth and positioning of tree is achieved, hold the tree upright.

Blessing

If Planting:

While the tree is being held upright in place, ask the participants to place offerings one by one into the hole. Invite them to share a few words about the symbolism of their offering. When all are finished, have one person continue to hold the tree as you shovel dirt mixture into the hole. Once dirt is filled into the hole, covering the roots, and at the height directed by the tree planting instructions you were given by your nursery, you can proceed to the next step of the blessing. (Section labeled "For Planting a Tree and an Existing Tree.")

For an Existing Tree:

Ask participants to one by one place their offerings at the bottom of the tree, then touch their third eye gently against the trunk of the tree and commune with the spirit of the tree. (An existing, more mature tree can tolerate this much better than a young, freshly planted tree.) Invite them to share a few words about the symbolism of their offering.

For Planting a Tree and an Existing Tree:

Proceed to do a thorough smudging of the tree, as high up as you can reach with your arms, and let the smoke waft upward into the branches if the tree is taller than you are. Circle the tree while smudging three times.

Next, circle the tree three times while drumming, rattling, or bell ringing. Hold the intention of both cleansing and awakening the tree with vibrant energy.

Fill your chalice or drinking horn with your libation of choice. Pass the horn among participants. Have them offer a small pour to the base of the tree. Have them take a drink themselves, and then offer any prayers or blessings either silently or aloud that they'd like to confer for both you and the tree, and for the coming spring.

Now you may close the ritual by releasing sacred space in accordance with the protocols of your tradition and releasing any entities on which you may have called.

After the Ritual

If you have just planted a tree, be sure to give it a good healthy watering. Also, many trees benefit greatly from mulching around their base. You've probably gathered by my frequent mentions in this article that I suggest becoming good friends with a local nursery. They're going to be able to offering you suggestions on how often and how much from here on out to water your tree, and if it would benefit from mulch.

Whether you have just planted a tree or blessed an existing one, you now have your very own consecrated prayer tree to work with. I hope that the spirits of the trees enchant you not only this spring, but the whole year long!

Notes

Beltane

Beltane Beyond the Maypole

JD Hortwort

MAY DAY—OR, FOR THE Celts who are reading this, Beltaine—is one of the most ubiquitous celebrations in the northern hemisphere. As a celebration that definitely finds its roots in Pagan traditions, it continues to be marked with festivals, parties, bonfires, and more, especially in Europe and many Third World countries. In fact, it could almost be said to rival the Winter Solstice and Samhain for its acceptance in the mundane world.

Even the stodgy old Communist Party in the late nineteenth and early twentieth centuries seized on the date. Of course, they first changed the name to "the International Workers' Day." In Russia, that name changed again in the 1990s to "the Day of Spring and Labor," which has a much gentler ring to it.

It seems people everywhere in the northern hemisphere can find an excuse to honor this day, which, for all intents and purposes, has some pretty randy origins. For our ancestors, this was the time to celebrate the creative energies of the universe, in the field and in the barnyard. Our ancestors weren't too averse to taking part in the action, either.

Is it Beltane or Beltine or Beltaine or Some Other Word?

Modern Pagans have always known if you're going to be in this tradition, you're going to do a lot of sorting out. When it comes to Beltane (or however you like to spell it), it really depends on the country of origin.

The Irish might spell it Beltine, Beltaine, or Belltaine. A Scotsman might say Cetamain. The Manx word is Boaldyn. Most modern writers spell it Beltane. Other spellings include Beltaine, Bealtaine, Beltain, Bealteine, and Bealltuinn.

Regardless, the first day of May is celebrated with bale fires, handfastings, the gathering of herbs, and general randiness—if you have a field of wheat that needs a little encouraging.

Beyond the Maypole

Mention Beltane and most people will immediately think of the Maypole—that very masculine symbol of the holiday. Beltane certainly would not be the same without it, any more than you can have a Beltane celebration without colorful ribbons, bright clothing, and flowery headdresses.

At the House of Akasha (a Celtic spiritual organization in Greensboro, North Carolina), our Maypole is a permanent fixture at a special spot on our meeting grounds. There's no fixed height for a Maypole that we have ever determined, but I would caution against making it too tall.

Before we made our permanent pole, we raised an ambitious one of about fifteen feet. It was beautifully festooned with multi-colored ribbons and took what seemed like forever to braid in our Maypole dance. Let me just say, nobody needed ale or May wine for the next hour or so after it was complete. We were all too dizzy from the dance!

Fewer folks in the modern world mark the holiday with balefires today, but fire is a central focus of Pagan May Day observations. The lighting of the balefire is done to celebrate the growing strength of the sun and to purify those who can jump over it of any lingering diseases from winter.

In the modern world, candles can be an acceptable alternative, especially if weather keeps the ritual celebration indoors or if no private space outdoors is available. Plus, the older members of our group, myself included, find it much easier to hop over a candlestick than to jump over a balefire.

Beltane has been important in Ireland since the Sons of Mil were believed to have arrived there on May 1 to engage the Tuatha de Danaan. Irish Celts were accustomed to mark Beltane with a ceremony to open the pastures. Great fires would be built and the herd animals shepherded between them to gain the blessings of Bel or Belanus. Bel (Bile—Irish; Beli—Welsh; or Belenus—Gaul) was the name European Celts gave their sun god.

Fewer folks still in the modern world pick up on the association of sacred waters and trees with this time of the year. We are blessed at the House of Akasha to have a place to worship that includes both running water and an abundance of trees. We don't call our stream "sacred," but we do find it to be a special place.

Sacred Waters

Hundreds of years ago, people made pilgrimages to sacred waters in hopes of cures for illness or blessings for good fortune at important times of the year, such as Beltane, Midsummer, and Lughnasadh.

Sacred wells and springs abounded in Ireland and throughout Europe. Every country had its sacred rivers or bodies of water too. Invariably, beside most wells there were important trees or shrubs suitable for leaving messages on to entice the gods to intervene on one's behalf.

No one could be surprised that water, most often associated with goddesses, might be venerated by ancient people. In so many senses, it was the "elixir of life." Safe, fresh water could insure survival for people and livestock. If that water came bubbling up from a mysterious opening in the earth, it provided a natural attraction. If it was naturally heated, as some thermal springs were, and blended with healing minerals, how could one deny the presence of a divine force?

Although many wells and springs sacred to the Celts were later rededicated to Christian saints, the practices that went on around them to coax that divine force into action remained for a long time rooted in Pagan ideas. Visitors still came to light candles, pay a token, or leave portions of bandages for themselves or sick friends too ill to travel.

Veneration of waters wasn't limited to wells and springs. The Danube River in Germany is sacred to Danu. The Seine River in France gets its name from the Celtic goddess Sequana, honored for her healing gifts. Sinainn gave her name to the River Shannon in Ireland. Like her, Boann gave her name to the River Boyne in Ireland.

Archeologists have found major rivers in the British Isles and Europe to be literal treasure chests. The faithful brought offerings to toss into the waters in exchange for favors. Warriors who had pledged a percentage of their battle bounty to one deity or another would sometimes deposit their pledge into rivers to be carried to the otherworld. Likewise, the heads of leaders and important members of the Tuatha might be taken to an important river as a final resting place.

Sacred Trees

Beside these wells, springs, and rivers were trees. Trees, with their obvious masculine association, played an important part in the lives of ancient people. Tribal names were frequently tied to specific trees. For example, the Eubron tribe in Gaul were the people of the yew.

If you really wanted to demonstrate your military prowess and strike fear in the hearts of your enemy, you and your troops would sweep into the center of the opposing side's settlement and cut down their sacred tree or bile (be it yew, oak, ash, birch, etc.).

The name of the site of Cill Dara (or Kildare for modern folks) in Ireland, sacred to St. Brigid, translates into "the church of the oak." Nine magical hazelnut trees were said to stand at the head waters of the River Boyne. From them dropped nuts that conferred the knowledge of everything. Or you could just eat the salmon that swam in the waters behind the tree. They had been feasting on the nuts all their lives.

Some trees, like the alder and the ash, were so revered they could not be cut down. The ash tree bestowed protection from fairies and bad magic to those who carried a bit of it with them. Although not limited to ash trees, the Maypole was said to have been frequently made of ash.

When any of these trees grew beside a sacred well or river, they were considered a direct connection to the otherworld where deities and other magical creatures dwelt. People visited the waters to wash away their illnesses, everything from fever to arthritis. Other folks made wishes for fortune and, in some cases, misfortune. The misfortune, of course, was usually directed at someone else.

To mark their visit, they would tie bits of rag onto the tree. In some cases, they left monetary tokens embedded in the tree bark. Who was going to steal it and risk the ire of the otherworldly denizens!

The concept of the sacred water and sacred tree comes together in the love story of Boann and the Dagda. Boann is the goddess of the River Boyne that flows beside Newgrange, the home of the Dagda. Some evidence suggests the root of his name means oak. Together, they gave birth to the Celtic god of love, poetry, and youth, Aengus mac Og. It's the age-old story of water supporting the tree that bears the fruit that sustains the people of the Tuatha.

In this story, Aengus eventually tricks the Dagda out of his home and Boann may or may not have been drowned when she released the waters that became the River Boyne, but nobody ever said the old stories all come to a happy ending.

Honoring with Water and Tree

In an effort to honor what we understand are Celtic traditions, we can mark our Beltane celebrations with more than just a Maypole to symbolize the divine male. Beltane is a time to celebrate both the masculine and feminine energies. After all, it takes both to procreate!

This is a time when both energies are vibrant. They are joined by a common passion and goal: the perpetuation of the species. In the case of the god and goddess, it is the perpetuation of all species, plant and animal.

In the House of Akasha, we have done our celebrations in several ways. Sometimes, members have gathered in the running waters of the stream adjacent to our ritual area to let the waters renew us. We have included plants or planting exercises to mark the importance of the growing season to our ancestors.

But, perhaps most importantly, we take time to relate to the natural area around us. We have conducted meditations in which we see ourselves rooted in the mundane world but connected to the Otherworld. Our spot has one particular beech tree with roots that have grown in the general shape of a human body. It's a good spot to recline, enter into a meditative state, and feel your body being absorbed for a brief time into the very essence of the tree. Where the journey takes you after that is up to you as meditator.

At Beltane, just as at Samhain, the veil is thin. It invites us to respectfully acknowledge that which we cannot see, that which we cannot explain, and that which can enrich our lives throughout the course of the year.

References

McCaffrey, Carmel and Leo Eaton. *In Search of Ancient Ireland: The Origins of the Irish from Neolithic Times to the Coming of the English*. Chicago: New Amsterdam Books, 55, 83–84. 2002.

Ellis, Peter Berresford. *The Druids*. London: Constable and Company, 121–135. 1994.

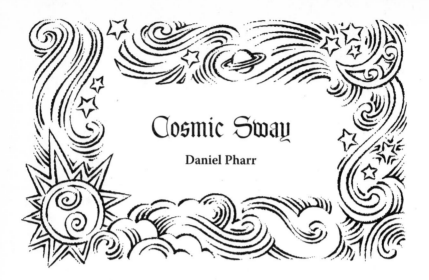

Cosmic Sway

Daniel Pharr

ORIGINALLY ONLY TWO SEASONS were recognized by the ancient Celts: winter, beginning on Samhain, and summer, beginning on Beltaine. Samhain also marked the new year. So as darkness came before light and night before day, winter came before summer. Beltaine, the first day of summer, is a lunar holiday occurring on the Full or dark Moon nearest the mid-year lunar cycle. Beltaine has remained the second most prominent high holiday after Samhain, even after adding Imbolc and Lughassadh, and later the solstices and equinoxes. If only two high holidays in a year can be celebrated, rightfully those two holidays would be Samhain and Beltaine.

Like every other sabbat, Beltaine was fixed to a particular day on the calendar in an effort to convert the celebration from a lunar-based holiday to a solar-based holiday. Thus Beltaine landed on May 1, six months after Samhain's solar date, and since night comes before day, the celebration begins at sundown on April 30 and ends at sundown on May 1.

Beltaine Sun

Beltaine on April 30 will occur under a waxing first quarter Moon in Leo. The first quarter of the lunar cycle can manifest as a period of increased stress brought on by an intense yearning to achieve and be seen. Leo multiplies these desires by furthering the need for attention and being noticed. Trying to accomplish something, anything, to quench the thirst of recognition, can be quite nerve-racking, as mistakes are made and complications increase. However, the Leo need to be the center of attention also provides vibrance and lets shine an inner light of vitality. This is a wonderful time to be on stage, to perform, to be in the public eye. Utilize this energy to act out a Beltaine ritual, lead the singing of the ancient songs around the balefire, dance wildly, or call down the deities and directions for the night's work. Self-expression in any positive manner is appropriate at this time.

The Leo Moon influence will be around all night on April 30 and until 12:04 p.m. on May 1 when the Moon goes void-of-course and moves into Virgo on May 2 at 1:35 a.m. Before the Moon goes void-of-course, consider making any large purchases, especially a car, truck, motorcycle, or other form of transportation. Leaving on a longer journey is also recommended at this time. Traveling is good for the Celtic soul, as the ancients were always searching for adventure. This Moon will open the door to the inner dragonslayer.

Gardening

The month of May is the height of planting season. The earth has been collecting heat and light from the sun for months and has warmed to the point that naturally sown seeds are popping open and sending forth all manner of May flowers. Plant everything, sow all seeds, transplant from under glass into the earth all day on May 6 and through the night to sunrise. A waxing Moon moves into Scorpio at 3:04 a.m. on the sixth and becomes a Full Scorpio Moon on the seventh just after sunrise. A waxing water Moon nearing fullness in May auspiciously marks the perfect time for planting, transplanting, and sowing. Likewise, planting is advised on the evening of May 24, and all night and day on the twenty-fifth and twenty-sixth, under a waxing Cancer Moon.

Beltaine Moon

The more historically correct lunar Beltaine occurs on May 7 under the Full Scorpio Moon at 6:45 a.m. The Beltaine balefire and celebration is most appropriate on the evening of the sixth under a nearly Full Scorpio Moon, and dancing by the Maypole might well happen in the daylight hours of May 6. Although Beltaine does not officially begin until sundown, festivities leading up to Beltaine, like the Maypole, can certainly occur earlier on the warm summer afternoon. The Maypole is usually constructed some days ahead, as time permits, and erected just prior to the dance by the women in the celebration, provocatively holding, carrying, and caressing the pole until it stands on its own fully erect. The men usually dig and prepare the hole in the ground to receive the pole in a similarly provocative manner.

Be sure to make offerings of milk and bread when calling down the deities, and ideally place them into the hole before receiving the shaft. The dance around the pole in opposite directions can be confusing at the start, so a dance conductor of sorts is very helpful in starting folks on the right foot. Music or at minimum a drumbeat are essential to fuel the frolicking interweaving of dancers.

The jubilant festivity on this first night of summer, a warm night around a substantial blaze, can be exhilarating. Light and breezy ritual clothing is best, or choose to enter the circle only partially dressed or skyclad. In many celebrations, Beltaine is synonymous with debauchery. Decorate braided hair with picked flowers. Decorate face and body with henna or charcoal, smear symbols on the body using carbon black from the fire, to aid in energetic flow and spiritual release, self-protection, and proclaiming the future. Decorate the ritual area with ribbons, candles, and hang garlands of flowers. Serve egg dishes, oatmeal, and lamb. Build a great fire. Place boughs of cedar or other sacred trees on the fire and use other boughs to waft the smoke onto the revelers as a blessing and a banishing of evil, evil intent, or malady. Set plenty of drummers to a beat, move and dance around the fire, jump the fire, build the energy to climax in the enactment of the sacred union of the goddess and the god.

Dark Moon

The dark Moon in Gemini occurs at 1:38 p.m. on May 22. This will be a playful time for the esbat. The dark Moon is always in support of divination. In the sign of Gemini, jollity and affability will add some spicy cheer to the work of divining the future. Further lubricate the process with some of the last remaining store of mead, if desired.

Green Man

Have a volunteer become the Green Man for the celebration. The Green Man is a representation of the spirit of the land, emulating the God bringing forth the abundance of the earth. The Green Man's enduring benevolent presence metaphorically fertilizes minds and bodies with the mischievous lifting of skirts, pinching of posteriors, and other such Scorpio trouble-making.

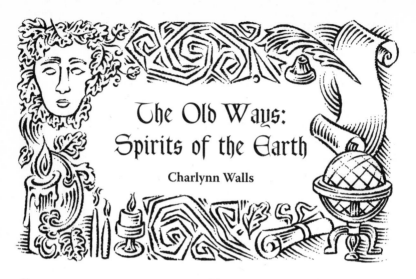

The Old Ways: Spirits of the Earth

Charlynn Walls

EACH YEAR AS THE seasons turn I become more and more attuned to the natural world around me. One Beltane I awoke to find a large faerie ring in my front lawn. There were two distinct rings in the yard: the outer ring where the grass was green and the inner ring made of toadstools. It was clear that the Fae had been working hard to bring themselves to my attention on this sacred day. I mentioned the sight to my husband so that he and the children would be sure not to disturb the rings. I also made sure to reciprocate and left them an offering of food and drink. I was also careful not to disturb the circle, laying the offerings right outside the circle.

Beltane is observed on May 1 and is a cross-quarter day that separates Ostara and Midsummer. This festival is opposite Samhain on the Wheel of the Year. Therefore, it mirrors the thinning of the veil and is a between time when we can connect with other spirits. Since the realms collide on this night, the Fair Folk are more active with the mortal realm.

The Fae

The Fae, or the Fair Folk, are a race of human-like beings that have magical powers. They typically have a tall, slight build and fair complexion. They tend to be of nobility and act as such, with exacting manners. They can shape-shift to make it easier to blend in with mortals. Their realm simultaneously exists with ours but is separate. They occasionally step into our realm to walk among us. And like humans there are many races. Some are benevolent, but the intentions of others are not always pure. It is always wise to be cautious when dealing directly with one of the Fae.

Beings identified as Fae are often recognized in other areas of the world as well. They are more commonly found in Ireland, Scotland, and Wales. The Faerie are intrinsically linked to the land, making them highly attuned to the elements and the earth. So if the land is damaged, they feel the impact as well, because this is where they get their strength and power. Some of their sacred sites of long ago are still known today. Some of the sites noted by Sirona Knight are "the Faery hill in Donegal, the Faery woods in Sligo, and the Sheeauns, the Faery mounds" (Knight 2000). These areas are such a part of the local lore that even in modern times they are often avoided. In Ireland, for example, they have re-routed roads to avoid taking out a faerie mound. Other areas that may not be as well-known but have frequent visits from the Fae are areas that lead down into the ground, away from the world as we know it.

Walking Among the Fae

The realms between the worlds can be breached under the right conditions. Our realm and that of the Fae are easily traversed on any of the sabbats, but especially on Samhain, Beltane, and Midsummer. They can be accessed readily during transition times such as dawn, noon, twilight, and midnight. Accessing the realm of the Fae can be accomplished through a Faerie ring, groves of trees, glades, caves, or other openings into the world below.

Walking among the Fae does carry some risk. There are stories of individuals accidently walking into the Faerie realm, never to return. Of course, there are some suggestions that can keep you safe. Be aware of your surroundings and who you are with. If you happen upon one of the Fae, be courteous. If you make promises, be sure to carry through on your end of the bargain. If you should arrive in the otherworld, avoid eating or drinking there. Carrying an item to barter with may also save you a headache.

There are rewards too, of course. The Fae can be great magical allies. They can help increase your own knowledge of the elements, especially the one that they are personally attuned to. They can shift your vision to what is usually beyond perception.

Honoring the Fae on Beltane

Here are a few ways you can work on cultivating a relationship with the Fae. Remember to be a good host, be consistent, and be respectful. Doing so will gain their trust.

Offerings of Milk and Honey

Take time to familiarize yourself with your own property, local walking paths, or parks. Get a feel for the land and look for the areas that would make excellent portals to the realm of the Fae. Make yourself known to them by leaving a small token or an offering of milk and honey. Avoid anything made of iron. Leaving an offering will show the Fae that you want to interact with them and will make it more likely that they show themselves to you.

Creating Sacred Spaces

The Fae appreciate a good host. So if you are able to make a space for them on your property, do so. It can be something as small as placing or creating a Faerie door at the base of one of your trees where they can easily enter or leave your part of the world. Or you could be clearing a part of your yard that is overgrown, making it more hospitable. You could also plant a small garden specifically for them, including herbs and flowers that have correspondences with Faerie lore and magick. Make sure you keep it tidy with regular upkeep and you will forge a strong relationship with them.

References

Knight, Sirona. *Celtic Traditions: Druids, Faeries, and Wiccan Rituals*. New York, NY: Citadel Press, 2000.

Marquis, Melanie. *Beltane: Rituals, Recipes & Lore for May Day*. Woodbury, MN: Lewellyn Publications, 2015.

McCoy, Edain. *The Sabbats: A New Approach to Living the Old Ways*. St. Paul, MN: Lewellyn Publications, 1994.

Morgan, Sheena. *The Wicca Book of Days*. London: Vega, 2002.

Nichols, Mike. *The Witches' Sabbats*. Albany, CA: Acorn Guild Press, 2005.

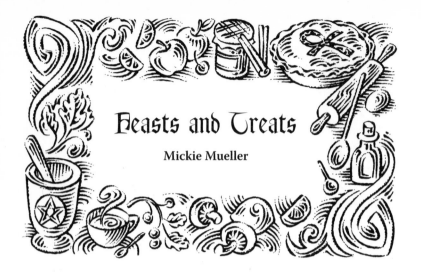

Feasts and Treats

Mickie Mueller

It's time to celebrate the lusty month of May. The world has burst into life and we're surrounded with sensuality, love, and passion. This menu delights the senses while keeping it light, so that whatever your Beltane celebration entails, you'll be ready for it. With foods associated with both the faerie realm and sacred sexuality, you'll have a lovely feast for Beltane as you welcome in the season of growth.

Breaded Portobello Mushrooms

Mushrooms are often associated with Beltane due to their connections to the fairy realm and sexuality. A local bar and grill my husband Dan and I like to go to serves some great breaded portobello mushrooms, and he challenged me to make some at home. Of course I accepted the challenge and what resulted is one of our favorite appetizers for company. You can use the recipe for small mushrooms too, but the big slices of portobello make a great presentation.

Prep time: 15 minutes
Cooking time: 25 minutes
Servings: 4

4 large portobello mushrooms
½ cup all-purpose flour (gluten-free flour mix works fine)
1 egg
¼ cup milk
2 cups of square rice cereal such as Rice Chex or another brand
1 tablespoon paprika
1 teaspoon salt
1 teaspoon pepper
1 teaspoon cayenne
1 tablespoon olive oil
Nonstick cooking spray

Preheat air fryer or oven to 400° F (200° C). Pour rice cereal into a gallon-sized zipper storage bag and zip it closed. Roll over the rice cereal with a rolling pin or large glass until crushed into small pieces that resemble breadcrumbs. Clean the mushrooms and slice them about ¾-inch thick, then rinse the slices.

Prepare three shallow dishes: one for the flour and one for the egg and milk (beat these together with a fork). In the third bowl, mix the crushed cereal, paprika, salt, pepper, and cayenne. Add the olive oil and mix it into cereal and seasoning with clean fingers. Be sure to mix it in well. Toss each mushroom slice in the flour and coat. Next, dip in the egg and milk mixture, then roll it in the cereal mixture.

Bake on a sheet pan for 25 minutes, turning mushrooms halfway through baking time. These can also be cooked in an air fryer at 400° F (200° C) for 10 minutes.

Mushroom Dipping Sauce

Here's a great dipping sauce for those breaded mushrooms that will get your heart pumping. It's quick and easy; everyone here loved it!
1 cup plain Greek yogurt or coconut Greek yogurt
1 tablespoon horseradish
2 tablespoons lemon juice
1 tablespoon sriracha

Combine all ingredients in a bowl and stir. Serve with your breaded portobellos.

Penne Puttanesca

Pasta is a pretty sexy dish, and as pasta goes, one that's light and fresh is even sexier. When I do spaghetti night, I often just open a jar of sauce and jazz it up with extras, but for a special Beltane meal, this traditional Italian dish isn't much more work and it's fresh and made with love. Many people do a puttanesca with spaghetti noodles; I usually opt for an elegant penne.

Prep time: 10 minutes
Cooking time: 30 minutes
Servings: 4

12-ounce package of penne pasta
    (you can also use gluten-free pasta)
2 tablespoons olive oil
6 cloves of garlic, minced
6 anchovies, rinsed and minced (optional)
¼ teaspoon crushed red pepper flakes
2 tablespoons tomato paste
5 cups diced roma tomatoes (about 8 tomatoes)
½ cup kalamata olives, cut in half
¼ cup capers
¼ cup chopped parsley
Salt and fresh pepper to taste
Freshly grated parmesan to garnish

Boil water and cook the pasta according to directions on the package. Heat olive oil in a large skillet over medium heat, then add garlic, red pepper, and anchovies. Cook about 2 minutes, then add tomato paste and stir. Next add tomatoes and reduce to simmer. Simmer about 10 minutes, allowing the tomatoes to break down and the dish to become saucy. Add olives, capers, and parsley and simmer 5 more minutes. Toss with the cooked penne pasta until coated. Top with parmesan to serve.

Asparagus with Lemons and Capers

Asparagus is a very sensual side dish for Beltane. Add capers to that, with their magical properties of both luck and passion; garlic, which banishes negativity and promotes lust; and lemon juice, which not only brings bright notes to this dish, but is used in magic for love and friendship, and Beltane magic has arrived at your dinner table. If you don't love asparagus, this recipe works well with green beans also.

Prep time: 5 minutes
Cooking time: 15 minutes
Servings: 4

1 pound fresh or frozen asparagus
2 green onions
2 tablespoons capers, plus one tablespoon reserved liquid
2 garlic cloves
1 teaspoon salt, divided
½ cup water
¼ cup fresh lemon juice
1 tablespoon olive oil

If using fresh asparagus, wash and remove the woody ends of the asparagus. Slice the green onions thinly and at an angle. Mince the garlic cloves. Place the asparagus, green onions, capers, garlic, a tablespoon of the liquid from the capers, ½ teaspoon salt, and ½ cup water in a skillet over medium heat, and cover with a lid. Steam the asparagus for 8–12 minutes, stirring occasionally to ensure even cooking. Once they're tender but still have their bright green color, remove them from the pan and set on a plate. Add lemon juice, olive oil, and the other ½ teaspoon of salt to the skillet. Return the asparagus to the pan, and toss gently to coat, then place back on the serving dish and serve.

Ellie's Strawberry Pie

Strawberries: to me they're as beautiful as roses but taste much better. This pie is easy to make and always impresses guests. My mother-in-law Ellie makes this one. I love its fresh flavor; it's not as sticky and sugary as traditional strawberry pie. You can make it with sugar-free gelatin and pudding mixes if you wish. You can use traditional pie crust made from scratch or from the refrigerated section; I won't judge. It's also good made with a graham cracker crust or gluten-free cookie crust if you prefer. If you're vegetarian or vegan, replace regular gelatin with a strawberry-flavored vegan gelatin.

Prep time: 10 minutes
Inactive: 3 hours
Cooking time: 10 minutes
Servings: 6

Baked pie crust, cooled
4 cups strawberries
1 3-ounce package strawberry gelatin mix
    (feel free to substitute vegan strawberry gelatin)
1 3-ounce package of vanilla pudding mix
    (not the instant kind, the kind you cook)
2 cups water

Add both pudding mix and gelatin to a sauce pan along with 2 cups water and stir while bringing to a boil until the gelatin is dissolved. Chill the mixture in the refrigerator until it thickens a bit. Clean and cut the strawberries in slices. Fill the pie crust with the sliced strawberries. Once the gelatin mixture is slightly set, pour over the strawberries. Chill pie in the refrigerator at least 3 hours before serving.

Crafty Crafts

Ember Grant

BELTANE IS TRADITIONALLY THE time to celebrate the full blooming of nature—a time of fertility and growth. Take advantage of the abundance of plants and flowers to create some lovely items you will treasure for years to come.

There are so many things you can do with pressed flowers! These are just two of my favorite projects for the season—we're going to use the decoupage technique to "paste" flowers and leaves onto stones and glass. But before we can make anything, we need to press and dry the flowers and leaves.

Dried Flowers

Pressing and Drying Materials
Assorted flowers and leaves—picked or purchased
Sheets of plain paper and paper towels for drying
Books or heavy items for pressing, or a heavy mug
    or other microwavable container

You can press flowers the old fashioned way, or you can make "instant" dried flowers in the microwave. Experiment with different flowers and leaves to see how they dry. Some, such as those with very thin, delicate petals, still work best when dried inside the pages of a book. To do this, find several very heavy books. You'll also need some plain printer paper or parchment paper. Open one of the books and lay a sheet of paper on one side. Arrange the flowers and leaves on the paper, and place another sheet on top. Then close the book. Put more heavy books (or bricks) on top of this book and leave it alone for about a week to ten days. Caution: moisture from the plant material could seep through the paper, so make sure you're using a book that you don't mind getting messy. An old phone book is a good choice.

To dry leaves and flowers in the microwave, first lay them on a sheet of plain paper, then cover with another. You can fold them between one sheet if you'd like—that may fit better in smaller microwaves. Then place a paper towel on top of the paper. Next, you need something to hold the paper down. A good item for this is a glass or ceramic mug—the heavier the better. Place the papers inside the microwave and set the mug on top of it, pressing down on the flowers and leaves. Microwave for 30 seconds, then take a peek. If they're not dry, try another 30. It probably won't take longer than 60 or 90 seconds at most (for very thick items). Be careful when removing the mug—it will be hot. Use a hot pad to grab the handle. This takes some experimentation. Use tweezers to remove the flowers and leaves from the paper.

Small, delicate flowers and leaves work well—but nothing too delicate; they will disintegrate in the microwave. Your choice of plant material makes a big difference in the drying method you use. Remember: select small flowers and leaves that are not too thick or too thin for the microwave. If you do want to press a thin flower, the old fashioned way is best.

I've had a great deal of success using the microwave method for rose petals and small leaves. I've even used tiny, individual verbena flowers—just pinch off the long white part of the flower after you remove it from the plant (and don't over-cook them!). Little fern-like leaves work really well; I like to use the feathery leaves of yarrow.

Decorative Stones with Decoupage Pressed Flowers

Materials
Decorative landscape stones (price varies depending on size)
Small paintbrush to apply the glue
Mod Podge glue ($3–$7)
Pressed flowers
  Cost: $3+
  Time Spent: 1 hour or less

You should be able to find smooth stones at any garden center. These are often used in fountains and rock gardens. Wash and dry them thoroughly. The size you use depends on what you want to do with your finished pieces. You can use small stones that fit in the palm of your hand, or larger ones. You can put several small stones in a bowl for decoration or arrange them on your altar, or you can choose a large stone and make a paperweight.

Depending on the type of glue you use, however, these will most likely not be durable enough for outdoor use.

Decide which flower or leaf to put on which stone. For large stones, you may be able to add more than one. First, brush a thin layer of glue onto the stone. Then quickly add the flower or leaf. Carefully brush another thin layer of glue over it.

Be sure to read the directions on the Mod Podge container for exact specifications. I like to use the satin finish for my stones. Repeat as directed, until you have applied the required number of coats. Making these little stones is also a fun project for kids. You can make dozens of them and give them as gifts. These make lovely symbols of the earth element on an altar as well.

Glass Candle Holder or Vase

Materials

Clear glass jar of any size
Mod Podge ($3–$7)
Pressed flowers or leaves
    Cost: $3+
    Time Spent: 1 hour or less

This is essentially the same procedure as making the decorative stones, but this time we're using glass. You can create elegant candle holders or make a beautiful vase by using the decoupage technique, just as you did with the stones—it just takes a little more planning and practice.

First, choose a glass container and be sure it's clean. If you're new to this process, you may want to start with something small. You don't need to purchase an expensive piece—just recycle a jar from your kitchen.

Press and dry the flowers just as you did with the stone project. This time, however, you may want to use larger pieces. You can plan how you want the flowers, petals, and leaves to be arranged, but don't worry too much about this. In fact, a somewhat chaotic look is more natural, like leaves and flowers being tossed on the wind. Again, consult the directions on the Mod Podge container. I used the satin finish for this project as well. Apply a layer of glue, add the flowers and leaves, and apply glue again. Work on one section at a time. Don't worry if you think your finished product looks "messy"—you can add a final coat of Mod Podge when you're done. Besides, a "rough" look is actually nicer; it looks natural and hand-made. Streaks and lines will even give the glass a frosted look. Your jar will look even prettier with a candle glowing inside it. I used the satin finish glue. You can use matte or glossy too. There's even a hard coat style for outdoor use (it's still not completely waterproof).

Suggestions: Use only one type of leaf and completely cover the glass or arrange the leaves in an ordered way, such as long leaves all pointing upward around the base of a jar. Or go for the wild look and just add a variety of colors and styles sprinkled all over the container. For an elegant vase, add one simple flower to a glass bottle.

No matter your style, you will end up with stunning candle holders or vases for a Beltane celebration! Plus, this is a great way to preserve your favorite flowers and leaves. These projects can be adapted for a variety of seasons as well.

A Crystal for Every Season: Carnelian

Charlie Rainbow Wolf

THIS IS THE THIRD festival of the wheel and is traditionally a festival of fertility and light. It falls halfway between the equinox and the solstice, and in the northern hemisphere it honors life and growth and renewal. The word *Beltane* means bright fire, so it's no surprise that fires and light play a great part in this festivity. Marriage is also associated with Beltane, as this is the ceremony when the Horned God took the Lady of the Land in marriage. I have some friends with children who were conceived at this time of year—it's powerful energy!

The stones linked with Beltane are those that look fiery and passionate. Any bright red or orange stone works—symbolizing the fires—as do most green stones, symbolizing life and growth. Amber, bloodstone, carnelian, emerald, garnet, malachite, and tiger's eye are all very suitable stones for including in your Beltane festivities, and of course, if you have a favorite not listed in this group, use it! It's intent that is the most important part of any ritual.

Carnelian

I like to use carnelian as a Beltane stone, because nothing says "fire" to me more than its glow of translucent flame orange. I have a polished carnelian that emerged from the tumbler in a natural heart shape. I use this a lot, for both the color and the shape of the stone make me think of life and vitality, and the fire of passion that burns within anyone who's awakened into their being, anyone who is dedicated to manifesting their bliss.

Carnelian is a form of chalcedony that comes in the palest of milky flesh colors to the deepest translucent red. It's a member of the quartz family, quite common throughout the world, and its molecular structure is roughly 47 percent silicon and the rest oxygen. It's quite robust, a 7 on the Mohs scale. Beads made of carnelian have been found dating back to the Neolithic period, making it one of the oldest stones used for adornment and other purposes.

Carnelian is a sacral chakra stone, and one that helps you to increase your personal empowerment while keeping your ego in check. This energy center also deals with conception and fertility— not just physical conception, either, but also ideas, plans, and projects. The association with creativity in all senses of the word is one more reason why this is such an appropriate Beltane stone.

Divination

If scrying is a part of your ritual, carnelian makes a good companion. When my little heart-shaped gem is chosen from my bowl of stones in a crystal reading, I always ask the querent where their passion lies and what is inhibiting them from their authentic empowerment. This isn't a time to retreat, nor is it a time to hesitate. Carnelian is all about action and adventure!

It's possible that this stone is an indication that a troubled relationship has reached make-or-break time. Either the passion is still there and there's something to work with (which gets into sacral chakra stuff) or the passion that once ignited intimacy has now turned to anger, in which case it's time for a break. The surrounding stones will reveal a lot about which way this situation should be steered, although it's not carved in stone (ha, see what I did there?)

and nothing can take away a person's free will if they're determined to make something work.

Healing

Healers use carnelian in a variety of ways. Massage eggs and wands are popular because of the soothing feeling of the round and polished surface of the stone. Carnelian stimulates energy, so its presence is valuable when you want to stimulate someone or something.

An easy way to use carnelian in healing is to place the stone over the pulse points of your body. Wrists, ankles, the bends of the knees or elbows, over your heart, or on your neck are popular positions, and ones you should be able to reach easily when you're treating yourself. Gently massage the stone in clockwise spirals over these points to increase your energy and raise your vibration.

Another way carnelian assists in healing is in a gemstone layout. You don't have to work with a full grid—in fact, that could be tricky to do by yourself, because you have to place the stones on yourself, and that is often hard to do without previously placed stones falling off! Placing a carnelian stone over your sacral chakra, the energy center that's between your navel and your pubic bone, will work in a similar fashion, and Beltane is one of the best times to do it; after all, it's a festival of passion and creativity! Simply quiet yourself, lie comfortably, place the stone, and envision it balancing out the areas of your life that deal with emotions, confidence, nervous energy, affection, joy, and focus.

Ritual Ideas

Even though Beltane is thought of as a fire festival, there are areas that celebrate it as a water festival, honoring the spirits of the lakes and streams nearby. Decorating village wells—known as well-dressing—is practiced in some English towns and villages. If you choose this to be a fire festival, you might want candles or a bonfire; if you prefer it to be a water festival, maybe choose a small fountain, or even just a chalice filled with water.

A bowl of carnelian pebbles makes a relevant base for either a candle or a water feature. Because it's a hard stone and one that is fairly inexpensive, think about getting an inexpensive tabletop fountain and replacing the feature stones with carnelian. Add any food offerings you wish to make to your deities; select foods that honor the fruits of the earth. Cakes made with oats and milk are served in some communities. Or perhaps make some traditional May wine, made with white wine, sweet woodruff, and strawberries.

Reference

Barthelmy, Dave. "Quartz Mineral Data." Mineralogy Database. http://www.webmineral.com/data/Quartz.shtml#.W2r4hNJKhQA.

Ritual: Spring Dance of the God and Goddess

JD Hortwort

THIS RITUAL WAS WRITTEN for the House of Akasha, where we have the luxury of private property on which to conduct our ceremony. That is key here because the ritual involves having a tree or shrub that will be planted in the ritual area.

For those who don't have access to a place to plant the tree or shrub, you can still conduct the ritual. Your group can purchase a containerized tree, do the ritual, whether indoors or outside, and then donate the tree to a local school or park. You can also nominate a member who will receive the plant for their home landscape. Or you can use a houseplant for your ritual and then pick a member who will take care of the plant going forward.

Altar Decorations: Flowers, candles (red, white, and purple), incense, chalice, athame, cakes and ale, red and white tablecloth, offering bowl, censor. A containerized tree or shrub sits beside the altar.

During this ritual, members will be writing a wish or goal for the coming months on a piece of paper, preferably a handcrafted paper. That paper will be tied to the tree or shrub in the circle that will then be planted at a later date on the ritual site. To allow the ritual to flow more smoothly, the wishes or goals can be written beforehand and carried into the circle.

You can write the goals on paper, but you can also use natural material. Sometimes we have used bay leaves or sycamore bark as writing paper. That way you can be assured the wish will be released into the universe as the writing material degrades. If you can't leave the notes to degrade on the tree, gather them after the ritual and ceremoniously burn or bury them.

The Ritual

Members are smudged and asperged as they arrive at the ritual area. When the group has assembled, call your guardians for the circle according to your tradition. In the House of Akasha, these are the calls we use. One person is assigned to call each quarter and each spirit; however, for small groups, one person can go deosil around the circle and call each elemental.

(East) Spirits of East, Ancient Ones, Spirits of Air; please be with us and guard our Beltane celebration. Hail and welcome.

(South) Spirits of South, Ancient Ones, Spirits of Fire; please be with us and guard our Beltane celebration. Hail and welcome.

(West) Spirits of West, Ancient Ones, Spirits of Water; please be with us and guard our Beltane celebration. Hail and welcome

(North) Spirits of North, Ancient Ones, Spirits of Earth; please be with us and guard our Beltane celebration. Hail and welcome.

(Spirit) Akasha, Divine Spirit. Present in all things and all people; please be with us at this, our Beltane celebration. Hail and welcome.

High Priestess (HPS): *Lady Boann, she of the fair bosom, lady of the River Boyne, mother of Aengus, ruler of the Milky Way, consort to the Dagda, we ask that you be with us for this, our Beltane ritual. Hail and welcome.*

High Priest (HP): *Lord Dagda, lord of the cauldron, strong and wise, master of Uaithne that sings so sweetly, King of the Tuatha and* lover of Boann, we ask that you be with us and guard us for this, our Beltane ritual. Hail and welcome.

HPS: *This is the time of surging growth and great expectations. Today, we celebrate the union of the Lord and Lady. Since awakening at Yule and Imbolc, the Lord and Lady have toyed and flirted with each other. Even as the deer of the forest and the sheep in the fields have come together to procreate, they are drawn to each other by a force that is as old as time.*

HP: *All around us we see the fresh energy of the Universe in the vibrant leaves on the trees and the first fruits from the fields. This energy is there for all to tap and not just for procreation. This is the time for us to "make hay," to build our plans to improve our lives and to put those plans into action. As we celebrate the rising vitality in the universe, listen to our Beltane song:*

(We have set this original poetry to music for our bard to sing, but it can be recited, as indicated here, by the HPS and HP.)

HPS: *Maiden pretty, maiden fair, running fingers through her hair,*

Dreaming of a lover's snare, on one fairy morning.

Sings, "Who will come and dance with me, dance with me, dance with me?

Who will come and dance with me, on this fairy morning?"

HP: *Now comes a laddie, brave and strong, skin of tan, hair so long,*

Taken with the maiden's song, on that fairy morning.

Says, "I will come and dance with thee, Dance with thee, Dance with thee

I will come and dance with thee, on this fairy morning."

HPS: *T'was in the spring and on May's eve, by rushing brook, on gentle leaves,*

That fiery passion they did weave, on one fairy morning.

HP: *Grasping now with all their might, bodies heaving, hearts in flight*

Loving madly though the night, 'til next fairy morning.

HPS: *Then in his arms the maiden lay, asked, "Will you go or will you stay?"*

With softest breath, the lad did say, on that fairy morning.

HP: *"Until death will I stay with thee, stay with thee, stay with thee.*

This vow I do make to thee, on this fairy morning."

HP picks up the athame, the HPS picks up the chalice.

HP: *As the blade is to the Lord.*

(Holds the athame above his head)

HPS: *As the cup is the Lady.*

(Holds the chalice in front of her)

HPS: *Today we celebrate the sacred union.*

All say: *Blessed be this sacred union.*

(The chalice is held up and the athame is plunged into it. These are returned to the altar. The HP and HPS carry the tree/shrub to the center of the circle.)

HPS: *Now that we have raised the energy, let us utilize it to send our personal goals out into the universe. Everyone take a moment to meditate on your heart's desire. When you are ready, step up and tie your wish on our Beltane tree.*

HPS: (After the tree ceremony)

Now we shall bless the cakes and ale.

HP: *We ask the Lord and Lady to bless these cakes, the ingredients with which they were made and the labor that went into making them. Blessed be!*

All say: *Blessed be!*

HPS: *We ask the Lady and Lord to bless this drink, the sweet nectar that makes it pleasing and the fellowship that arises when we share it. Blessed be!*

All say: *Blessed be!*

(Cakes and ale are shared all around. Members are asked to put a little of their cake and ale into the offering bowl on the altar. This will be placed in a separate spot for the deities and elementals after the ritual.)

HP: *As Beltane draws to a close and the ritual prepares to end, carry with you the strength that comes from fellowship and community.*

HPS: *Now the Lady grows from Maiden to Mother and prepares to bring forth bounty in the coming months. Carry with you the love of the Mother and the love of your fellow members as we leave the circle.*

HP: *Lord Dagda, Lord of the cauldron, strong and wise, master of Uaithne that sings so sweetly, King of the Tuatha and lover of Boann, thank you for being with us and guarding us for this, our Beltane ritual. Hail and farewell.*

HPS: *Lady Boann, she of the fair bosom, lady of the River Boyne, mother of Aengus, ruler of the Milky Way, consort to the Dagda, thank you for being with us and guarding us for this, our Beltane ritual. Hail and farewell.*

(Spirit) Akasha, Divine Spirit. Present in all things and all people. Thank you for being with us in this our Beltane celebration. Hail and farewell.

(North) Spirits of North, Ancient Ones, Spirits of Earth; thank you for being with us and guarding our Beltane celebration. Hail and Farewell.

(West) Spirits of West, Ancient Ones, Spirits of Water; thank you for being with us and guarding our Beltane celebration. Hail and farewell.

(South) Spirits of South, Ancient Ones, Spirits of Fire; thank you for being with us and guarding our Beltane celebration. Hail and farewell.

(East) Spirits of East, Ancient Ones, Spirits of Air; thank you for being with us and guarding our Beltane celebration. Hail and farewell.

Open circle.

Notes

Notes

Litha

The Season of the Summer Solstice

Laura Tempest Zakroff

THE SUMMER SOLSTICE IS commonly observed on June 21 in the northern hemisphere and has many names, including Midsummer, Litha, St. John's Day, Kupala Night, and more. From Bulgaria to Brazil, Wales to Wyoming, you will find a wide array of festivals and traditions celebrating the Solstice. The actual technical date of the Solstice can vary from as early as the nineteenth to as late as the twenty-fifth. Yet many of these events go beyond just a single day and the night before—they may last for several days or upwards of a whole week or more. Some of them even take place weeks before or after the actual Solstice!

These longer festivals often have roots that go back centuries. The practices span all of the elements: collecting water from sacred wells; blessing fleets of ships; lighting bonfires and burning effigies; gathering medicinal herbs and wearing wreathed crowns of flowers and ferns for fertility; the sounding of horns and cleansing with smoke; and of course feasting, drinking, and dancing. All of these activities speak to the culture of the land itself: the daily lives of its people and their connection with the cycles of nature.

So if we simply acknowledge a fixed date and go by the book, are we really tapping into all of that rhythm? When we get too wrapped up in the modern calendar and focus on just the numbers, we can lose sight of what it really means to celebrate the changing of the seasons. Let's explore how you can shift your brain from simply seeing dates to enabling yourself to resonate more deeply with the world around you.

The Experience of a Season

As a child, the beginning of summer happened when school year wrapped up and we had nearly three months of free time to enjoy. At the parochial grammar school I attended, the yearly parish carnival fundraiser also coincided with that final week of school. The arrival of the trucks bearing colorful rides and games, along with the erection of striped tents over the schoolyard, heralded that summer was within our reach.

For that whole last week of school, every night as the sun began to set, what had been a big, boring, paved parking lot and church grounds came alive with twinkling lights and the sounds of merriment. Trailer doors would pop up to reveal games of chance with their tantalizing backdrops of stuffed animals and amazing prizes. The aroma of fried dough, cotton candy, and pizza filled the air. Each following day, the students would be abuzz with who managed to sneak on to the bigger rides, who got sick on the Zipper or Tilt-a-Whirl, who won what prizes, and how many times they went down the giant slide without getting friction-burned by the fiberglass.

I attended the same school from kindergarten through eighth grade, as did my older brothers, so there are years of memories tied into that carnival, even from my earliest years. There are the goldfish that lived long lives in our household, from the game where you had to get ping pong balls in certain bowls of water. (Yes, I know this is not an acceptable or humane thing nowadays, but it was the 70s and 80s—there weren't even laws for wearing seatbelts in cars for much of that time.) There's the giant stuffed unicorn that was bigger than me, which my father won for one of my birthdays. I later found out that he didn't leave it up to chance—he put a quarter down on every possible square in the roulette wheel game! Numerous nights of my brothers being tasked to have me tag along with them while my parents worked volunteer shifts in the big tent. There was the year I was finally tall enough to ride the Gravitron with my brothers—and I felt so cool and grown-up! Later I could go and hang out with friends without parents or brothers. Then when I was (newly) thirteen, I went on my very first date to the carnival with a boy named Scott, and had my first kiss. (So much awkward!) The carnival was just a week every year, but in my memory, it stretched on forever.

Once school was out and the carnival finished, my family would head down to the Jersey Shore. Falling on the Solstice or not, this migration to the beach meant that summer had truly begun. The days would become a blur of soft sand, ocean waves, and salty air, filled with hunting seashells, playing in the dunes, surfing, reading books, and walking the boards. When I was fourteen, I got a summer job on the boardwalk, so that got added into the mix through my eighteenth year.

After that year, I was away at college, starting a new life, and working multiple jobs—so summer didn't feel like a distinct season anymore. Instead I celebrated the Summer Solstice by following rituals in the books I read, then later started to create my own rituals and gatherings. It was a day I marked to follow the path, yet I had lost track of what the season felt like.

The Summer Solstice as a Day

The Summer Solstice simultaneously marks the longest day of the year and the shortest night. If you envision the year as a turning wheel, then the Winter Solstice stands opposite of it, with its corresponding longest night and shortest day of the year. Situated between them on either side of the wheel, you will find the Spring and Fall Equinoxes, with their equal balance of both night and day.

When I was growing up, each of these special days were considered to be "the first day of" whatever season they preceded. But for a moment, step back from the hardline association of the day with the tilt of Earth's axis in combination with the position of its revolution around the sun. This astronomical alignment and arrangement is definitely the reason for seasons. Yet there's no hard switch that is flipped turning spring into summer, or fall into winter. The facts prove that this is a gradual shift, so the extremes and equal points simply make a good point of measure. Which is why our ancestors often built monoliths, temples, and other landmarks to help keep track of the days in correlation to the sun's journey across the sky.

So unless you are meticulously counting the seconds from sunrise to sunset, the days on either side of the Solstice will feel just as long, the nights just as short. The shift is so slight, most people don't even notice. To further complicate things, if you follow the observed dates for a Solstice versus the actual date (though occasionally they do line up), you might miss the Solstice entirely!

Our society has gotten so used to putting everything into neat boxes—be it celebrations or cubicles! You have this obligatory thing on this holiday, then the clock turns over and the next thing you know, everything is 50 percent off! And you'd better start getting ready for the next big commercial whatever. Such a mindset tends to be counterintuitive to the practice of Witchcraft. There's no need to rush or cap off every celebration by the hours. Rather we should sample and savor the rise and fall of the pattern. I suggest breaking your sabbats out of their date boxes to start viewing them as larger experiences.

The Meaning and Feel of the Season

For me, despite the fact that I'm generally a positive and optimistic person, I can't help but think that once we hit the Summer Solstice, it's going to get a little darker each day. This shouldn't get me down because autumn is one of my favorite seasons, and I'm happiest when I'm wearing boots and scarves versus trying to douse myself in sunscreen and battling sweat. (I still love the beach though!) But still, the lessening of the light affects me. The shortening of the days makes me feel like there's less time to be fully active. I'm more likely to get a move on when I wake with the sun, and less likely to hunker down when there's more light in the evening.

Our ancestors felt the changes both gradually and acutely as well, as they tended to live closer to the land than we do now. They were also more at the mercy of the whims of the weather than most of us today. If a rainy summer ruins your tomato plant or a storm cuts power to your storage freezer, it's fairly easy to go down to the grocery store and restock. But you don't have to work in agriculture in order to connect to the land. We just need to pay closer to what's going on around us: What animals are around? What's in season? What plants are blooming or bearing fruit? What does the air taste like?

There's the science behind how the seasons affect us, but there's also the spiritual sense as well. This is why we often turn to myth and metaphor to find our place and deeper meaning. Personally I've never connected with the symbolic rise and fall of the Holly King and Oak King, which some traditions use to explain the seasons. As much as I love myth, it's hard for me to find a spiritual connection to that particular story when I'm observing the world around me. But it might strike a chord for you. Or maybe you'll find something more familiar with the myth of Persephone because her story echoes something in your own life. You would be hard-pressed to find a culture that doesn't have a myth that correlates with life patterns of the planet, and in particular one that's relative to your region or in tune with your world view.

If tales of deities don't work well for you, there are other ways to consider the progression. You could approach the Summer Solstice like climbing a mountain. We slowly ascend, day by day, working through the dark of the forest until more and more daylight appears. When we finally reach the pinnacle, the world is bright and illuminated. We take time to catch our breath and take stock of the landscape spreading out before and after us. Then we begin our trek down the other side and the light begins to fade as we get further down the way. We know that we shall rest when we reach the time of the Winter Solstice.

The Summer Solstice is an active time. We see the world around us blossoming, growing, rising, maturing. The earth is coupling and bringing forth life all over. Summer is often also marked by storms and extreme weather too—hurricanes, tornados, high winds, and monsoons. Though sometimes devastating, the active weather clears the way for new growth. It's like the sun is shining light on a giant live-action movie!

On a personal level, with the longer hours of sunlight and warmer weather, we can spend more time outside finding the right amount of active for us. We can choose to do it alone in our own backyards, travel the world, or gather together with family and friends. Take advantage of the sun's rays to grow a little garden— whether it's in the windowsill of an apartment, a community plot, or your own yard. Go explore your local parks and natural area features. Try a new sport, drop in on a community class, have picnics. Whatever is within your budget and ability to go do, get into motion!

Lastly, we can use the season of the Summer Solstice to grow ourselves. What sort of activity do you need to stir within you? Is there an achievement you need to recognize and celebrate? Do you need to make some big changes and clear out some debris from your life? Perhaps there's a project that you've been wanting to tackle, but have been putting it off. Now is an ideal time to let it take root and tend to it so that you can take advantage of this active time to grow.

Just remember that you don't have to do it in a single day. You've got a whole season!

Cosmic Sway

Daniel Pharr

MIDSUMMER—THE HEIGHT OF THE summer season, not the warmest day but the longest—marks the midpoint of summer, halfway between the first day of summer at Beltaine and the last at Lughnassadh, and occurs on June 21 at 11:54 a.m., ten hours after a dark Cancer Moon. Bidding the waxing sun farewell and welcoming the waxing darkness should be done on the evening of June 21 under a barely waxing dark Moon that moves into Cancer at 2:01 a.m.

Litha Sun

The Litha sunrise was observed by the ancients, just as was the Yule sunrise. The actual sunrise is at 5:25 a.m.; honor the moment and wake for it. Make your morning beverage, bundle up, and sit outside. Experience the moment of sunrise, observe the light and its quality, smell the air. Early mornings have a different wonderful quality about them, a clean, calming, undisturbed quality that is strangely energizing. The hours around dawn are a magical time to be in nature. Have a walk. Feel how nature adjusts to a new day.

Organize your evening celebrations. Prepare meals, select the music, set out drums, and honor the seasonal shift with a bonfire, or any sort of blaze, as fire is the central representation of the sun in all its glory. Cook with the fire, have a barbeque, put candles around the house for light, purify the house and family with the smoke from burning herbs. Given that Litha is occurring under dark Gemini and Cancer Moons, divination is an appropriate party activity. Toss the stones, stir the coals, see the future. Begin the festivities in the daylight hours so that the celebration is well underway at the 8:30 p.m. sunset. Have the circle cast, the fire burning, drums beating, and charcoal tattooed dancers dancing. The mead racked last Samhain is ready for sharing. Open the first bottle of mead to loosen the dancing and divinatory energies around the fire.

Gardening

Vegetable plants and herbs are blossoming, unripened tomatoes hang on the vine, pea pods are engorged with peas, corn stalks are knee-high, ripe red cherries are eaten off the trees, and the days are warming but still offer an occasional misty morning. Warm and moist is the perfect environment for growing food. From this day until mid-winter, the days will gradually diminish in both length and light, first becoming hotter to the point of sizzling and then colder with increased darkness. The most notable shift happens after Lughnassadh. The final plantings for autumn and winter harvest should be sown between Litha and Lughnassadh on Full water and earth Moons. Adding symbolism pertaining to the farming of crops is most appropriate in any Litha celebration. The metaphor is the feeding and nurturing of life sown at Beltaine, as we would do any new beginning, weeding the garden to keep the beds free from unwanted pests and noxious plants, as is done in the home and in relationships, and affirming the intention for a bountiful harvest by staying focused on that which is important.

Handfasting

Litha is the day for a traditional handfasting, although Full Moon handfastings were also considered proper. Some modern-day wedding traditions came from the handfastings of old, such as the June wedding. One tradition that wasn't carried forward was the optional year-and-a-day trial marriage, in which marriage was only entered into for one year and one day, for a particular purpose or to simply check compatibility. There might be many less divorces and many happier couples if this tradition had been passed down through the ages. Other traditions did stick with us, like the expression "tying the knot," which literally came from the handfasting practice of binding the couple's hands together as a symbol of their union. During the ceremony, a rope or cloth was wound about the clasped hands of the couple being wed. Today when people get married, we say they "tied the knot."

Litha Moon

After the sunset on June 21, Litha will be celebrated under a dark Gemini Moon that will have gone void-of-course at 5:47 p.m. The Moon will still have an influence of sorts, a bit of Gemini and a bit of Cancer. Typical of Gemini, the energies will fluctuate back and forth, making the merriment more dependent on the emotional state of the partygoers than the actual lunar sway. Gemini brings much merriment to any festivity. Quick-wittedness, sociability, excitement, flirtation, and general cheerfulness are the hallmarks of the Gemini Moon, but being void-of-course will weaken the energetic pull and loosen the astrological grip.

By 2:01 a.m. on June 22, about the time the celebration will be winding down, the Cancer New Moon will come out to play with its favorite toys: nurturing, moodiness, compassion, insecurity, caring, and sensitivity, all presented in positive and negative fashion. Say goodbyes, bid fond farewells, do the merry meets and merry parts, and head to the relative safety of your home and bed, unless processing with the few remaining revelers seems appropriate as everyone comes back to their emotional base, raw from the ceremony and life. In this case pour another mug of mead, find a comfortable spot, knees drawn up on the couch, and get down to it.

July 4

The waxing Moon moves into Capricorn at 12:47 a.m. and twenty-four hours later turns full. The Full Moon will diminish the viewing of fireworks and weaken the crowd's response to the fireworks. The practical Capricorn Moon will help folks remain reserved in the face of explosions and bored with the crackling. A Capricorn Moon can also be hard on the knees, so sit rather than kneel, should taking in the local fireworks display become the evening's entertainment.

Full Moon

The Capricorn Moon will become full on July 5 at 12:44 a.m., just after the fireworks display from the fourth is finished. A Full Moon intensifies the energies present, and this Full Moon will strengthen the Capricorn influence. Make sure everyone is wearing seatbelts on the drive home. Take the most expeditious route. Brush teeth and place the day's clothes in the laundry basket. Rules are made for a reason.

Dark Moon

A dark Moon in Cancer occurs at 1:32 p.m. on July 20. Twenty-two minutes later, at 1:54 p.m., the Cancer Moon goes void-of-course, which will immediately feel improved. At 4:16 p.m., the newly waxing Moon enters Leo with an unconscious but audible sigh of relief from the Cancer emotional intensity. This Cancer Moon will actually be good for relationships, but the Moon will also promote healing, and as they say, the first step in solving a problem is admitting one exists.

The Old Ways: Cerridwen

Charlynn Walls

THE FIRST SUMMER THAT I had unequivocally dedicated myself to the old ways I was startled one afternoon when driving toward my grandmother's home. I was blessed with a vision of the Goddess. She was breathtaking. She was the embodiment of all the elements. Her hair was copper-hued and flowed around her like water, her skin smooth and fair like porcelain, her eyes the color of the sea and flowing between blue and green, and dressed in the softest green earth. Years later the vision would lead me to the specific goddess who would become my patroness: Cerridwen.

Midsummer, or the Summer Solstice, is observed around June 21. This is the longest day and shortest night of the year. It is a time when the world is in all its lush glory. The Goddess is full of ripe potential and is depicted as heavily pregnant at this time. The God is at the height of his power. The focus of ancient peoples was on keeping the fields tended and herds healthy.

The Goddess: Cerridwen

Cerridwen is a Welsh goddess that is often honored during Midsummer for her ability to tend to the cauldron from which the God will be reborn. She nurtures, protects, and guides those through spirituality. Though she is most often portrayed as a crone in stories and visual depictions, she is also a mother and witch.

She is like any other mother, putting the needs of her children before her own, worrying about their prospects in life, and doing what she can to help them along the way. While one child is a beauty, her son is not. In order to see her son married, she concocts a potion that will give him wisdom. This will make him a more desirable suitor. She creates this potion in Awen, her cauldron of creation and inspiration. However, three drops of the potion are ingested by Gwion who receives the gifts of inspiration, prophecy, and the ability to change form. Cerridwen's own son dies as a result. She feels a mother's guilt and seeks revenge. She pursues Gwion and matches wits with him by shifting forms. When at last Gwion changes into a piece of corn, he is eaten by Cerridwen. She becomes pregnant through this act and thus embodies the nature of Midsummer as she begins the act of protecting and nurturing life (McCoy 1994).

The Cauldron

The cauldron is a traditional witches' tool, having three legs and made of cast iron. It is associated with Cerridwen. The cauldron had a place of honor in many ancient homes, occupying space in the center of the house at the hearth. In its most simplistic form the cauldron was used as a tool in the home to provide food, adding meat, vegetables, water, and heat in order to transform basic ingredients into a sustaining and filling meal to be enjoyed with the family.

When wielded by a witch, the cauldron becomes a vessel for transformative magick. The most prevalent way to transform oneself would be to gain wisdom from the gods. By doing so, the practitioner is changed on a most fundamental level and therefore emanates that change into the world.

It also represents the womb and element of water. The divine feminine gave birth to the world and all its inhabitants. That birthing process was reflected on the earth itself and recognized by ancient peoples in the natural formations near their homes. Places that held the power of birth included the caves, cenotes, canyons, and wells that became the areas visited by the people with offerings and by the shamans in order to harness those powers.

Ritualized practice called for a more portable representation of those sacred places. The cauldron bears a resemblance to them, as they are vessels that hold or contain the unseen. If the vessel is dark or filled with water, it holds infinite possibilities. Used in a capacity to represent the goddess, the cauldron allows life to come forth from the primordial expanse. It transports and manifests our desires and hopes into the world. It is the embodiment of the celebration of Midsummer, as it is about creation.

Awen is Cerridwen's cauldron and one of her sacred symbols. Awen represents inspiration and change—including physical, mental, and spiritual. The cauldron is made of the ore of the earth and forged in fire (Hughes 2012). The connection between the cauldron and practitioner helps bring to life all that is possible.

Celebrating Midsummer

Cerridwen tends the cauldron and it is symbolic of life, death, and rebirth at the time of Midsummer. She is able to nurture and bring inspiration and wisdom to those who seek her council and drink of Awen.

Cerridwen's Cauldron

Seek your own inspiration from the cauldron of Awen during the Midsummer sabbat by using it a scrying mirror. Take a cauldron and pour water into the vessel. Use the light from the bonfires lit on Midsummer, or the candles from your rite, to guide your vision. Stare into the pool and see what the flickering light brings into focus. See what Cerridwen has to offer as insight for the coming months.

Elixir of Awen

In the lore, Cerridwen creates a potion to instill inspiration and wisdom to her son. Recreate the elixir by taking mead or apple juice and pouring it into a cauldron during the ritual. Stir in your intent and visualize the outcome. Drink the elixir that now symbolizes the potion that Cerridwen concocted in the cauldron in order to instill wisdom.

References

Franklin, Anna. *Midsummer Solstice: History, Lore & Celebration.* United Kingdom: Lear Books, 2009.

Hughes, Kristoffer. *From the Cauldron Born: Exploring the Magic of Welsh Legend & Lore.* Woodbury, MN: Llewellyn Publications, 2012.

Knight, Sirona. *Celtic Traditions: Druids, Faeries, and Wiccan Rituals.* New York, NY: Citadel Press, 2000.

McCoy, Edain. *The Sabbats: A New Approach to Living the Old Ways.* St. Paul, MN: Lewellyn Publications, 1994.

Morgan, Sheena. *The Wicca Book of Days.* London: Vega, 2002.

Nichols, Mike. *The Witches' Sabbats.* Albany, CA: Acorn Guild Press, 2005.

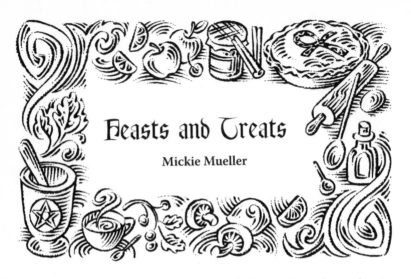

Feasts and Treats

Mickie Mueller

THE HEIGHT OF SUMMER brings a plethora of produce; this is a great time of the year to enjoy bounty from the earth. Do you have fresh herbs, tomatoes, or cucumbers growing in your garden or from a neighbor? I have some great recipes to highlight your delicious produce from Mother Earth. You can prepare much of this meal ahead of time so that there's minimal time in the kitchen and more time with friends and family in the sun. Because it's probably pretty hot out, I'm providing you with a meal that doesn't heat up the house too much and is light and delicious for your Midsummer full of magic.

Salad on a Stick

One of my coven sisters brought this seasonal appetizer to a gathering years ago and I've made variations of it ever since. This is perfect for Litha with fresh tomatoes in season, basil growing like gangbusters, and cucumbers ripe on the vine—this one is summer at its finest. You can prepare this one a couple hours before your guests arrive, just keep them covered in the fridge and add the dressing right before serving.

Prep time: 15 minutes
Servings: 4–6

1 cucumber
Pint of grape tomatoes
Can of pitted black olives or kalamata olives
Bundle of fresh basil
Feta or mozzarella cheese cubes
2–3 tablespoons olive oil
1–2 tablespoons balsamic vinegar
Salt and pepper to taste
Pack of bamboo or wooden kabob skewers

Peel the cucumber and cut it into slices, then cut those slices in half. Assemble the skewers: wrap a tomato with a basil leaf and spear it on the skewer so that the basil leaf is pierced through both the top and the bottom. Next add feta, olive, 2–3 cucumber slices, and then repeat the order once. Arrange the skewers on a plate and drizzle with olive oil, balsamic vinegar, salt, and pepper, or a vinaigrette dressing of your choice.

Falafel Pita Sandwich

This is a summer favorite at our house; you don't have to heat up the oven and it's a real crowd pleaser. I usually make the falafel mix in the morning and refrigerate it all day. You can even slice up the sandwich toppings ahead of time. Then when it's time to eat, all you need to do is shape and cook the falafels. Do not use canned chickpeas for this recipe; the texture is wrong and it won't work.

Prep time: 30 minutes
Inactive: 12 hours
Cooking time: 30–40 minutes
Servings: 6

1 pound dry chickpeas, soaked in water overnight
1 chopped onion

¼ cup fresh parsley

2 teaspoons all-purpose or gluten-free flour

5 garlic cloves, peeled and chopped

2 teaspoons salt

1½ teaspoons ground coriander seeds

1½ teaspoons cumin

½ teaspoon cayenne pepper

½ teaspoon ground pepper

Dash of ground cardamom

Choice of oil for deep frying or cooking spray to make patties on a griddle

Pita bread (if you're going gluten-free, these are also great in a lettuce wrap)

Sliced tomatoes, onion, and lettuce for topping

Tahini (recipe follows), hummus, or another sauce

Drain the chickpeas that you've soaked overnight and put them in a large bowl. Add in all the rest of the falafel ingredients (everything in the list besides the oil, pita bread, and toppings) and mix with a large spoon. If you can't fit all of it in your food processor at one time, don't worry; I can't either. I just mix the rough-cut ingredients in a big bowl and then I pulse half of the mixture at a time.

Add the mixture to your food processor and pulse it until it becomes a coarse consistency, scraping the sides occasionally with a rubber spatula. Keep blending until you can take a handful, press it together, and it holds its shape. Remove mixture to a large bowl and repeat the blending process with the other half of the mixture. Add both halves of the mixture together in the bowl and mix with a fork to make sure the texture is consistent. Cover and refrigerate at least one hour.

Form the mixture into balls and fry in a skillet in about 2 inches of cooking oil at medium-high heat until golden brown on the outside, or deep fry at 350° F (177° C) for 5 minutes. Alternately, if you prefer not to deep fry, I like to form the mixture into patties, about 3 inches in diameter and about ½-inch thick. Make sure the edges are packed and smooth. Cook them using nonstick spray in a skillet or on an electric griddle set at 375° F (245° C) for about 4–5 minutes per side. Slice the pita bread in half and open the pocket in the pita. Fill with falafels, tomatoes, lettuce, and onion, and top with tahini sauce, hummus, or other sauce of your choice.

Tahini Sauce/Dip

Tahini is a sesame seed paste, and it's used to make this lovely creamy sauce that's great with falafels, but also a dip for raw veggies, chips, pretzels, or pita chips.

Prep time: 5 minutes

½ cup tahini
¼ cup fresh lemon juice
1–2 garlic cloves
½ teaspoon salt
⅓ cup lukewarm water

Blend all ingredients in a blender until smooth and creamy. If you have a Bullet blender or Ninja, these work great for making tahini sauce. If you prefer a thinner consistency, just add a bit more water until you're happy with it. Serve with your favorite veggies or chips—or veggie chips! Yum!

Sparkling Raspberry Lemonade

We love making sparkling drinks! If you have a sparkling water maker, use it for the recipe. If not, a bottle of club soda works just as well. This is a nice way to make a sparkling drink with real sugar and fruit instead of all the corn syrup and chemicals you get in commercial soft drinks.

Prep time: 10 minutes
Cooking time: 10 minutes
Cooling time: 15 minutes
Servings: 4-6

2 fresh or frozen raspberries
1 cup sugar
1 cup fresh lemon juice (5–6 lemons)
½ cup water
32 ounces sparkling water or club soda

Add raspberries, sugar, and ½ cup of water to a saucepan and bring it to a boil. Stir until the sugar dissolves. Once it reaches a boil, maintain its boil for 3 minutes. Remove from heat. Use a potato masher to mash up the raspberries, releasing more of the raspberry juice. Once the mixture is cool, strain it into a large pitcher with a tight-fitting lid. Add lemon juice and sparkling water and mix gently, so as to not disturb the bubbles too much. Serve over ice. Garnish with a fresh raspberry and lemon wedge if you wish.

Tip: Before juicing lemons, keep them at room temperature. Roll them on the counter while pushing down and squish the heck out of them. Now when you cut the lemon in half, it will be much easier to juice.

Crafty Crafts

Ember Grant

MY FAVORITE IMAGE OF Midsummer is that of a deep forest with the twinkling of fireflies among the branches. I often wonder if this is what has inspired the popularity of string lights used as decoration—they certainly evoke this magical atmosphere.

More than just a backyard trend, lighting up the night has served a practical function for centuries. Many Pagan holidays are celebrated with fire. Midsummer fires have been traditionally used to invoke blessings, ward off evil, and provide purification. In addition to fires, there are accounts of people centuries ago celebrating with lamps and lanterns—sometimes hundreds of them at once—on this night in various parts of Europe. Often the lanterns were adorned with floral garlands of white lilies, birch branches, and fennel.

Tissue Paper Lantern

In the spirit of these traditions, and to honor the longest night of the year, it seems a fitting time for light-inspired projects.

Materials
Balloons—one for each lantern ($1–$3)
Tissue paper—at least three sheets for each lantern ($4)
Glue ($2)

Yarn or string for hanging
Brushes or sponges for applying glue
Bowl for mixing glue and water

    Cost: $8+

    Time spent: several days, allowing for drying time

This project uses the classic process of papier-mâché. In this case, however, instead of using thick paper or newsprint, and then painting it, we're going to use colored tissue paper. To make these lanterns especially magical, choose tissue paper with celestial themes such as stars or spirals. If you can't find these patterns, choose something else with symbolic significance— flowers, for example—or just use plain colors. You can paint symbols on them when they're finished, if you'd like. Blow up a balloon to your desired size and tie it. Set it aside for now.

For best results, you'll need three layers of tissue—depending on the size of your lantern, you may only require two sheets of paper. Begin by tearing the tissue paper into manageable pieces—approximately a couple inches wide (tearing gives a more natural look than cutting). Once you begin working, you may want to apply a solid

color, or white, for the first two layers, then use a patterned sheet for the final layer. It's up to you.

Pour a small amount of glue into a bowl and add water; mix well. If you like to measure it, a good ratio is three parts glue to one part water. However, I usually just pour some glue into a bowl and add a little water at a time, while stirring, until the mixture reaches a spreadable consistency that isn't too runny. If you don't use all the glue, you can cover the container with plastic wrap and place it in the refrigerator until you need it again.

Dip pieces of tissue paper into the glue and stick them to the balloon. Focus on a small section at at time until you completely cover the balloon with one layer of tissue. Allow this layer to dry completely before adding another layer.

This process can be time-consuming and may stretch over a couple days. You can make it go faster by applying a layer early in the morning and then another at night. Just make sure the first layer is dry before adding another. Three layers should be enough. You may be able to get by with only two layers, depending on how transparent you'd like your lantern, but three layers will give you a stronger shell.

When the lantern is dry, cut a small tear in the balloon to release the air. You'll see the sides of the lantern shrink in during this process, but that's okay. You will then be able to peel the balloon out from the paper shell. If you dislike the jagged edges of your lantern, just use scissors to cut the edges and make them smooth.

Use a three-hole punch or just the point of a pair of scissors to make a hole in each side of the paper shell. String ribbon through the holes and tie knots to secure. You may also want to use tape around the holes for a tighter hold. Hang the lanterns from tree branches or plant-hanging hooks or just place them in the grass. Be careful, though—they're not waterproof.

Variations: make your lantern using only white tissue paper, invert it over a battery-operated candle instead of hanging it, and you have a glowing paper crystal ball. You can also decorate your lantern with dried leaves and petals (using the technique from the

Beltane projects). Simply decoupage them on with last layer of the tissue paper. You can also add glitter after applying your last layer. Just sprinkle it over the wet glue.

Fairy Garden in a Jar

Fairy gardens can range from simple to elaborate, but either way they can be expensive to create. They're also typically made to remain in a permanent location. With this project, you can make one on a small scale and move it to any location at any time.

You may already have some of these supplies lying around the house. Since I work with silk and dried flowers a lot, I only had to buy one small sprig of leaves to add to mine.

Materials
Silk leaves and small flowers, moss, etc. (price varies)
Small strand of string lights ($3–$10)
Fairy house—there are premade varieties in craft stores ($5)
Clear glass jar or other container (price varies)
Optional: crystals, stones, shells, or other decorative items
> *Cost:* $15+
> *Time Spent:* several hours

I happened to have a glass container in my closet that looks like a giant, decorative brandy snifter—it's essentially a large glass bowl on a small pedestal. This turned out to be perfect for this project. You can buy one of these at a craft store, but it's certainly fine to use whatever you have available or, if you do need to shop for this item, buy whatever size or shape suits your situation. Just be sure it's large enough to put your hand inside and that it's tall enough to hold everything.

I found a little fairy house that looks like an acorn with a door and windows painted on it; the craft store had several options to choose from. In addition, most craft stores sell bags of moss or small "mats" that you can cut to fit your project.

Put the moss in the jar first and then start adding the lights. Don't wait to put the lights in last—they need to be integrated into the arrangement. Just let the cord drape over the back of your jar so the battery box can sit on a tabletop. If you can find a set of lights that is remote-controlled, you can try to hide the battery box inside the jar if you want, but this may take up too much room.

Next, position the house. You don't need to use any glue. Don't worry too much about using floral foam or wire, or making it too perfect. Let things move around—it looks more natural that way. Layer leaves around the edges inside the jar to mute the lights and give the house some shade. Add some small silk flowers if you like and any other things—I put a small quartz crystal in mine. Just keep adding things until you reach your desired effect. If necessary, use a fork or other tool to reach into small areas and move things around.

These little fairy gardens can light up dark corners of a room or a bookcase, or can be used as table centerpieces. They keep the magic of Midsummer alive all year long.

Reference

Hutton, Ronald. *Stations of the Sun: A History of the Ritual Year in Britain*. Oxford: Oxford University Press, 1996.

A Crystal for Every Season: Citrine

Charlie Rainbow Wolf

IN THE NORTHERN HEMISPHERE, this festival celebrates the height of the summer. Even though modern calendars herald it as the first day of summer, traditionally this is the height of the season, and the longest day. Tomorrow the nights start to draw in, and the daylight lessens, as we head toward autumn and harvest.

Standing stones and stone circles play a large part in many Litha celebrations. There's the annual gathering at Stonehenge in Wiltshire, the Almendres stones on the Iberian Peninsula, and the Grange stones in Limerick. Shrouded in ancient mystery and folklore, these stones make an enigmatic setting when it comes to celebrating the turn of the year.

Smaller stones are also associated with Midsummer. Baculite, citrine, fire opal, gold stone, iron pyrite (fool's gold), orthoceras, sunstone, and topaz are all suitable crystals to include in your Summer Solstice ritual. Baculite and orthoceras connect you to the ancient ones, while the others reflect the light of the sun. It's worth noting that gold stone isn't actually a stone as such—it's actually a form of glass—but that doesn't take away from its charm.

Citrine

My favorite stone for Litha is citrine, because it just seems such a sunny and happy stone somehow. It's a form of quartz, translucent or transparent, and comes in all shades of yellow, from the deepest amber to the lightest lemon. In fact, it gets its name from the French word *citron*, meaning lemon. Some citrines contain inclusions, and I've even seen enhydros—a stone that has ancient water trapped in it.

Like other quartz stones, citrine is found in natural points, druse, tumbled, or carved and polished into different shapes. Its molecular structure is silicon and oxygen, and it is pretty hard, a 7 on the Mohs scale. It's often confused with yellow topaz, but the hardness of the two stones is quite different, with topaz being much softer.

Natural citrine is usually light in color. It's formed in nature when amethyst or quartz gets too hot. Be careful when choosing your stone, as a lot of the citrine on the market these days is man-made, and doesn't have quite the same healing and magical properties as natural citrine. The darker colors usually come from heat-treated amethyst or quartz. Natural citrine is mostly light in color, with a natural cloudiness and minus the telltale lines that usually appear on artificially heat-treated stones.

Magic and Meditation

Citrine has long held a reputation for being "the merchant's stone," and carrying or wearing it was thought to bring good fortune to traders. We have one in our coin jar at home, to help attract wealth and encourage it to hang around. It seems to work; we've had ups and downs but we've never really had to go without!

Citrine in my bowl of divination stones always represents new beginnings and good fortune. I actually have several in there, ranging from the large natural point to little tumbled stones. It's fascinating how some querants will pick up that big point then put it down, then pick it up, then put it down—usually reflecting that they're on the verge of an exciting adventure, yet hesitant about embracing it.

The yellow hues of citrine make it a very suitable solar plexus chakra stone. This is the energy center that is associated with your moods, emotions, and creativity. When this area is out of balance, you'll feel restless and down on yourself. Thoughts of unworthiness or guilt permeate your day, and you find yourself overthinking things and being touchy and temperamental with others.

Fortunately, it's easy to get things back on track. Place the citrine over your stomach below your navel. Close your eyes and take cleansing breaths in through your nose and out through your mouth. Envision your life going smoothly and things that you want to happen coming to pass. Picture yourself as confident and able to easily deal with the daily challenges that life throws to everyone. When you feel your center returning, open your eyes, get something to eat or drink, and put your citrine away in a safe place until you need it again.

Make a Mini Megalith

You don't have to visit one of the ancient stone monuments to celebrate Litha with standing stones. It's possible to do this in your own garden, your own room, even on your own desktop! Obviously with citrine being the featured stone it would be awesome to work with that, but any stones will do. I have a small bag of clear quartz points, but there's no reason not to use other stones you've collected, or even pebbles from the road! You may fancy using several different types of stones too, assigning each one a position and a meaning. Go with what feels comfortable.

Start by determining where you want to place your stones. One method of doing this is to use twelve stones, one for each Sun sign, placing them in a circle starting with Aries and going around to Pisces. If you're particularly interested in astrology, this might appeal to you. A variation on this would be to assign a sabbat for each stone, and place eight of them in a wheel. The stones could also represent a particular totem or spirit guardian, as Sun Bear describes in his book *Dancing with the Wheel* (1991).

Stones with symbols on them are another possibility. If you are a rune caster, or have a bag of witch stones, then by all means use these. In this way, not only are you erecting a stone circle, but you're also tapping into the vibration of the glyphs on the stones, giving you a double dose of magical energy.

If you have the room, and you've never done a ceremony inside a stone circle, try it for Litha—and be sure to note any difference in the energy levels you notice. For group workings, your stones need to be small enough to handle, but large enough that you won't lose them! Group or solitary, placing small stones on a tabletop gives you a focal point for your ritual. Placing the stones creates a sacred space, one that has just as much potential as the giant monuments of old. In this case, size really doesn't matter; focus on your intent and know that you're partaking in something that is ancient and special.

Midsummer Embodiment Ritual

Laura Tempest Zakroff

When the season turns toward Midsummer, I think of Pan, the satyr-shaped Greek god of nature, wild things and border places, shepherds and flocks, music and merriment. As spring rises into summer, there is a charge to the air that reminds us to live and to love. A song on the wind that calls us to go get out in the wild and find ourselves. In ancient times, you would not find Pan's places of worship housed in grand formal temples. Instead his sacred spots could be found in locations of a liminal nature: groves and grottoes. Pan didn't dwell in the city—you had to go out to the rural areas to find him. Nowadays, the trick isn't so much about going out into wooded lands as it is about finding the heart of the wild within ourselves.

On the surface, Pan may seem to be a pretty simple deity to figure out. He's got goat parts aplenty, has his signature flute on hand, and always seems in the mood for love. But dig a little deeper and you'll see his inherent connection with nature and the rhythm of the land. He may be mischievous at times, to the point of being called a trickster. But it is not because of ego or from bravado—like other beings who receive the trickster label. Pan is a mixture of mayhem and melancholy, merriment and mysticism. His very name means "all." A vessel of wisdom in his own way, Pan pushes those who encounter or call upon him to experience life more fully, more intimately. Rarely is that push a comfortable one, but there is much to learn in the process.

Note that we find Pan within the word *panic*—meaning stirred to a frenzy or causing terror—which has also long been an attribute of the god. This makes sense when you consider that Pan rules the borders between the wild lands and civilization. The further we step away from the light of the fire (our ordered world), the more we become fearful of the unknown, the beings that lurk in the dark, and the sounds they make.

So wait, why do a Midsummer ritual involving Pan? If you're afraid of the dark, then there's no better time of year to face it than when the nights are short. Understand that I'm talking about more than just physical darkness, but the shadow aspects of ourselves that we need to embrace. We can use the light of Midsummer to illuminate our paths and see ourselves more clearly. Who better to lead the way than a goat-footed god with a carnal understanding of what makes us both wild and wise?

Pan encourages us to embrace our bodies, to find pleasure in the physical world around us. He reminds us that sometimes we can live a little too much in our heads, and that we should embrace life with our whole being—mind, spirit, and body. The energy of the Summer Solstice calls us to tune in on being both physically and spiritually active, so this is an ideal time to work with Pan to encourage that growth.

For this ritual, we're going to delve a bit into ecstatic rites by using movement to get us into our bodies. This is not about performing dance or looking pretty or coordinated—no one is judging you but you. (Pan will laugh both at and with you, regardless.) The goal is stop thinking so hard and feel through your body. If you have mobility issues, move as much as you feel comfortable with—even if it's just tapping your foot or fingers.

You can also use trance meditation to transport yourself to a place where you can dance in spirit form, if physical movement is not an option for you.

Time of Day: I recommend performing this ritual within an hour of the impending sunset. It should be a sunny day so you can really tell the changing of the light.

Location: Can be indoors or out. Make sure it's a space you can move around in without tripping or bumping into things. If you're indoors, then the space needs to have windows that let in enough light.

Preparation

Dress: Loose, light attire, fit for freedom of movement. Some folks may opt for skyclad, but personally I like the additional action that fabric brings to dance. If you feel inspired, earlier in the day, collect flowers and greens that you can make into a wreath for your head. Before the ritual, freshen up with a quick shower and anoint your body with a favorite scent, or a soothing lotion if you have allergies to scent. The point is to activate more of your senses—through smell and touch.

Music: Choose some light and airy instrumental flute music to start off with, followed by a song or songs that have a good rhythm that make you want to really dance. Depending on your ability and stamina, you could choose one song, or go for a ten to fifteen minute stretch of songs. Listen to your body. Make sure it's easy to access your music player/phone, to turn it on/off, etc.

Altar & Offerings:

If you have a statue of Pan, or something goaty, place that on the altar

A cup of libation for him—honey mead, wine, or juice

White or green candle

Incense blends: pine, cedar, balsam, or earthy musk scents

A fresh sprig of pine, cedar, or similar evergreen
A string of bell chimes

The Ritual

Prepare the space by making sure it's clean and setting up your altar according to your path. If you have a specific way to craft your sacred space—by casting a circle or other method—do that now. Start the flute music.

(Shake the bells)
> *Pan, great goat-footed God of the wild, I call to you!*
> *Being of borders, maker of music, lover of life,*
> *Come share your ways of wisdom with your child!*

(Light the incense)
> *Pan, the sound of your pipes fills the air and awakens the world.*
> *Help me breathe in the winds of change.*

(Light the candle)
> *Pan, may your laughter and wisdom illuminate this place.*
> *Help me embrace both light and shadow.*

(Raise the cup and take a sip, then hold it up)
> *Pan, I offer this libation in your honor. As it flows through me,*
> *may it flow through you.*

(If you're outside, you can pour it on the earth. If you are indoors, do this after the ritual.)
(Pick up the sprig of pine)
> *Pan, you invigorate the earth with your touch.*

(Touch it to your forehead)
> *May my mind be opened.*

(Touch it to your heart)
> *May my heart find your beat.*

(Touch it to your feet)
   May my feet move to your rhythm.

(Put down sprig and start dance music)

   IO Pan, I dance for you.
   On this longest day,
   IO Pan, I dance with you.
   On this shortest night,
   Pan, great god of all, come dance with me!

Start slowly moving your head from side to side to stretch your neck, move your shoulders back and forth, and allow your arms to move freely, all the way down to your hands. Next pick up and put down your feet, finding the rhythm and moving your weight from side to side. Focus on how it feels to move your body, and release any censoring thoughts from your mind. Just listen, feel, and channel the music. Be in your body and allow it to dance.

Once the music is finished, remain standing and take three slow deep breaths in and out. Listen to the world around you. Be present in your body as you feel your heart beating and limbs tingling. Face the altar and say:

Great God Pan, I thank you for sharing your ways with me. May your wisdom light the path before me as we descend into the dark half of the year. May the work of my mind, body, and spirit do you honor.

Conclude the ritual as your practice deems appropriate.

After Ritual Care: After you are done, be sure to hydrate properly. Drink some cool water, and have a light snack—perhaps dark chocolate and strawberries? (Bonus points if you've prepared or acquired strawberries dipped in chocolate.) Pay close attention to your dreams, and write down what you can remember in the morning.

Note: If you've never worked with Pan and would like to discover more about him, I highly recommend reading *Jitterbug Perfume* by Tom Robbins. It's an incredibly metaphysical story that gives one of the most spot-on depictions of Pan I've come across. Sometimes fiction is able to capture the core of reality better than any formal list of historical tidbits.

Notes

Lammas

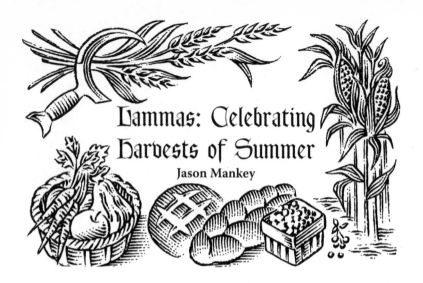

Lammas: Celebrating Harvests of Summer

Jason Mankey

IN MY EXPERIENCE, LAMMAS has never been the most popular of holidays. Between the summer heat and family vacations, it's often difficult to find the energy for ritual and to get the coven together. When asked about their favorite sabbat, most Witches reply with Samhain, or possibly Beltane or Yule. Lammas has a few supporters out there of course, but not enough to ever give our local open Lammas rituals the same draw that our Samhain rituals have.

Part of the reason for this may be the confusion that often surrounds Lammas. Unlike many of the other sabbats, Lammas has several different names. "Lammas" is the name of an Anglo-Saxon early harvest celebration, and was later used by Catholic Christians to celebrate the first harvested grain (which they also called Loaf Mass Day). In addition to bread, in medieval times Lammas was associated with fairs, local elections, paying rent, and the opening of public lands (Hutton 1996, 331).

The other three greater sabbats (Samhain, Imbolc, and Beltane) all have Irish-Celtic names, and it's become more and more common to call Lammas by its Celtic alias, Lughnassa (also spelled Lugnasa, Lughnasa, and Lughnasadh, with some of these being pronounced differently depending on location). *Lughnassa* is certainly the older of the two words, and there are some who wonder if the Anglo-Saxon *Lammas* is an appropriated version of *Lughnassa*.

Lughnassa is often linked to the Celtic god Lugh. It's become common to associate Lugh with the harvest or the sun, but there's no concrete evidence suggesting that he had dominion over such things. Lugh himself is a god of many skills, and was most often compared to the Roman Mercury, who is a god of commerce, thieves, travelers, and honeyed words. *Lughnassa* might come from several different Celtic root-words, including *lug* (raven), *leu* (dark place), and *lou* (an oath or vow). Regardless of where the word *Lughnassa* originated, it's become common to honor Lugh in Lammas circles.

Just to make things more complicated, Lammas is sometimes called by a few other names. In medieval times it was known as the "Gule of August," which possibly translates as the "Yule of August" but is more likely to mean "feast of August," from the Welsh word *gwyl*, which translates to feast (Hutton 1996).

Since the Welsh celebrated their own Gwyl Aust at the start of August, this becomes even more likely. Though rarely heard today, Lammas is also sometimes called "First Fruits," a reference to its position as the first of the three harvest festivals.

Lammas can be difficult for another reason; its date will vary depending on who you ask. In most Llewellyn annuals and in the work of Witch Scott Cunningham, its date as given as August 1. However, some Witches choose to celebrate the sabbat on July 31 (which is why in some quarters it's also known as "August Eve"). Still others prefer August 2, a date that shows up in the book *The White Goddess* by poet and author Robert Graves. (I'll admit to being one of those Witches who prefers the August 2 date.)

Despite its rather low popularity, Lammas (or Lughnassa) offers all sorts of different ways to celebrate! It's a holiday that probably deserves a more prominent place in the calendar of most Witches (or at least a little more attention) and is an essential spoke on the Witch's Wheel of the Year. What follows are some of my favorite ways to celebrate the season.

Bread

One of the most traditional ways to celebrate Lammas is with bread. There are obvious ways to incorporate bread into a Lammas ritual, such as using it during the mini-thanksgiving celebration of cakes and ale (sometimes also called cakes and wine), or throwing small pieces of it into a ritual fire. But there are even more creative ways of incorporating bread into Lammas, and one of my favorites is to bake it during ritual.

"Bannock bread" or "camp bread" is surprisingly simple to make and requires nothing more than these ingredients and steps:

3 cups flour

1 teaspoon salt

2 tablespoons baking powder

1½ cups water

¼ cup oil or melted butter

Mix all the ingredients together. Then wrap your dough around a stick and cook over a low fire (or better yet, just the coals) like a marshmallow. Ta-da, instant bread! Alternatively, the dough can be placed in a well-greased cast-iron skillet, which is then set over coals. In this case, the bread needs to be flipped after about ten minutes. (Too many ingredients? Bannock bread only really requires flour and water!)

Cooking bread during ritual is a great way to connect with the various powers often honored by Witches. I find that it links me to my ancient ancestors who probably baked bread in a similar way in early August. It's also a way of connecting with the natural world since very few of us cook outdoors anymore (and even then it's usually on a grill). It's also a way to draw closer to the goddess and god, especially when honoring harvest deities.

It's also possible to "drink bread," provided one is of legal drinking age. Beer is not much different from bread, and in its ancient form utilized the same ingredients: water and grains. The earliest beer was simply grain that was allowed to naturally ferment for a couple of days in water and was then consumed. Because this resulted in husks of grain being left in the beer, the earliest beer drinkers consumed their brew with straws!

Fresh Fruits and Vegetables

There's a tendency among many Witches to ignore what's actually going on around them during the sabbats, and instead build their rituals around the weather and agricultural activity of other areas. Lughnassa or Lammas was originally an Irish-Celtic holiday, but there's no reason to tailor your rituals for the British Isles if you are living in Canada or California. Where I live, there's no grain harvest in August, but there are several other harvests worth celebrating.

In Northern California, Lammas season is a time for fresh tomatoes, green beans, sunflowers, blackberries, summer squash, and cucumbers. Many of these vegetables I grow in my garden, and others are welcome sights at my local farmer's market. Finding a way to incorporate these fruits and vegetables into my Lammas celebrations (even if they just end up being used as decorations on my altar) makes the sabbat more real to me in some ways. Grain harvests are more a hypothetical where I live than a reality, and I want to put my boline to actual work in late July.

It's possible to celebrate the first fruits of the late summer harvest by simply thanking the deities you honor for their gifts in a ritual setting. Alternatively, they can just be consumed at a pre-Lammas meal or even during ritual itself. I often think of my personal harvest activities in the backyard as small, intimate acts of Witchcraft. Harvesting food that I've personally grown brings me closer to the natural world. And for those not in a position to grow their own food, local farmer's markets are more like county fairs than boring trips to the grocery store. I treasure those moments as well.

Corn Mother

The Lammas rituals of many Witches are presided over by the "Corn Mother" or "Goddess of the Grain." The phrase *Corn Mother* is sometimes used as an honorific for harvest deities such as the Roman Ceres and Egyptian Isis, but it can also refer to a representation of the Great Goddess made from cereal crops such as corn (maize) or wheat. Handmade Corn Mothers can be elaborate or simple. In some cases, they are nothing more than an ear of corn crowned with a couple of flowers. Grain Goddesses constructed from wheat can be made with nothing more than a couple of rubber bands (see *Ancient Ways* by Pauline and Dan Campanelli for more information).

Even those of us who aren't near a local grain harvest are still affected by it. So much of what we eat comes from cereal crops that a severe draught or blight affecting those crops would have devastating consequences nationwide (and beyond). Thanking the Goddess of the Grain for an abundant harvest is probably in everyone's best interest!

Though we don't often think about it today, cereal grains are in many ways responsible for modern civilization. Our very ancient ancestors left behind their hunter-gatherer ways to raise wheat, barley, maize, and rice. Without the gifts of the grain, it's very likely that our world would be very different right now.

Height of Summer (Make It Seasonal)

In many Pagan and Witch circles it's commonplace to think of Lammas as an "early autumn" festival, but for many of us, Lammas-time is the height of summer. Incorporating summertime activities in your Lammas rites is a great way to connect with friends, family, and the season. Pre- or post-ritual sabbat feasting might take place around the grill instead of the kitchen stove, for instance. And August is a great time for an outdoor ritual, especially in a location that might be too cold to visit the rest of the year.

Traditionally, Lammas was a time of county fairs and community get-togethers. Though not as possible as they once were, county and state fairs still exist, and many of them take place in August. Coven activities don't have to take place in a circle; why not visit a county fair and grab a corn dog? In many places, county fairs still have agricultural competitions and exhibits, and this is another great way to learn about the harvest season where you live.

For those who like to really break with tradition, why not have your Lammas ritual in a pool? Pools and summertime are long-time friends, and it's an easy way to beat the heat of early August. Most of us don't have access to a private pool, of course, but ritual could take place around a wading pool or even a water sprinkler. Witches are often a serious bunch, but the sabbats were also made for celebrating!

John Barleycorn: The Dying and Resurrecting Harvest God

One of the most cherished myths in many modern Witchcraft traditions is the story of the dying and resurrecting Harvest God. In this tale, the God of the Grain sacrifices himself before the scythe in order to ensure a bountiful harvest for all. Depending on the location and exact tale being told, the Harvest God "dies" anytime from Lammas to Samhain, though an earlier death during the reaping is more common. He's then reborn in the spring when his seed is put into the soil and grows anew.

The most well-known tale of the Harvest God isn't found in myth, it comes from the eighteenth century English folk ballad John Barleycorn. The song tells the tale of how barley is grown, harvested, and turned into beer and/or whisky. Beginning in the 1940s, the song began to be linked to Witchcraft, and was assumed to be an ancient ballad telling the story of the dying and resurrecting Harvest God (Young 2011, 126–127). (Some early Witches put the lyrics to John Barleycorn in their Books of Shadows, making it an oathbound secret!)

The story of the fallen grain god is more of a modern myth than an ancient one. It rose to notoriety in Sir James Frazer's (1854–1941) *The Golden Bough*, a multivolume work that attempted to draw parallels between a whole host of male deities. In the ancient world, most gods died and then went to live in the realm of the dead, or perhaps a place like Olympus. What most of them didn't do is annually die only to be born again. However, the myth makes so much sense and is such a poetic metaphor that it's hard to escape from. Despite its rather dubious ancient origins, the story still resonates and is a welcome one at many Lammas rituals.

References

Hutton, Ronald. *Pagan Britain.* Cornwall, UK: Yale University Press, 2014.

——. *Stations of the Sun.* Oxford, UK: Oxford University Press, 1996.

Young, Rob. *Electric Eden: Unearthing Britain's Visionary Music.* London: Faber and Faber, Inc, 2011.

Cosmic Sway

Daniel Pharr

AUGUST, THE HOTTEST MONTH of the year, feels like summer and is thought of as summer—school is still out, vacations are still on, and shorts, t-shirts, and flip flops are appropriate wear. Lughnassadh is the first day of autumn, landing halfway between Beltaine and Samhian, between summer and winter.

Gardening

The arrival of Lughnassadh heralds the first major harvest. Tomatoes, potatoes, garlic, onions, lettuce, carrots, kale, cabbage, beans, zucchini, cucumber, and strawberries are picked and served fresh, garden to table. Nature is filling the great Horn of Plenty for all to thrive. As the harvest is reaped, so must the winter beds be sown to maintain balance. Harvesting root vegetables leaves room in the garden for the next crop. Under the waxing Capricorn Moon, sow one last round of radishes, greens, lettuce, and beans. Plant cabbage and cauliflower for a winter harvest.

Lughnassadh Sun

The solar celebration of this Celtic lunar high holiday was attached to the evening of August 1 and extends through to the next sunset.

This year, sunset on August 1 will be at 8:10 p.m. The Capricorn Moon will provide plenty of light for the evening's merriment, and will bring some amount of earthly sensibility to the Lughnassadh festivities and a certain Capricorn practicality to the preparations. Pragmatism may prove to be a positive influence, making this event one of the better organized in recent memory, but the festivities themselves may be tedious or dreary, and the practitioners may feel a little sluggish, lacking the fire that Lugh, the God of Fire, would expect from devotees. If a solar celebration is the choice this year, plan for some spontaneity, movement, and a bit of fun; avoid any activities that might cause embarrassment or self-scrutiny. Attendees may be more self-conscious than normally expected, as this Capricorn Moon offers emotional awareness.

Lughnassadh Moon

Lughnassadh is a lunar holiday, like Samhain, Imbolc, and Beltaine, this year falling under the Aquarius Full Moon of August 3, and more precisely at 11:58 p.m. In the daylight hours, build the balefire of one or more of nine sacred woods—birch, apple, rowan, ash, grape, fir, alder, willow, beech, hawthorn, oak, holly, hazel. Do not burn elder wood as it curses those who do. Start the fire and get it burning. Each tree provides a particular influence for the celebration; for example, birch and oak bring the knowledge of the goddess and the god, respectively, fir provides the influence of immortality, and rowan adds magical power. This balefire formula is the ideal mix, but all is not lost if the many woods are not used. Experience a glimpse into the future regardless of the types of wood burned.

Bless the fire with herbs and plants. Place bundled herbs in the fire to bring the herbal energies into play, honoring Lugh and the element of fire. Place one or more coals from the fire on a stone or flat wood and sprinkle the fiery coal with herbs and spices. Walk deosil around the ceremonial area, smudging and blessing the ritual space and the participants.

The games of Lughnassadh are excellent energy-raising fun. Organizing the revelries around the "three Ms"—movement, music, and mead—will help get everyone in the mood and focused on the evening events. Play games. The ancient Celts were competitive, and their Lughnassadh games reflected their desire to be the best, to seek adventure, and to be a hero, or heroine, as the case may be. Women were equal to men in all respects.

Jupiter in Capricorn, Mars in Aries, and the Sun in Leo will enhance the competitive nature, the motivation to physically play, and the ability to go that needed little extra to shine. The games of Lughnassadh, much like those of Beltaine, can become loose and spontaneous, verging on out of control, but worry not and have fun—the Aquarian rules of decorum have not been fully banished and lie in wait for the opportune moment to settle everyone down if need be.

The feast of Lughnassadh will appropriately feature fresh fruits and vegetables, and fresh protein from nature if possible. The God of Fire will expect a festive blaze after sunset. The Moon moves into Aquarius on August 2 in the afternoon, offering fun-loving energy in full force for the evening. Drums, fire-dancing, games of skill and chance, and divination are all fitting activities for this evening under the shining Moon. The Aquarius Moon is about friendship and passion, idealism and imagination, humanitarianism and community. There is significant interest in communicating with like-minded folks, exploring the science of nature and the nature of science, and spiritually learning, practicing, and growing. But there is also a pervasive need for freedom and independence under this Moon. More than just being seen, this Moon brings the want of recognition, so don't get bogged down with details or rules or expectations of others, and be sure to take note of personal accomplishments and performance rather than expecting others to do so.

Aquarian energies always begin slow and softly build. Set the drums or music to a slow beat. Walk deosil about the fire. Feel the drumbeat inside the body. Find a chant if it feels right, or speak the ritual incantation over and over, for to speak it is to manifest it. Slowly hasten the beat and the steps. Faster and faster, dance the drumbeat around the fire, building the energy for the final festive ecstatic release.

Divination

Finish the evening with divination. The balefire has burned all evening, sacred wood has powerfully embraced the celebration and activities, and the heap of coals glows invitingly. The evening has spawned a sweet and seductive creative charisma that hovers about. Add some ocean driftwood if available and let it rest in the fire until burning well. Add cedar, juniper, and sandalwood, most likely sandalwood chips, to the blaze. These woods of fire and masculinity with water and femininity are perfect for divination on this high holiday ruled by the Aquarian aspect of air. Colors and scents of the burning woods will fuel the exhilaration of uncovering the mysterious in the coals and flames. Look deeply into the shimmering embers and flickering flames with eyes and mind wide open. The Moon is firmly rooted in Aquarius and will show in the fire the ideal and the innate, and through inspiration, imagination, and invention, will manifest a vision of the path leading into the future.

Dark Moon

The Leo Moon is darkest at 10:41 p.m. on August 18. With Taurus rising and Leo Mercury, the next few hours will be all about self-indulgence, self-aggrandizing, self-importance, self-emphasizing, self-exaggerating, and self-convincing. Sadly, few folks will be around to witness the selfishness as the Moon moves into Virgo in six hours at 4:20 a.m.

Full Moon

The Full Pisces Moon appears on September 2 at 1:21 a.m. The third harvest Moon will bring with it sensitivity, moodiness, self-confidence, protectiveness, meticulousness, and plenty of emotions. Draw down the Moon for a strange combination of lunar energies. The light of this Moon will penetrate deeply, drawing out that which is seldom seen or heard.

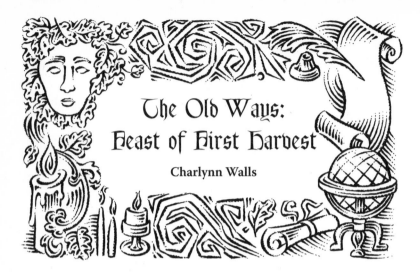

The Old Ways: Feast of First Harvest

Charlynn Walls

GROWING UP, IT WAS all hands on deck when it came time to bringing in the first of the harvests from the family gardens. Both my great-grandmother and grandmother had large garden plots that had a variety of vegetables and grains. The first grain that had to be harvested was the corn. We spent time picking the ears off the stalks. We could sit in front of the garage and shuck the corn, making sure that all the silk was off every piece. Then we would prepare and store the food for the coming winter.

Lammas is traditionally observed August 1 and 2. As the first of the harvest festivals, Lammas corresponds with the harvest of corn, but it can also relate to the first grains and fruits that are ready for harvest. Where you live will determine what will be harvested first. It is also referred to as Loaf Mass, which shows how important harvesting and using the first grains were.

Domestication of Corn and Green Corn Festival

During my archaeology courses we discussed the domestication of corn. Maize was originally a small grain similar to wheat, rather than the starch we now know with the large kernels. Years of selective breeding developed the corn we now eat. Jessica Saraceni noticed these changes in the genes of the plant, which meant "maize adapted to the arid climate of the Southwest and to the preferences of the local people" (Saraceni 2015). Native peoples made a tremendous impact on the productivity of corn harvests.

Native American peoples would celebrate the time when the corn would become ripe and ready for harvest. Corn was an important staple and one of the three sisters, along with beans and squash. The festivals surrounding the harvest of this grain honored the Corn Grandmother. The time of harvest was determined by the elders of the tribe. Since the time the corn would ripen would vary, so did the actual date of this festival. Once the corn was ready for harvest the community could move forward.

The community would hold feasts of thanksgiving for the bounty received. It was also a time to purify the community and the individual. A ritual purge would begin so that they could let go of old grudges that persisted over time. By letting go of what no longer served the purpose of the whole, they made room for a new outlook on life.

Baking Breads

Often, corn was referred to as the first grain of harvest, though in reality there could be differing grains that could be harvested first depending on the area you lived in, including wheat and barley. So one of the first goods that was created from the harvested grain was bread.

Bread could be created throughout the winter months from the stored grain. The loaves generated throughout the winter could be made and shared with those in the community. This could create a more thankful and united people if the harvest had been plentiful. These loaves became a central part of the Lammas festival.

Taking Time to Prepare for the Winter

There are numerous ways that we can begin to prepare for the coming winter months. If you are unable to harvest your own grain, you can purchase it from a store. Once the grain has been procured you can do a few things to prolong the life of the grain.

Food Storage Preparations

Corn can be saved in a variety of ways for the coming winter. Fresh corn can be shucked and frozen on the cob for a quick meal later on. If you are able to, you can shuck the corn and cut the kernels off the cob to create your own frozen sweet corn.

For corn kernels that have been dried, you should keep your newly acquired grain in a cool, dark, dry place. The grain will last longer in a place where it cannot germinate. Keeping it in an airtight container also prolongs the life of the grain and prevents molding. The corn can then be ground into corn flour or cornmeal.

Other methods of food storage include the pickling and canning of vegetables and meats. Pickling requires placing the food in a vinegar solution. Pickled vegetables are an excellent example of this technique. Canning requires the application of heat to create an airtight seal and preserve the food. You will be familiar with jams and jellies that are available on store shelves throughout the year. It is a great way to preserve food and make it last through the winter. You can find canning supplies in most supermarkets. The main tools are a stock pot, wire rack, tongs, and canning jars. Find a recipe from one of your relatives and create a lasting treat.

Ritual Food

Work to create a loaf of bread. Mix together the flour, water, yeast, and other ingredients. Knead the dough, being mindful of all that happened to get the grain to this point. Let the dough rise, envisioning the abundance of the harvest. Bake the bread and serve during ritual. As each person consumes part of the loaf, they can give thanks.

A freshly baked loaf of bread can also be made into an offering. If you are near a creek, stream, or river you can place the loaf into the water. Decorate the loaf with candles or stuff with pieces of paper that say what you are thankful for and send it downriver.

References

Franklin, Anna, and Paul Mason. *Lughnasa: History, Lore & Celebration*. United Kingdom: Lear Books, 2010.

"The Green Corn Festival." Mexican Holidays. Accessed June/July 2018. http://web-holidays.com/native/2012/03/11/the-green-corn-festival/.

McCoy, Edain. *The Sabbats: A New Approach to Living the Old Ways*. St. Paul, MN: Lewellyn Publications, 1994.

Morgan, Sheena. *The Wicca Book of Days*. London: Vega, 2002.

Nichols, Mike. *The Witches' Sabbats*. Albany, CA: Acorn Guild Press, 2005.

Saraceni, Jessica E. "The Origin & Evolution of Corn in the Southwest." *Archaeology Magazine*. 2015. https://www.archaeology.org/news/2879-150108-southwest-corn-dna.

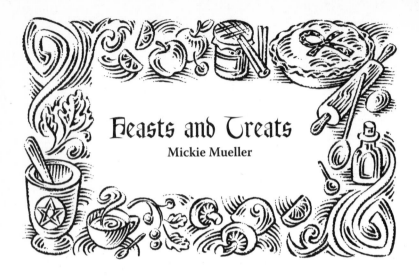

Feasts and Treats

Mickie Mueller

THE SUMMER HAS MATURED, and we move into the season when we acknowledge the harvest of grains such as wheat, corn, or barley. As these grains are harvested, we also notice the days shorten a bit; even as we still enjoy warm summer days, the spirit of the Sun King wanes. This festival is sometimes called Lughnassadh, in honor of the Celtic god Lugh. Games are traditional, as are bread, beer, mead, and honey, along with the harvest of summer vegetables that are still in abundance. This feast of the first harvest is sure to fill your heart with the spirit of the season and summon up blessings of joy and happiness.

Easy Beer Bread

We enjoy beer in our house, so I like cooking with it sometimes too. When I saw a beer bread mix, I had to try it. It was so easy to make and everyone loved the flavor. Then the store I got it from stopped carrying it; I hate when that happens! I went on the search for recipes and found that it's really easy to make from scratch. Self-rising flour makes it even easier. If you want to go dairy free, substitute coconut oil for the butter. I'll never buy a mix again.

Prep time: 5 minutes
Baking time: 1 hour
Servings: 6–8

3 tablespoons honey
3 cups self-rising flour (or all-purpose or gluten-free flour with 1
    tablespoon baking powder and 1 teaspoon salt mixed in)
1 12-ounce can or bottle of beer (you can substitute NA beer or
    club soda if you prefer)
Half stick of butter, plus a bit to grease the pan
Optional: diced, sautéed onions and/or shredded cheddar cheese to
    mix into the batter before baking.

Preheat oven to 350° F (177° C). Prepare a loaf pan by greasing it
with butter. Warm the honey a bit in the microwave; this helps it to
mix in more easily. Measure the flour into a large mixing bowl, then
add the beer and honey and mix with a wooden spoon until well
blended. Spoon the mixture into the loaf pan. Melt the half stick of
butter and pour it over the top of the loaf. Bake for 40–50 minutes
until the top is golden brown and a toothpick inserted into the center comes out clean. Cool in the pan for 2 minutes, then turn out
onto a wire rack. You can slice and serve it warm.

Zucchini Pizza Boats

My mom has made stuffed zucchini with the oversized zucchini
from our garden since I was a kid. If you've ever grown zucchini,
you know that one day they look almost ready to harvest and then
two days later they're so big that they might take over the yard. The
seeds get pretty tough at this point, so many people just scrape out
the seeds and make zucchini bread. I have another recipe, though,
that turns that monster zucchini into a wonderful meal. This is a
slightly different version than my old family recipe; we made this
version recently and it was so good I just had to share it. Yeah, I'm
in Missouri and we're weird and love the St. Louis classic, melty,
sweet, processed Provel cheese on our pizza around here, but mild,

stretchy mozzarella is also delicious. No judgment; use the pizza cheese of your choice.

Prep time: 15 minutes
Cooking time: 40 minutes
Servings: 4–6

2 ridiculously large zucchinis or 4 average-sized ones
1 pound Italian sausage or vegan sausage
1 jar marinara sauce
1 cup Provel, mozzarella, or provolone cheese

Preheat oven to 350° F (177° C). Using a sharp knife, cut off the stem of each zucchini and cut in half lengthwise. Using a large metal spoon, scoop out the seeds and the soft middle of the zucchini. If the seeds aren't large and tough, you can put the seeds and other parts you scooped out into the freezer to use in zucchini bread at a later date. Place the zucchini on a rimmed baking sheet. Brown the sausage in a skillet, chopping it up into small pieces. Fill the cavity in each zucchini with sausage, then spoon the marinara sauce over the top of the sausage. Bake in the oven for 20 minutes. Sprinkle with cheese and then cook 10 more minutes.

Sandy's Spinach Salad

This great summer salad is the specialty of my old roommate, artist and photographer Sandy Wright. If you've ever had croutons tear up the roof of your mouth, you'll love her innovation to add a bit of crunch without the pain in the form of crispy chow mein noodles. Spinach is a food associated with prosperity magic. I suggest using locally sourced tomatoes if you can; it's a great way to connect with the spirits of the land.

Prep time: 10 minutes
Servings: 4

8 ounces fresh spinach
Half a red onion
2 medium tomatoes

1 cup chow mein noodles (they do make gluten-free ones if you prefer)

½ cup provelone cheese, mozzarella, or feta (shredded or chopped into desired size)

Tear spinach into bite-size pieces. Slice the red onion into desired size. Chop tomatoes into bite-size chunks. Combine all ingredients in a large salad bowl and toss with dressing.

Creamy Italian Dressing

This is not the healthiest salad dressing ever, but it is very delicious and decadent.

1 cup mayonnaise

½ small onion, minced

¼ cup olive oil

2 tablespoons red wine vinegar

1 tablespoon sweeter of your choice—sugar, agave, stevia

¼ teaspoon garlic powder

¾ teaspoon Italian seasoning

¼ cup grated parmesan cheese

¼ teaspoon salt

¼ teaspoon pepper

Combine all ingredients in a blender and blend until it reaches desired creamy consistency. Refrigerate at least 1 hour. Stir it all up well before serving.

Sparkling Floral Honey Nectar

This is a nice way to enjoy a mead-like flavor in either a non-alcoholic beverage or in some spirits if you wish. Honey is a powerful magical ingredient that brings sweetness to any situation and is also a wonderful offering to the gods. Honey is appropriate for magic involving love, healing, and prosperity.

Prep time: 10 minutes

Cooking time: 10 minutes

Cooling time: 15 minutes
Servings: 4-6

1 cup water
1 tablespoon dry or fresh lavender flowers,
    rose petals, or elderflowers
½ cup honey
1 liter sparkling water

Bring water to boil, then reduce to a simmer and add flowers. Simmer for 10 minutes. Allow to cool for 5 minutes, then strain. Return to the pan and heat on low. Add the honey and stir until dissolved. Cool and bottle. Store the honey syrup for up to a week. To make the Sparkling Floral Honey Nectar, add ½ cup of the honey syrup to one liter of sparkling water and serve over ice. You can also add the syrup to white wine or bourbon if you want a delicious summer cocktail.

Crafty Crafts

Ember Grant

THE FESTIVIAL OF LUGHNASADH originates in Irish myth with the heroic figure of Lugh. He was often called "Lugh of the Long Hand" or the "many-skilled" because of his diverse abilities. Since Lughnasadh involves celebrating "first fruits"—the beginning of harvest season—both of these projects feature seeds.

Natural Acorn Pendant

You can use a natural acorn to make a lovely pendant by simply giving the nut a coat of paint and a hook. It's very simple.

Materials

Small acorns with caps (gathered for free)
Acrylic paint ($3)
Paintbrush
Hypo-Cement jewelry glue or super glue ($3–$7)
Jump rings or wire ($2–$5)
Chain or cord (price varies)

> *Cost:* $10–$20
> *Time spent:* about 3 hours

First, you need to find an acorn—or several. If you don't happen to have easy access to these, go for a walk. You can probably find them in a public park or even in a parking lot. I once found some beautiful acorns beneath a tree in a shopping center.

Before painting them, you should be certain they're clean—and that they don't contain worms. One easy way to accomplish this, rather than waiting a few weeks for them to dry, is to dry them yourself. Rinse them with water and dry them on a towel. Don't use any that have holes in them. Place the acorns on a cookie sheet and literally bake them in the oven (or even a toaster oven) at 175 degrees for about an hour to an hour and a half. Turn them over at least a couple times. Let them cool for an hour or so before proceeding with using them in crafts. If any of the caps fall off, you can simply glue them back on with super glue or tacky craft glue.

Metallic gold looks very nice on the acorns, but if you prefer a more natural look, mix gold metallic paint with light brown. Paint the top, then the cap after the top is dry, so you can hold onto it. Experiment with colors if you wish. You can paint the top gold and

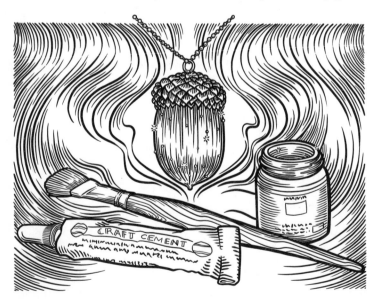

the cap a mix of brown and gold, or try silver, or even bright colors like red or orange.

Once the paint is dry, you need to decide which technique to use—a jump ring or wire wrapping. You could also try both. Securing the jump ring to the acorn can be challenging. I used Hypo-Cement, but super glue works as well. Use tweezers to hold the jump ring and attach it. It also helps if your acorn cap has a joint on it or other feature that allows a place for the ring to sit.

For wire wrapping, it's okay if the wire fits loosely—think of it as a little cage around the acorn. It won't fall out. But, if it does, at least you're not losing an expensive pendant! Practice wrapping the wire in a spiral around the acorn. Be sure to make a loop for the chain to go through. I had a small acorn, so I wrapped the wire around my finger first, so the coils would be smooth. If you've never wire-wrapped anything before, this can be a nice introduction to the process. Either method will give you a lovely, natural pendant.

Seed Art

I remember making projects like this in school when I was a kid. The end results were always surprisingly lovely, even when put together by inexperienced hands. It's still just as much fun as an adult! Plus, you end up with a lovely piece of framed art you can display in your home.

Materials

Frame ($5–$20)
Assorted dried beans and seeds (approx. $7)
Tacky craft glue ($3)
Mod Podge ($3–$7)

Cost: $20+
Time spent: several hours to several days, depending on the size

Choose a variety of dried beans and seeds for your project. You may be limited by what you can find in your local supermarket. Of course, you can purchase these online as well, so that's an option

to consider. Here are some good choices: white beans, pinto beans, corn, lentils, peas, rice, sunflower seeds, pumpkin seeds, red beans, black beans, black-eyed peas, and peppercorns. I used six different types of seeds, a 1 pound bag of each, and the price range was from 99 cents to $1.50 per bag. Your finished piece will resemble a mosaic-style piece of art, so choose a variety of contrasting colors for the best effect.

Just as important as your choice of seeds is your choice of frame. I used an 8 x 10 frame made of thick wood that was painted pale green with a hint of gold. I decided to highlight that color by using split peas in my design. You don't have to spend a lot of money here. You can use a frame you already have, or buy one in a secondhand store. Refurbishing an old frame is a great way to recycle it, too. It's probably best, however, to pick something at least 5 x 7. If you choose a frame that's too small, you won't have enough room to create your project.

I suppose you can glue the beans directly to the outside glass if you want, but I removed the glass and used sturdy cardboard as the base for my project. A perfectly sized piece of cardboard was included with the frame, but it was too flimsy; I traced around it onto a better piece of cardboard to ensure it was the right size to fit back inside the frame. If you do decide to glue directly onto the glass, you can insert the pattern or design you want to use inside the frame and use it as a guide.

As for the design, you can draw something—a sun or sunflower is perfect for this time of year—or just create as you go. I started by drawing a few circles like a mandala, but then just let my design evolve after that, by adding lines and spirals. There's no wrong way to do this. In fact, this type of art turns out quite well by simply using a blend of curving lines in a variety of colors. Of course, if you want to plan your design, you can draw it and decide which colors to use in each area.

Work in small batches, spreading glue with a brush and attaching the seeds; you may need to use tweezers for very small ones. When you've finished adding all your seeds, allow the entire piece to dry before adding the finishing touch—a coat (or two) of Mod Podge. I used the satin finish and it gave the piece a lovely shine. Plus, it helps secure all the seeds in place.

When the piece is completely dry, place it back inside the frame and hang it. In addition, now that you have several bags of dried beans and seeds, you can prepare a feast for the holiday with your leftovers!

Other Options: You can also use this seed technique to make smaller pieces—pentacles, for example, to use on your altar. And, if you want, use hot glue to attach a ribbon to small pieces of seed art and make things you can hang. Planning ahead for the Yuletide season, you can make ornaments for your tree!

A Crystal for Every Season: Moonstone

Charlie Rainbow Wolf

LAMMAS CELEBRATES THE FIRST harvest, when thoughts turn to grain and everything that can be made from it. It's the first of the thanksgiving festivals, when John Barleycorn must die so that others might live through the sustenance that his body provides. Artists Fairport Convention, Joe Walsh, Martin Carthy, and others have recorded the centuries-old folk song telling the tale of the killing of John Barleycorn. There's an unplugged version by Steve Winwood (from Traffic) on YouTube, and if you haven't heard it, you're in for a treat.

In the northern hemisphere, this is the time of year when the earth starts to look tired. The harvest loses it's green colors and becomes golden, and the light of the sun takes on a more amber hue than it had when at its peak in summer. It stands to reason that the stones for this season are also gold and brown, as well as the darker colors that imply the ever-encroaching darkness. Suitable stones are aventurine, botswana agates, flint, all shades of jasper, labradorite, peridot, sardonyx, and gold tiger's eye.

Moonstone is my pick of them all for Lughnassadh, even though it might seem an odd choice for a grain festival. Moonstone comes in a variety of shades, from the palest of white to murky and mysterious gray—there's even a beautiful rainbow moonstone that shimmers and shines with opalescent colors. I chose moonstone for the first festival of the harvest because to me nothing says cycles and seasons more than the the phases of the moon and the rhythm of the harvest.

Moonstone's molecular structure contains oxygen, silicon, potassium, and aluminum. It's quite a soft stone, only a 2.5 on the Mohs scale. It's easily scratched and damaged, although it is possible to coax it into cabochons and other shapes for jewelry, or items designed for healing or ceremony. Its use goes back over two thousand years.

All moonstones are soothing to the spirit. You only have to hold one in your hand to see why! They're soft to the touch, smooth to the skin, their color subtle and serene. Moonstones are a fantastic ally during Lammas, when the bustle to get the harvest gathered and prepared for the winter is at its inception. They help to calm the nerves and promote rest and relaxation.

White Moonstone

Like the color it reflects, this is a stone of purity and light. If you're incorporating dreamwork or guided meditations into this time of year, white moonstone assists you in seeing your work clearly, and remembering what you're doing in the other realms. Moonstone is known to benefit travelers—and that includes astral traveling as well as more mundane journeys.

Peach Moonstone

This color resonates with the sacral chakra and works with you to soothe any misgivings about your sense of self-worth. Shades of orange always indicate confidence or lack of it. The peachy orange of the moonstone works with you to help you to balance your desires in a positive and healthy way, so that you find your faith in yourself, without doubting your competence and without coming on too strong.

Blue Moonstone

Blue is a calming and cooling color and the blue moonstone is no exception. It's easy to rely too much on the opinions of others and lose yourself in becoming a people pleaser. Blue moonstone helps you through this, so that you can hear what they have to say without feeling obligated to do it if you don't want to. It also helps you to speak your truth quietly and clearly, so that you have more of a chance of having your thoughts and feelings heard.

Gray Moonstone

Similar to blue, gray moonstone is also calming and soothing, in the way that a morning fog brings an ethereal quality to the day. This is the stone to choose for your companion if you need to retreat and regroup. I also find this stone a welcome consort when I'm journaling out my thoughts at the end of any particularly difficult days.

Rainbow Moonstone

This is perhaps my favorite moonstone, which given my name, probably isn't surprising! I use it as a worry stone or a fidget spinner, helping me to burn off nervous energy when I'm feeling overwhelmed and to cultivate balance in its place. It's my buddy when I'm gardening, it's my muse in pottery. It takes all the qualities of the other colors and brings them together in one magical and mystical stone.

Lammas Moonstone Magic

This charm is done at sunset, and can be worked as a group or by yourself. It's a good way to celebrate the turning of the wheel at the time of the cutting of the first harvest. You'll need:

A glass jug

A glass dish

A white tealight candle and something to light it with

A bottle of water

Note: I prefer to use the glass that has either etchings or carvings in it; they can be obtained from the dollar stores or second-hand shops very inexpensively.

Pour some water into the glass jug. Light the tealight candle. Tip it up so a few drops of the melted wax land in the bottom of the glass dish, then secure the candle into the dish on that wax—that sometimes takes more than one try, but don't be discouraged. Gently pour the water from the jug into the bowl, taking care not to jar the candle loose from is wax anchor, nor to splash water on the flame and extinguish it. As you do this, say the following words:

Setting Sun says day is done
It's time for Moon to shine.
By the light of candle white
I claim this night as mine!

Now gently dip your fingers in the water surrounding the lighted candle and touch them to your head, between your eyebrows. Continue with your Lammas celebration or ritual, knowing that you have harnessed the power not just of John Barleycorn, but also of the Sun King and the Grain Mother. Let the candle burn out on its own, then return the water from the glass dish back to the earth, where it will nurture the soil for another turn of the wheel.

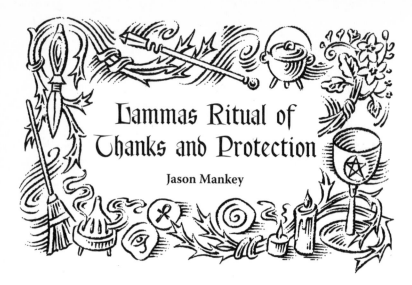

Lammas Ritual of Thanks and Protection

Jason Mankey

BESIDES THE USUAL ASSOCIATIONS with grain and the harvest, there are two other things I generally associate with Lammas: thankfulness and protection. Early August is a rather quiet time of the year on the Pagan turn of the wheel (it just doesn't quite have the party atmosphere of Yule, Beltane, or Midsummer, and is mostly absent of the gravitas that hangs over many Samhain rites), which makes it a great time for contemplation and to offer thanks for all that we've received in our lives. Thanks, of course, can be linked back to the harvest, but it can also be about the personal harvests and blessings in our own lives, and the lives of those around us.

Many ancient Lammas rituals were about protection. The first grains of the harvest were blessed, dried slowly over a fire, and then brought inside and distributed around the home to keep out negative energies and unwanted entities. Another way to accomplish the same thing was to offer pieces of the first Lammas bread to a fire as a sort of offering. Often, such offerings were designed to keep certain mundane critters such as foxes and crows away, but were also sometimes directed at more supernatural threats, such as malevolent spirits or fairy folk.

For this short ritual, all you'll need is a whole loaf of bread. Start by setting up your rite in your usual manner (casting the circle, calling the quarters, etc.) and then calling whatever deities are important to you and your practice. At harvest time I often focus on deities such as Demeter and Dionysus, or sometimes larger figures such as the Harvest Lord or Corn Mother. Whomever you call, just be sure their energies resonate with you and the rite.

After your container is set up and your chosen deities invoked, take your loaf of bread and hold it, reflecting on the energy and ingredients that went into making it. When finished, hold it comfortably and say:

Great Goddess (or insert name of a specific goddess here), I thank you for this bounty.
Your gifts are what keep me and my loved ones strong and walking upon this Earth.
Through the powers of soil, sun, rain, and wind I hold this bread!
May it be a source of protection and thanks on this sacred sabbat day! Blessed Be!

Next, break your loaf of bread into two somewhat equal halves. The half in your left hand will be used for protection magick, the half in your right hand as a show of thanks to the gods and the earth for all you've received in life. Set the half loaf designated for thanks aside, and place the remaining piece of bread in your non-dominant hand. If you are inside, have a libation bowl for your offerings ready; if you are outside, stand near a secluded liminal space (such as near a tree or a shady spot in your yard or local park) or near a small fire or charcoal grill and then state your intention for this part of the rite:

May these first grains of my Lammas harvest serve as a shield against all wickedness, misfortune, and any maladies that may come for me or my loved ones. This bread, nurtured and blessed by the Lady and Lord (or specific deity names), shall be a source of magick and might on this Lammas night! So mote it be!

Now think of those things you want to be protected from over the coming months. As you contemplate each idea, pull a chunk of bread from your half loaf and hold it for a moment. If you are asking for you or a loved one to be free of sickness, picture yourself (or them) healthy and whole and moving around. Once that picture has been formed in your head, place your intention into the bread and then say it aloud and throw your small piece of bread into the fire or down onto the ground. Repeat this as many times as necessary. If you are doing this as a group ritual, simply pass the half loaf around and let everyone have a turn.

When you are done with this part of the rite, thank the grain and the harvest for looking out for you, and place any remaining bread onto your altar. Follow this by picking up the remaining (until now unused) half loaf in your non-dominant hand and address the gods:

As the gods and the earth so share with us, I now also share with the gods. Though our Lord and Lady do not demand sacrifice; I honor them for their gifts. Life can be hard, but I'm thankful for home, hearth, friends, family, the Craft, and the love of the gods.

Gracious Lady, Great Lord, O beautiful Earth, please accept these gifts from this first harvest as I praise all that I am thankful for.

Think of all the things you are thankful for in life, and for each one remove a chunk of bread, verbalize your thanks, and then share that small morsel of bread with a part of the earth. You could leave it near a tree, in some bushes, or in a body of water. Wherever you place it, make sure that the gratitude inside of you flows outwards into the bread and from there into the earth. If you are doing this with a group of people, pass the bread around the circle and have everyone verbalize what they are thankful for. Once the bread has been passed around the circle as many times as necessary, let everyone disperse to leave their offerings.

If this is a ritual you are doing inside, place your small pieces of bread in a libation bowl, and later, take it outside to a secluded spot when your rite is over. The best places for offerings of any sort are secluded or isolated areas where your offerings and magick won't be disturbed by mundane forces. If you are stuck in a very large city, just near a tree outdoors will work too.

If there's something left over from the half loaf designated for protection, it may be used for cakes and ale (adding a little extra protection to your insides never hurts). The half set aside for thanks should be saved and given to the fair folk/nature spirits at the conclusion of your rite. It's considered "bad form" to eat anything designated as an offering. After bread and drink have been consumed, dismiss any powers you've raised, close up your circle, and thank your gods for a blessed first harvest.

Happy Lammas!

Notes

Mabon

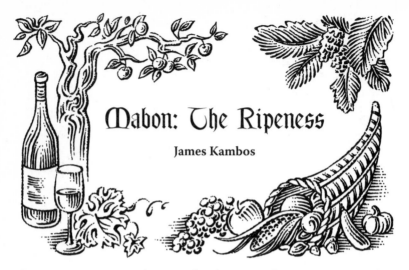

Mabon: The Ripeness

James Kambos

OUT ON THE LAND, where a calendar or an almanac is not needed to tell you what time of the year it is, Mabon is more than a day or a sabbat. It is a season. I learned this lesson as a boy during the time I spent on my grandparents' Ohio farm. There, you didn't need a calendar to tell you it was September or the autumn equinox or the harvest sabbat, Mabon.

You could see it, you could smell it, you could hear it.

On the farm, Mabon was all about ripeness and fulfillment. The urgency of planting and growing were over. The rhythm of the natural world slowed down. The promise of Beltane, Litha, and Lammas were finally realized in the ripeness of this sabbat's harvest. The miracle of the harvest spilled forth in a cornucopia of achievement known as Mabon.

This is my story of Mabon.

The ripeness of Mabon settles softly on the farm. You can see it. Here and there a tree on the edge of the pasture flames into color. Pumpkins in the garden ripen to orange. During the afternoon, the sunlight slants at a different angle. In the barn, I catch a glimpse of little velvety field mice as they scurry to find a home before the first frost. In the twilight of evening, as day melts into night, the fingers of dusk draw a little earlier across the orchard. At night, the fireflies are gone. But now, with the humidity of summer over, the fireflies are replaced by a Mabon night sky full of sparkling stars.

What I can't forget are the scents of Mabon. Out on the farm, the air carries the fragrances of Mabon. The breeze coming down from the upper meadow is soft as a baby's breath and still carries the perfume of the last hay cutting. From the fields comes the unmistakable scent of ripeness. The air in late afternoon has a tinge of that corn pollen sweetness, leftover from August and Lammas. Then, in the gloaming, as the sun sets, the windfall apples perfume the air coming from the orchard with a cidery tang.

Even today, the scent of a freshly harvested field in September takes me back to Mabon on the farm.

On the morning of Mabon, the sun rises almost due east, to the sound of the rooster's crow. Now the sounds of nature are more muted. There is no longer the pre-dawn chorus of birdsong, but Mabon brings us other sounds on the farm that tell us it is upon us. The early morning mist rises and swirls; suddenly it opens and above it reveals a brilliant deep blue September sky. Off toward the horizon I hear one of Mabon's most memorable sounds. It's faint at first. Yes, it's the gabble of wild geese. Finally, I see them flying by in a V formation. Following an instinct older than time, they glide across the early autumn sky, headed to warmer climates. They leave behind one of the most haunting sounds associated with Mabon. I pause and listen until the sound fades beyond the southern horizon.

In the afternoon light of Mabon, there is a golden haze lingering over the fields and the lane leading to the back woods. I'm lured into taking a walk. I walk slowly with the spirit and the sounds of Mabon. Some of the leaves have begun to fall; they crunch underfoot. A breeze rises, and the leaves make a clicking sound as they skitter along the fence. In the tall grass along the pasture, field crickets fiddle. It won't be long before the first frost will silence them.

As dusk deepens I head back to the old, white farmhouse. Now the only sound I hear is the corn rustling in the field.

The pulse of the season changes. The ripeness, the achievement of another year is almost complete. Just as nature begins its decline into darkness, Mabon, the Great Son, walks softly into the shadows where he'll learn the Mysteries before returning to us at Yule.

Now, let's take a closer look at the stories, legends, and beliefs surrounding this dark sabbat known as Mabon.

Mabon and the Equinox

As the golden days of September drift by, we arrive at the Fall Equinox, which occurs somewhere between September 21 and 23. This is also known as the Pagan holiday of Mabon, a time of balance and change. On this day, the hours of light and dark are about equal. Also, at about this time, the sun enters the zodiac sign of Libra, symbolized by the scales, which echoes one of Mabon's themes of balance. At Mabon we are at a point when, briefly, the light and dark are equal. But almost at the same time, we tip toward the dark part of the year.

Mabon is the second of the harvest sabbats and the first dark sabbat.

The Legend of Mabon

According to Welsh lore, Mabon was the son of the Great Mother Goddess Modron. The name Mabon means "Great Son." In some traditions it's translated as the "Great Sun."

As an infant, he was abducted and imprisoned. Later, he was freed and returned to his Great Mother as a youth in his prime, or as the Young God. This story is appropriate for this time of year. Just as Mabon disappears into the darkness and later returns, nature also begins to enter the dark season, which begins to overshadow the light. Then, at Ostara, when the Spring Equinox arrives, the light once again gains control and growth begins anew.

The Mabon legend parallels the ancient Greek story of the agricultural goddess Demeter and the abduction of her daughter, Persephone, into the Underworld. This was used by the Greeks to also explain the changing of the seasons.

The Meaning of Mabon

Mabon is one of the most mysterious of the sabbats because it celebrates the dual nature of life and death. At Mabon, the past and future are united. The seed that was planted in the past has sprouted, grown, and now at the harvest, has produced the grains, vegetables, and fruits that will sustain us. But as the crops are harvested, the natural world, like Mabon, begins to descend into darkness, eventual decay, and death. But we must remember, in the crops that are harvested are next year's seeds, which will begin the cycle of life/death/life all over again. This life, death, and rebirth cycle is one of Mabon's most important messages.

So, at Mabon, we mourn the passing of the Great Son as he returns to Mother Earth; however, he doesn't enter the darkness of complete death. It's the darkness of rest, regeneration, and eventual rebirth, which will occur at Yule when he returns to us as the newborn Sun God.

For now, we too must say farewell to summer and light, and enter the dark season. This is our time when the spirit can be nurtured, and personal growth can begin.

As the Great Son ages, he becomes wise. In some traditions he is Lord of the Shadows, and we are drawn to him because he is the keeper of the Mysteries. He knows the secrets of the seed, of growth, of death, and rebirth.

In some traditions, Mabon becomes the Huntsman, the rider of the storm. In this aspect, he leads the Wild Hunt. He and his spirit riders who follow him come from the shadows of the otherworld on windy, moonlit autumn nights when clouds scud across the sky. With them ride the spirits of those whose life cycles have just ended. But, as the Huntsman, he should not be feared; he offers peace, renewal, and unconditional love.

Another key message of Mabon is sharing. The Great Mother Goddess has not only shared her son with us, but she also shares with us the bounty of the harvest. She gives us so much and asks for so little in return. The least we can do at Mabon is give thanks for the abundance she has provided us with to sustain us during the lean months that lie ahead.

Ripeness and Fulfillment

You can't talk—or think—about Mabon without mentioning two key elements of this sabbat: ripeness and fulfillment. Interestingly, both words are linked with the harvest time and plenty. The root word of *ripeness*, ripe, can be traced back to an early Germanic word for *reap*, meaning "to harvest." The word *plenty* is actually linked to Latin for "full," which brings us to the word *fulfillment*.

At Mabon, ripeness and fulfillment are everywhere, and it isn't just confined to the farmer's field or a backyard garden. Apples are now being harvested in orchards, nut trees are also ripening. Summer's flowers are now producing seed heads to the delight of birds everywhere.

Plants now store their futures as they produce seeds for their tomorrows. Squirrels store their nuts in preparation for the dark season, and chipmunks line their cozy dens with grain.

Mabon is the ripeness, fulfillment, and achievement, brought together in a triumph known as the harvest.

The Witches' Thanksgiving

In many Pagan traditions, Mabon is known as the Witches' Thanksgiving. Indeed, this is a fine time to gather with family, friends, and coven members for food and the giving of thanks for all that we have. During these celebrations is also a good time to remember and raise a toast to our ancestors. As we give thanks, I like to take the time to help share my bounty with others. This is a good time to give food to a food bank, so they can be ready for the dark months ahead. Also, give to or organize a winter clothing or coat drive.

Don't forget to remember the wild folk who share your space. Do your pets have a safe, warm place to spend the winter in your home? Buy corn for the squirrels. At Mabon, I usually begin stocking my bird feeders, too. Above all, give thanks for your food, family, and home.

Plant for Tomorrow

Keeping in mind Mabon's theme of life, death, and rebirth, there is no better way to experience this than to plant some spring-flowering bulbs now. They say that by planting spring bulbs, you are showing that you believe in tomorrow. From Mabon through the rest of the autumn is a perfect planting time for many bulbs, shrubs, and other plants.

Planting spring bulbs makes you very aware of regeneration and the concept of renewal. All you need is a small amount of space in a flower bed, or at the base of a tree or shrub, and a few bulbs. Daffodils, crocus, and tulips are good choices. Loosen the soil and compost if you wish, and plant. Firm the soil over the bulbs and enjoy them next spring.

As you plant them, be aware that you are returning a dormant, lifeless-looking bulb back to the womb of Mother Earth. Then after resting in the Underworld, the bulb will surge back to life next spring.

What better way to experience one of Mabon's lessons!

Now, nature begins to pause. Each of us is surrounded with the ripeness, the achievement, of our own harvests. You don't need to be a farmer to reap a harvest, or to appreciate Mabon. Take pleasure in your own achievements and harvests at this time. It could be success in your career, the love of your family, or the attainment of your educational goals.

The great wheel of time continues to turn, and the never-ending pattern of the seasons continues.

Cosmic Sway

Daniel Pharr

MABON OCCURS WHEN THE days have shortened and nights have lengthened, coming to equilibrium on the morning of September 22. The equinox is traditionally celebrated as the second harvest festival, the middle of the harvest season. The start of harvest was at Lughnassadh and the end will be at Samhain. This high holiday is a time to recognize the waning of the Green Man and the vitality of nature, and to celebrate the bounty that was received from this cycle of the wheel.

Gardening

Ancient harvests usually occurred on or around the Full Moons for greater light in the dark hours. The Moon will be waxing from New for only a few days before the twenty-second, so the harvests should occur on the preceding Full Moon of September 1 (actually at 1:21 a.m. on the second) and the following Full Moon on October 1. Harvest after dusk is often done because the life-energy of the plants is fully circulating from solar exposure in the daylight. The fruit of the harvest is filled with life-enhancing benefits. Working under a Full Moon also adds a sense of the sacred.

Mabon Dark Moon

Following a lunar based calendar, the midpoint between Lughnassadh and Samhain is calculated to be September 17 at 8:19 a.m.—in essence, the night of the sixteenth, which is also the night of the dark Moon and suitably celebrated as an esbat. Give a nod to Mabon during the methodical ritual of the dark Virgo Moon. The fastidiousness and critical nature brought by the Virgo Sun and Moon will be somewhat offset by the peace and harmony of the rising Libra. The evening's ritual should generally be a cheerful event, even though the dark Moon is a time of low energy requiring the forfeiture of older projects yet unfinished and provisions made for the new ones. Decline is in all aspects of life preceding a dark Moon, including emotions and physical activities. Staying in bed doesn't seem to be an option, nor does expressing enthusiasm for anything. This is not a great day for any activity that *must* be done rather than joyfully chosen to be done. Attitude will turn the dial until the dark Moon shifts from decline to growth during the day of the seventeenth.

Mabon Sun

Although the Autumnal Equinox is a solar event, the Moon will have an influence on the experience of the holiday. The moment of Mabon's equipoise will occur under a Sagittarius Moon at 9:30 a.m. on September 22. The Sagittarius Moon will also be present on the evening of the twenty-first, having moved out of Scorpio at 3:31 p.m. that very afternoon. This should be a better choice for the Mabon festivities. The celebration will likely be well-attended and not as raucous as other sabbats, leaning toward gracious and uncomplicated, simple sophistication with a bit of playfulness.

Mabon Celebrations

Often these festivities are more formal in dress and more relaxed in ritual. This evening is the Wiccan Thanksgiving. A feast is a usual accompaniment to the giving of thanks for the bounty received from that which was sown last spring, actually and metaphorically. The spiritual symbology is that of the cornucopia, the ever abundant Horn of Plenty. Root crops like carrots and onions, breads and nuts, and fruits like apples are all abundant at mid-harvest. Use plenty of apples to adorn and spice pork, and for pies, sauce, and serving fresh. Slice the apple across the midpoint to expose the pentagram. Grapes are also harvested at this time of year, so wine is appropriate if desired. The Sagittarius Moon will help to counteract and open the secretiveness of the rising Scorpio, and create a space of optimism and freedom along with warmth, sociability, and friendly banter.

A fun ritual of thanks can be had by asking each attendee to write down their individual bounties for which they wish to give thanks, bounties that were received over this last growing season, positive or negative, naughty or nice, on several small pieces of paper, one bounty per paper. Consider setting a maximum number of papers to keep the thanksgiving game limited in time. Categories of bounties could also be requested, like one bounty each concerning spirituality, family, fitness, sex, work, or other similar aspects of life. Each person should then fold the papers in half and place in a cauldron, pot, box, or other container to be drawn at dinner.

After the ritual, prayer, or when appropriate, spin the bottle to see who goes first and proceed widdershins, as this holiday marks the coming of the end and waning of the year. Mix the papers, draw one, say aloud, "We give thanks for," then read that which is written on the paper and pass the cauldron. The game might come off as thoughtful at times, such as, "We give thanks for friends and family"; or individualized like, "We give thanks for my belly dance instructor"; or bawdy like, "We give thanks for having had sex at Beltaine." One person's desire to offer thanks is embodied by all. The game is most fun when the thankfulness includes those things not often spoken. Add a physical dimension by having the reader mime or act out a representation of the bounty on the paper. On other sabbats, this game could get out of hand, but playing under this Sagittarius Moon will help keep a level of decorum and balance.

Full Moon

A week later, the Moon will be Full and under the influence of Aries on October 1 at 5:05 p.m. With a Libra sun, a rising Pisces, and Mercury in Scorpio, there is no strong earth to ground the emotional. Aries will bring the fire, the push, the urgency, courageousness, independence, and recklessness. Scorpio will add an element of sarcastic investigation and secretiveness. Libra will have a harmonious and affectionate texture, and Pisces will aid the empath and encourage self-sacrifice. That which is figuratively harvested on this night could be anything, from anywhere, for any purpose. The esbat ritual will be interesting, with secret and reckless courageousness juxtaposed to harmonious self-sacrifice. The ritual will come down to the good of the one versus the good of the many.

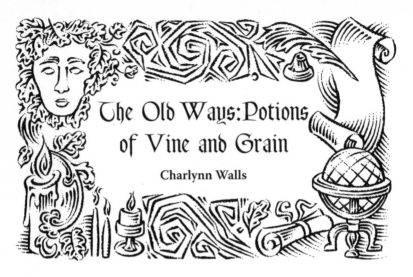

The Old Ways: Potions of Vine and Grain

Charlynn Walls

Growing up in the Midwest, we had several causes for celebration, usually associated with the varied harvests in the area. One time we celebrated was after the harvest of the grapes. I have fond memories of marching in the parades and even participating as a bunch of grapes on a float through town. The Fall Festival, a Harvest Home celebration, became synonymous with the harvest of the grapes that were to be made into wine.

Mabon, or the autumn equinox, is a time when day and night are equal and occurs between September 20 and 24. It is sometimes referred to as Harvest Home and is a time of thanksgiving which occurs in conjunction with the final harvest of the year. Mabon is the second harvest festival in the Wheel of the Year and sees the harvest of grapes, barley, and hops.

Fruit of the Vine

Winemakers spend the growing season tending their vines with care, using the knowledge passed to them from their predecessors, hoping that the harvest will be good. They want the vines to struggle a bit, to create deep rich aromas and tastes, but if the vines struggle too much, the fruit withers on the vines. So they look for the perfect time to bring in the harvest.

The harvests begin in the Midwest during the month of September. Local festivals celebrate the end of the harvest with celebrations that reach out to the community. They incorporate the beginning steps of the winemaking process into the festivities. Winemaking processes have changed over the years, but we still have evidence of wine being present throughout the ancient world. *Archaeology Magazine* reports that some of the oldest wine we have record of is nearly seven thousand years old. A piece of pottery retained residue from the wine and was found in the Zargos Mountains of Iran.

The grape stomp is a popular event and local folk rite where the participants line up and race one another to produce the most juice from the fruit by stomping on it with their bare feet. This may have been among the ways the first winemakers would have produced the juice to make wine. Another event that fascinates festivalgoers is juice pressing. According to Berkowitz, "Grape presses dating to the late third millennium B.C. have been found at Titris Höyük in southeastern Turkey." This is the more "modern" approach to the grape stomp, in which either a small or large press is used to squeeze the juice from the fruit. It is also the first step in turning juice into wine.

Viticulture has been a part of many cultures around the world, including Italy, France, Spain, and the United States. Italian winemaking dates to Roman times with Baccus (the god of the grape harvest and winemaking), when wine was an important part of the rites.

Homebrewing

Grains can also be brewed. The hops and barley that are the main components in beer are harvested in late September. Cultures around the globe have created alcohol in various forms as a safe and sanitary drink. Beer was also packed with essential nutrients that aided health. Osiris is often given credit for creating beer and bringing it to the ancient Egyptian people. Once it became established in the culture it became a part of important festivals and celebrations.

Beer even made its way to the continent of Asia. As reported by *Archaeology Magazine*, "The grain was first used by the ancient Mesopotamians for brewing beer." It is possible that when barley was introduced from western Eurasia into the Central Plain of China, it came with the knowledge that the grain was a good ingredient for beer brewing" (Berkowitz 1996).

Public celebrations continue today, like Oktoberfest, which originated in Germany in 1810. The festival features the beers of the region. Barring a few instances when the festivities were suspended, such as during WWI, it has been continuously ongoing ever since. Oktoberfest is celebrated during the last couple of weeks of September and into the first weeks of October. The beginning of the festival falls around Mabon. The celebration is mirrored in cities throughout the United States.

Celebrating Mabon

Winemaking

An easy way to celebrate this harvest festival is to make your own wine. Create this to use in your rituals and offerings for the coming year. The easiest wine to make is mead, or honey wine. You will need a glass bottle, or carboy, to hold the liquid. For a gallon of mead, you will need to mix a gallon of spring water, three pounds of honey, and a packet of yeast. You will mix the ingredients together and seal the bottle with an airlock. As the honey ferments, it will create gas that will need to be let off. The airlock will let it vent without allowing anything into the container. After two to three weeks, the fermentation process should be complete and you may bottle the mead into a clean bottle with either a cork or sealed cap. The mead may be consumed after two weeks bottling or may be aged for months before consumption.

Thanksgiving Offerings

During Mabon it is important to remember to give thanks for the bounty of the harvest that has been received. Take a moment to honor the god or goddess of your choice during this festival and leave an offering as thanks. Offerings of food, especially those that are fermented and are harvested during this season or drink that is created using the ingredients harvested during this time, would be appropriate.

References

Berkowitz, Mark. "World's Earliest Wine." *Archaeology Magazine* 49, no. 5 September/October 1996. https://archive.archaeology.org/9609/newsbriefs/wine.html.

Dugan, Ellen. *Autumn Equinox: The Enchantment of Mabon*. St. Paul, MN: Lewellyn Publications, 2005.

"History of the Oktoberfest." Oktoberfest. https://www.oktoberfest.net/history-oktoberfest/.

McCoy, Edain. *The Sabbats: A New Approach to Living the Old Ways*. St. Paul, MN: Lewellyn Publications, 1994.

Morgan, Sheena. *The Wicca Book of Days*. London: Vega, 2002.

Nichols, Mike. *The Witches' Sabbats*. Albany, CA: Acorn Guild Press, 2005.

Powell, Eric A. "Neolithic Chinese Beer Recipe." *Archaeology Magazine*. 2016. https://www.archaeology.org/news/4484-160524-neolithic-chinese-beer-recipe.

Feasts and Treats
Mickie Mueller

MANY THINK OF MABON as the Witch's Thanksgiving or Harvest Home celebration. This day of balance marks the autumn equinox, when the day and night are of equal length. This is the second harvest sabbat, and by now, the feeling of fall is in the air. Even if the weather is still a bit warm, the evenings are probably a bit cooler. We're starting to see the autumn harvest of squash and pumpkins come in at the farmer's markets, produce stands, and grocery stores. Many people love to go apple picking at their local orchard to celebrate Mabon. Our thoughts this time of the year turn to sharing fellowship and gratitude for our abundance. Creating a special meal crafted with loving care can fill our hearts and keep us focused on how much we have to be grateful for, thus magically creating more abundance in our lives.

Hungarian Mushroom Soup

My family loves this soup. It's got a perfect duality of warmth and creaminess, making it the perfect starter for a meal to celebrate this day of balance. This comforting soup warms the spirit.

Prep time: 10 minutes
Cooking time: 30 minutes
Servings: 4

6 tablespoons (¾ stick) butter or margarine, divided
4 cups sliced mushrooms
1 large onion, diced
1 teaspoon salt
1 teaspoon black pepper
1 teaspoon ground coriander
2 teaspoon dill
3 tablespoons Hungarian or smoked paprika
2 cups vegetable or chicken stock
3 tablespoons all-purpose flour or gluten-free flour blend
1 cup milk, coconut milk, or unsweetened almond milk
½ cup sour cream (or you can substitute Greek yogurt or dairy-free
   yogurt)
Juice of half a lemon

Melt 2 tablespoons of butter in the skillet and add mushrooms. Sauté until lightly brown. Remove mushrooms from skillet and set aside. Melt another 2 tablespoons of butter in the skillet. Add onion, salt, pepper, coriander, dill, and paprika, and sauté over medium heat for about 5 minutes. Return mushrooms to skillet and add ½ cup of vegetable stock. Reduce to a simmer, cover, and cook for 10 minutes.

Melt the last 2 tablespoons of butter in a soup pot. Stir flour into the melted butter to make a roux and cook while stirring for a few minutes. Add milk and cook while stirring constantly over medium-low heat until thick, which takes about 10 minutes. Pour the mushroom mix into the soup pot and add the remaining 1½ cups of stock. Cover and simmer about 10 minutes. Before serving, stir in sour cream and lemon juice.

Nut-Crusted Salmon

I think salmon is the perfect hearty fish for the season, for those who want to shake things up instead of sticking with roast chicken or turkey. This dish isn't difficult, with just a 10-minute prep time, but impressive enough to serve guests. If you can get fresh salmon, it's lovely; if not, frozen will do just fine. All nuts are associated with Mabon and you can use any varieties that you like or have easy access to when making this a lovely harvest meal. You can add the toppings to your salmon fillets and cover with plastic wrap in the fridge ahead of time so that it's ready to pop in the oven.

Prep time: 10 minutes

Cooking time: 15 minutes

Servings: 4

½ cup mayonnaise of your choice

2 tablespoons Dijon mustard

½ teaspoon salt

½ teaspoon black pepper

1 pound salmon fillet, cut into 4 pieces (or alternately, a pound of frozen salmon fillets thawed using instructions on the package)

½ teaspoon orange zest

2 teaspoons fresh chopped rosemary

½ cup chopped nuts of your choice: almonds, pecans, walnuts, hazelnuts

Preheat oven to 400° F (200° degrees C). Mix mayonnaise with Dijon, salt, and pepper. Spray baking sheet with cooking spray. Arrange salmon on a baking sheet. If your fillets have skin, place them skin-side down. Spread the tops with the mayonnaise mixture. Sprinkle with orange zest, rosemary, and chopped nuts. Bake 15 minutes or until the fish flakes easily with a fork.

Sun-Dried Tomato Polenta Acorn Squash

Acorn squash has a slightly pumpkiny flavor, which I love to season with savory flavors instead of sweet. My sister Robin first introduced my family to this dish and we fell madly in love with it. She found the original version on the *Vegetarian Times* website and made it for us on Thanksgiving. I've altered it slightly it over the years, as I'm known to do. It's rich, creamy, and delicious. We serve it as a side dish with salmon, but it can also be a main course with sides of green vegetables and some crusty bread. I always save the seeds; you can toss them in salt and roast them in the oven just like pumpkin seeds! You'll need a wire whisk and a wooden spoon for this one.

Prep time: 15 minutes
Cooking time: 45 minutes
Servings: 4

2 acorn squash, cut in half crosswise, seeds and loose pulp removed
2 ounces sun-dried tomatoes
¼ cup sunflower seeds
3 garlic cloves, minced
½ cup fresh, grated parmesan (Robin says to splurge on fresh, don't use that powdered stuff)
¼ cup olive oil
2½ cup chicken or vegetable stock
½ teaspoon salt
¼ cup polenta or substitute coarsely ground cornmeal

Preheat oven to 350° F (177° C). Spray a cooking sheet with non-stick cooking spray and place the four halves of the squash on it, cut-side down, and bake for 45 minutes. While the squash bakes, soak tomatoes in very hot water for 15 minutes. Add the sunflower seeds to a cold skillet (no oil is needed) and heat to medium, stirring often until aromatic, light brown, and glistening. Remove from heat. Remove the tomatoes from the water and coarsely chop them.

To make the sun-dried tomato pesto, put sunflower seeds, garlic, sun-dried tomatoes, and grated parmesan in a food processor and blend. As it's blending, slowly drizzle olive oil through the chute until well mixed into a pesto.

Bring the stock and salt to a boil in a saucepan. Beat with a whisk as you very slowly sprinkle the polenta into the pan, whisking constantly. Once all the polenta is added, turn down the heat to medium-low and switch to stirring constantly with a wooden spoon, being sure to scrape the bottom and along the edge of the pan. Continue for 20 minutes or until the polenta pulls back from the sides of the pan; it will be creamy when finished. Remove from heat and stir in the sun-dried tomato pesto.

Take the squash out of the oven and cut a bit off the tops and bottoms of the squash as necessary so that they have flat bottoms and form neat squash bowls that don't roll over. Fill the bowls of the squash with the polenta and pesto mixture. Top with fresh grated parmesan and serve.

Crispy Apple Pie Wraps

Apples are the quintessential Mabon treat. They are ripe and lovely, and full of the magic of love, fertility, healing, and immortality. I created this treat when I was trying to cut out sugar and gluten from my diet and I was dying for some dessert. I thought it wouldn't be too bad, but it was actually really good and perfect for fall! I made up one for each member of my family, using flour tortillas instead of the gluten-free wrap I used; they loved it too.

Prep time: 5 minutes
Cooking time: 6–15 minutes
Servings: 4

4 apples, cored and chopped
3 tablespoons honey
1 teaspoon cinnamon
Pinch of cardamom
¼ teaspoon salt
1 tablespoon coconut oil
4 flour burrito-sized tortillas or gluten-free wraps

Preheat oven or air fryer to 400° F (200° C). Mix cut-up apples, honey, cinnamon, and salt in a microwave-safe bowl. Microwave for 1 minute, stir, then microwave 1 more minute.

Melt coconut oil for less than a minute in the microwave and spread it thinly on both sides of each tortilla using a basting brush. Divide the apple mixture between the 4 tortillas. Roll each one like a burrito: fold one side over the apples, then pull the sides in to enclose the apples, while rolling it all the way up. Fasten it closed with a toothpick. Bake them either in the oven on a baking sheet for 15 minutes or in an air fryer for 6 minutes. Optional: dust the tops with powdered sugar.

Crafty Crafts

Ember Grant

AT THE AUTUMN EQUINOX we again mark a seasonal change; day and night are equal length once again, and the days begin to get shorter. While the process of harvest can occur at various times during the fall, this day marks the official transition to autumn—a time we celebrate by decorating with leaves, gourds, and other symbols of the changing season.

Clay Leaf Incense Burner/Trinket Dish

Naturally, autumn leaves are the classic symbol of the season. To celebrate the equinox, leaves are the focus of this easy and elegant project. These dried clay leaves can be used for stick or cone incense, as a small trinket dish, or even for burning a tealight candle. Either way, they bring images of nature into your magical work.

Materials

Acrylic paint—choose a combination of fall colors, green, or even a metallic shade ($2–$3 per bottle)

Molding clay—air dry ($5–$15, depending on the size of the package)

Paintbrush

Waxed paper or plate
Knife for trimming
Fresh leaf to use as a mold
Optional: a layer of gloss/shine to finish and seal—Mod Podge can
    be used for this
    Cost: $10+
    Time spent: about 1 day, to allow drying time

I used Activ-Clay brand craft clay. It's soft and easy to work with, plus it air-dries so there's no need for baking. Keep in mind that your item will not be suitable for food use.

Choose a leaf with clearly noticeable veins. Pick one off the tree so it's still flexible. Next, scoop out some clay and roll it using a rolling pin to achieve your desired size and thickness. Don't make the leaf too thin or too thick—aim for about ⅛ inch thickness. You can make it thicker, but it will take longer to dry. In addition, if you want to give the leaf curled edges for a natural look, leaving your piece too thick means it may end up with a wrinkled appearance. On the other hand, making it too thin means it will be more brittle and prone to breakage—especially if your leaf has fine points on the edges.

You can roll the clay on waxed paper if you wish, but I've found that a countertop works just fine. This clay is easy to clean and shouldn't make too much of a mess. If you have a glass surface protector for your counter, that works well too.

Press the leaf, backside down (the veins protrude more on that side), onto the clay. Apply light pressure with your fingertips to achieve the best transfer of the lines from the leaf into the clay. Gently pull the leaf away from the clay. Now you can pick up your clay leaf—carefully—and prepare to trim the sides. Laying it on a large serving platter or plate works well. Just be gentle when handling it. Be mindful of the backside—your fingertips can make dents and you can also accidentally cut into it with your fingernails. Use your palm. Use a spatula if necessary, and move the clay leaf to a large plate or tray.

This next step can be challenging, but it's still easy once you get the hang of it. Using a small knife, trim away the clay around the edges of the leaf, giving it shape. If your natural leaf has lots of tiny jagged points, as some oak leaves do, just smooth them out in a single line to avoid having lots of tiny edges. After the trimming, the edges will probably look uneven and sharp—simply use your fingertips to gently smooth out any rough areas.

Next, if you plan to use your leaf as a burner for stick incense, use an actual stick of incense (or a toothpick or paper clip) to poke a small hole at the end, near the place where the leaf's stem would be.

After the edges are trimmed, you're ready to let your leaf dry. If you'd like the leaf to have natural-looking curved sides, rest it in a bowl or other curved dish while it's drying. If your dish is too deep, put a block, lid, or ramekin in the center, under the leaf, to hold up

the middle so it doesn't fold in half. Otherwise, just set the leaf on a plate. Depending on the size and thickness of your design, it may take a couple days to fully dry.

When it's dry, you're ready to paint it. Choose your color, or colors, and add a bit of metallic if you wish, for a subtle shine. Paint both sides and don't forget to paint the edges as well. When the paint is dry, you can seal it with a coating such as Mod Podge. I like to use the satin finish, but it's your choice. A more durable finish may give your leaf extra protection. Either way, I do believe that having some type of finish on the leaf is a good idea. You may find that your leaf needs several coats of paint because the clay is porous. Add as many coats as you like. I usually find that two or three is sufficient, depending on the color. Also, be aware of the incense stick hole that you made and be sure to poke through it again to clear away any paint or sealant that may have accumulated there.

Experiment with fall colors on your leaf, or various shades of green. I like to mix in some gold, silver, or copper as well, to add a subtle sheen. Or start with a greenish-brown base, then add the colors for a more natural look. Try using a small sponge to dab on some red, yellow, or orange. If you don't like how it looks, simply paint over it and try something else.

Once your leaf is fully dry, it's ready for burning incense. If you burn a votive candle directly on it, it may be difficult to clean off the wax, so tea lights are recommended. Otherwise, clean-up of incense ash should be easy; wipe the surface with a damp cloth or paper towel and pat dry. Keep in mind that if you burn cone incense on these it may leave a stain—incense is made with sticky resin that can permanently leave residue on your container.

Alternative idea: While you have the clay handy, you can also use small leaves to make little imprints with holes that you can put a string or chain through to make a pendant!

A Crystal for Every Season: Tourmaline

Charlie Rainbow Wolf

THIS IS THE SECOND of the three harvest festivals. The first, Lammas, is the festival of grain; this is the festival of fruit. It's the time when the day and the night are of equal length, and it's the perfect sabbat for finding balance in your life. It's the time of the cutting of the last grain, the final culling of the god, while the goddess is in all her glory in her role as the Harvest Queen. In the northern hemisphere things are winding down for the winter, but there's still plenty to do to preserve food for the cold season.

It's no surprise that the colors of the season echo those of the harvest; gold and warm yellow, mossy green, shades of rust and russet. Look for stones that echo these colors, either in your favorite metaphysical shop or just while you're out in nature. Traditionally, some of the stones that are associated with this time of year include amber, hematite, lodestone, mookaite, petrified wood, two-toned shiva lingam, and topaz.

My favorite Mabon stone is tourmaline. Its energy signature represents protection, grounding, and focus—qualities appreciated by the farmer in the fields and the back-to-school student alike. When I first started working with crystals nearly three decades ago, tourmaline was the stone that brought discipline and development to my efforts. In fact, in my first crystal divination readings when I only had five stones, black tourmaline—also called schorl—was the stone that I used to indicate where the querent needed to pay attention, and bring back some balance and order.

Tourmaline doesn't just come in black, though. It's also found in blue, green, pink, red, and a blend of several colors in one stone. They all have their own nuances, but all tourmalines are good protectors and conductors of energy. It's fairly hard—7.5 on the Mohs scale—and is often carved into jewelry, healing wands, and more. It's versatile and reliable, and those are two of the qualities that it imparts to people who choose to delve into its personality.

Black Tourmaline

I've started with the darkest because this was the first tourmaline to introduce itself to me. I was taught that the shamans and magicians of old used this stone to protect them as they did their rituals and traveled between worlds. It's a root chakra stone, and useful to have around when you're working to overcome fears and insecurities about your physical needs. Healers believe that this stone helps to deflect negative energy, from both environmental influences as well as psychic attack.

Black tourmaline is also found growing as inclusions in quartz and other stones. Clear quartz acts as an amplifier in this instance. The tourmalated quartz blends the qualities of both minerals, and is thought to be quite powerful when used in crystal healing. It's said to balance the yin/yang energies. Wear this stone if you are apprehensive about a situation, or carry one instead of a fidget spinner to give yourself something to do when you feel anxiety creeping up on you.

Blue Tourmaline

This stone looks so very tranquil and peaceful, and that's the energy that it brings to your Mabon activities. If you're rushing around trying to get everything done, use blue tourmaline to help you relax and unwind. It resonates with both the third eye and the throat chakra, helping you to think before you speak, and to make sure your words are kind and helpful. Like all tourmaline, it's also a protective stone.

Green Tourmaline

You might also hear this stone called verdelite, echoing *vert*—the French word for green. It comes in all shades, from the palest lime to the deepest olive, and this is the tourmaline that is most associated with nature spirits and dryads. It's the color of life, and a very important crystal to healers. It's a heart chakra stone, and is used for balancing emotional issues as well as physical ones.

Pink or Red Tourmaline

Even though there's a slight difference in the energy between the pale rose and the deep magenta, both of these colors resonate on the same frequency. They're both heart chakra stones, with the red being more intense than the pink. The red color is called rubellite, but don't mistake it for a ruby! This is another energy neutralizing stone, protective like all tourmalines, and a valuable crystal when working to replace fear with love. Many people think that hate is the opposite of love, but it's not; fear is. Pink and green combined in the same stone is called watermelon tourmaline, and is thought to be a impressive healer when it comes to matters of the heart.

Mabon Reflections

Journaling is a wonderful way to mark the passing of Mabon, and it can be done as a solitary practice or group activity. Record your thoughts, then either keep them in your Book of Shadows or share them with others around a fire, or both! I've shared many a ceremony where we've written what we wish to see die and expire with the last breath of the Corn King as he gives up the final harvest and then fed those papers to the fire as we discussed what we hope to change.

Tourmaline is a sturdy ally on this journey of reflection. If you're fearful of change, write about that, and allow black tourmaline to protect your energy as you explore new ideas and concepts. If the summer saw relationships fade, work with pink, green or watermelon tourmaline to heal the hurt from this separation so you're able to lose the attachment and replace it with compassion and understanding. Blue tourmaline will help you leave the past behind without regret, making room in your life for new beginnings.

If you don't keep a journal and want to make this into more of a ritual than a reflection, try writing down your thoughts on something that is related to the harvest. Corn husks are large enough to hold several words and phrases. When your writing is finished, offer the husk to the fire. Another idea is to get a flower bulb and write onto it what you wish to bury, then plant the bulb. In this way, you give that energy to the earth, so that it might grow anew in the spring.

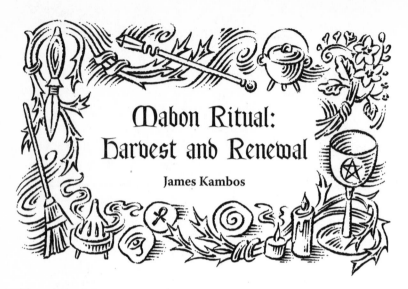

Mabon Ritual:
Harvest and Renewal

James Kambos

THIS MABON RITUAL IS about honoring the harvest. It's also about rest and renewal.

The Items You Will Need:

A sage and cedar smudge stick
A large brown candle for the altar
Seasonal decorations for the altar
Four burgundy or rust candles for each quarter
Incense such as myrrh or sage
Basket of pine cones, one for each person
A cauldron filled with spring-flowering bulbs such as daffodils
    (have enough so each person gets at least one)
Non-perishable food items to be donated to a local food bank

Food for Cakes and Ale:

Since Mabon is frequently referred to as the Witches' Thanksgiving, you may have a full buffet of autumn-inspired foods on hand. Naturally, this depends on the size of your coven and their desires. Or, you may keep it light and serve a spice cake and cider. Other suggestions include snacks such as nuts, apple slices, and caramel sauce for dipping.

Preparing for the Ritual

A Mabon ritual prepares us for the dark season that lies ahead. It should help us connect with our ancestors, which is our past. It's also a time to celebrate the harvest, our present. In addition, it makes us aware that decay leads us to renewal and rebirth, which is our future.

As part of the ritual materials list, I've included some small tokens participants will focus on during the ritual and take with them as a reminder of the ritual. These tokens are the pine cones and the flower bulbs. The pine cones represent our ancestors and eternal life. Each person will hold a pine cone as they think of a special person in their life who has passed to the Otherworld. The basket of pine cones may be set on one side of the altar.

The spring-flowering bulbs used in the ritual serve to remind us of Mabon's life/death/rebirth theme. They also remind us of our future and renewal since they'll bloom in the spring. I suggest placing them in a cauldron during the ritual because the cauldron represents the womb of Mother Earth. And of course, the earth is where the bulbs will rest before their rebirth. The bulbs may be set on the other side of the altar. I've suggested daffodils, but use what works best for your area.

Since one of Mabon's themes is sharing the harvest, I've also made a food collection part of the ritual. I hope your group or coven will donate the food collected to a local food bank. The food you collect may be placed outside the magic circle.

Preparing the Magic Circle

First, mark off the magic circle by lighting the sage and cedar smudge stick. Walk around the circle in a clockwise direction. Begin and end in the east. For Mabon, I like the altar to face west. Set the brown candle in the center of the altar with the incense beside it. Arrange seasonal decorations on and around the altar as you wish. Set the quarter candles at each direction.

The Ritual

The ritual should begin at twilight, as the sun loses the light of day. The leader will now light the incense and wave it about the circle. Once the sacred space is ready, the leader should stand at the altar, facing west. Everyone else should stand behind the leader. Now the leader lights the brown altar candle.

Together say:

Mabon, Great Son, now you must return to the shadows,
As darkness falls, one last time you walk the meadows.
The harvest is done, now the farmers store their golden hoard,
Farewell Young God, as you become the wise Lord.

Now the leader or someone who has been chosen will light the quarter candles beginning in the East and say:

Guardians of the East, help guide us as we enter the Season of Darkness.

Light the south candle and say:

Guardians of the south, help guide us as we enter the Season of Darkness.

Light the west candle and say:

Guardians of the west, help guide us as we enter the Season of Darkness.

Light the north candle and say:

Guardians of the north, help guide us as we enter the Season of Darkness.

The leader should now turn and face the group. The group may now stand or sit around the edge of the circle, facing the center of the circle. The leader now says:

Our time in the season of summer light is done,
Tonight, we say farewell to the Great Son, Mabon.
He must return to the womb of Mother Earth,
For rest, renewal, and rebirth.

We also remember our ancestors who've come before,
For they've passed through the otherworld's door.
As we are surrounded by the harvest of September,
Let us pause and take time to remember,
Our personal harvests that our own ancestors helped us achieve.
Think of the bounty they helped us receive.

The leader, going clockwise around the circle, will give each person one pine cone. The leader may explain that the pine cones symbolize eternal life, and each pine cone represents an ancestor. Then tell the group, or coven, that they should each meditate on an ancestor of theirs who helped them achieve a personal harvest, while holding their pine cone. Give them a couple of minutes. Next, ask for volunteers to share with the group who they thought of and why. This is usually a very moving experience. Allow about fifteen minutes for this remembrance activity.

At this point, the leader should move the cauldron containing the spring bulbs to the center of the circle. If it hasn't been made clear, the leader should explain that everyone will receive a bulb to take home and plant as a living token of this ritual. The leader should remain in the center standing over the cauldron. Together everyone should say:

Now leaves of gold begin to fly,
And wild geese sing their mournful cry.
The grasses will soon be bleached white as bone,
And the earth will soon be barren as a stone.
Flowers now turn to a sorry dust,
Weeds bow down and sere to rust.
But, no death is final or the end,
For the cycle of life will come again.
These bulbs contain the secret of life, death, and rebirth.
Like Mabon, they too will rise again from Mother Earth.

Everyone should step forward and receive a flower bulb, then return to their place. To end the ritual, all, including the leader, should stand, join hands around the circle and say together:

This circle was cast in peace,
This circle is released in peace.
Together we rejoice in the harvest and the land,
Forever, we're linked heart to heart, and hand to hand.

This concludes the ritual. For safety, extinguish all candles. Now enjoy the cakes and ale.

In a day or two, please deliver all the food you've collected to a food bank or to a charity of your choice.

Notes

Notes

Notes

Notes

Notes

Notes

Notes

GET MORE AT **LLEWELLYN.COM**

Visit us online to browse hundreds of our books and decks, plus sign up to receive our e-newsletters and exclusive online offers.

- **Free tarot readings • Spell-a-Day • Moon phases**
- **Recipes, spells, and tips • Blogs • Encyclopedia**
- **Author interviews, articles, and upcoming events**

GET SOCIAL WITH **LLEWELLYN**

Find us on [f]

www.Facebook.com/LlewellynBooks

[twitter] **@LlewellynBooks**

GET BOOKS AT **LLEWELLYN**

LLEWELLYN ORDERING INFORMATION

Order online: Visit our website at www.llewellyn.com to select your books and place an order on our secure server.

Order by phone:
- Call toll free within the US at 1-877-NEW-WRLD (1-877-639-9753)
- We accept VISA, MasterCard, American Express, and Discover.
- Canadian customers must use credit cards.

Order by mail:
Send the full price of your order (MN residents add 6.875% sales tax) in US funds plus postage and handling to: Llewellyn Worldwide, 2143 Wooddale Drive, Woodbury, MN 55125-2989

POSTAGE AND HANDLING
STANDARD (US):
(Please allow 12 business days)
$30.00 and under, add $6.00.
$30.01 and over, FREE SHIPPING.

INTERNATIONAL ORDERS,
INCLUDING CANADA:
$16.00 for one book, plus $3.00 for each additional book.

Visit us online for more shipping options.
Prices subject to change.

FREE CATALOG!

To order, call
1-877-
NEW-WRLD
ext. 8236
or visit our
website

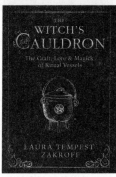